IMAGES
of America

MAURICE RIVER
TOWNSHIP

On the Cover: This Leesburg blacksmith shop was an active place of business in the late 1800s and early 1900s. It was owned by Argus Ferguson and then Sam Chambers. This photograph was taken around 1900. Though not pictured on the cover, the Maurice River is in the original photograph's background. (Courtesy of Drew Tomlin.)

IMAGES of America
MAURICE RIVER TOWNSHIP

Julie Ann Rumbold

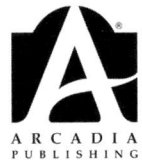

ARCADIA
PUBLISHING

Copyright © 2017 by Julie Ann Rumbold
ISBN 978-1-4671-2643-4

Published by Arcadia Publishing
Charleston, South Carolina

Printed in the United States of America

Library of Congress Control Number: 2016962723

For all general information, please contact Arcadia Publishing:
Telephone 843-853-2070
Fax 843-853-0044
E-mail sales@arcadiapublishing.com
For customer service and orders:
Toll-Free 1-888-313-2665

Visit us on the Internet at www.arcadiapublishing.com

This book is dedicated to the all previous residents, who created the stories and paved the way for every single one of us today, and to my father, Ronald Hampton Rumbold, for his deep family roots in Maurice River Township.

Contents

Acknowledgments		6
Introduction		7
1.	Port Elizabeth	11
2.	Dorchester	29
3.	Leesburg	47
4.	Working the Water	67
5.	The Lost Villages	87
6.	Heislerville and Matts Landing	101
7.	Delmont, East Point, and East Point Lighthouse	111
About the Organization		126
Bibliography		127

Acknowledgments

I am grateful to many people for their support in the development of this book. First and foremost, I wish to thank the Maurice River Township Heritage Society and Dennis Bailey, Karen Lee, and Bob Legg for sharing their time, ideas, and photographs with me and for scanning pictures. I appreciate Drew Tomlin, Leesburg resident and researcher, who visited with me, went on road trips, shared pictures, and provided data. Richard St. Aubyn pointed me to Arcadia Publishing. I enjoyed our visits and the stories and pictures that were shared. I am thankful for the Friends of East Point Lighthouse, especially Nancy Patterson, for the photographs that were contributed and for their tireless efforts to save a national treasure. Rachel Dolhanczyk, museum curator of Bayshore Center at Bivalve, was most helpful by contributing pictures, as well as her time and effort scanning photographs, and taking me on a museum tour. The staff there is doing a great job of preserving the history of those who made their living working the water. J. Roy Oliver, township committee member and lover of history, told me many interesting historical tales. I am also grateful for the following people: Vic Ballato, Louis and Kit Peterson, Nelson Klein, Terry Bennett, Joe and Donna Haase, Sonja Jordan, Mary Hagemann, Ed Krupa, Tom Wiechnik, and Leslie Ficcaglia. For everyone who contributed pictures, including photographs that did not make it into the book due to resolution or preservation issues, I am thankful for your willingness to contribute. I am grateful for the support and encouragement of my husband, John Barone, and our blended families including Kristen and Kimberly Barone, Adam and Megan Valenzano, Ryan McClellan, and Dakota Hafer. A thank-you is owed to my nephew Ronald Flynn; when I made many trips to Dorchester and surrounding areas in search of additional photographs and information, he provided me lodging. I thank my sister Christina Longley and my friend Amy Smith for their prayers and support. My Higher Power and Friends of Bill W. never once doubted me on this journey. Finally, thanks go to all the residents of Maurice River Township for their deep roots and long memories and for keeping such a beautiful place alive for future generations.

INTRODUCTION

Maurice River Township is in Cumberland County, New Jersey. The township was formed as a precinct in January 1748 and was incorporated in 1798 as one of the state's initial groups of townships. It consists of just over 94 square miles of beautiful rural land in the southeastern part of the county, bordered on the south by Delaware Bay and on the west by the Maurice River. The township includes Port Elizabeth, Bricksboro, Cumberland, Dorchester, Leesburg, Heislerville, Delmont, and part of Milmay. It is part of the Millville, Vineland, and Bridgeton areas for statistical purposes. In the most recent recorded population index, just over 7,900 residents lived in the township. It is located along Route 47, also known as Delsea Drive, which is a travel route to shore points. Delsea Drive follows the same pathway that was carved by early Native Americans.

Maurice River Township provides great recreational activities for outdoor enthusiasts. It is abundant in wildlife as well and was once well known for muskrat hunting and the sale of valuable pelts. It still offers excellent hunting, hiking, fishing, and crabbing opportunities. It is an area familiar to people with an interest in sighting rare and endangered bird species. There are several popular marinas for boaters and fishermen dotting the river.

The township is known as "the Gateway to the Wild and Scenic Rivers" due to the four waterways in its borders, including the Maurice River and Manumuskin, Menantico, and Muskee Creeks.

Maurice River Township played many important roles in American history. It was originally part of a great wilderness settled by the Lenni-Lenape. They called the Maurice River "Wahatquenak." How the river became Maurice is subject to some debate in the area. Most local legends and historians report that the river is named after the Manhattan-bound Dutch exploratory ship *Prince Maurice*, which was sunk by local Native Americans in 1657 in an area of the river nicknamed "No Man's Friend" because of its twists and curves. In fact, local resident and township committee member J. Roy Oliver is in possession of an egg-shaped cannonball typical of those made by the Dutch in the 1600s. Dorchester resident Joe Glasser, a friend of Oliver's, retrieved the cannonball from the river in the area where the ship was supposedly sunk. As a child, he and his brother were diving and digging in the muck at the bottom of the river, as children do, when he came up with a cannonball. An older gentleman suggested that he put the cannonball in a jar of oil to preserve it. He did that for about 40 to 50 years. Much later, Roy and Joe saw each other and Roy learned that his friend had a cannonball that he was willing to sell. One story surrounding the cannonball, though it has never been verified, is that it was fired from the ship at the Indians who sunk it.

Historian Lucius Q.C. Elmer reported in *History of the Early Settlement and Progress of Cumberland County, New Jersey*, first published in 1869, that the name was more likely given by Dutch captains Mey or DeVries who were in the area. In fact, Captain Mey founded Cape May. Elmer wrote that a map published in Amsterdam in 1676 included not only New Jersey but also the river at the entrance of the bay, which was identified as "Mauritius Revier." His book states that when the county of Cape May was established in 1692, it was bordered on the east by the "Morris" River. Clearly, there is still some mystery around how the river became Maurice.

The Dutch explorers settled along the banks of Delaware Bay and its rivers in the 1600s. They came to the area to establish trading posts with the local Indians. The Dutch settlers began to claim jurisdiction over the territory they settled, and unfortunately, the Indians were mostly displaced. Small towns were founded along creeks and the sandy banks of rivers. Some early Swedish explorers also settled in the region.

Maurice River Township was a place of significance during the Revolutionary War. The inhabitants of the county joined in the resistance that led to the war. According to *Maurice River Town* by Herbert Vanaman, written in 1976, there was only one conflict in Cumberland County during the Revolution in which blood was shed, known as the Battle of Dallas Landing. It happened in August 1781 at the site of Dallas Landing, or Ferry. It was a bloody battle in which all the Tories perished. A Philadelphia newspaper account cited in the book stated that the New Jersey militia, led by Capt. James Riggins, killed four or five of the enemy when they attempted to board his vessel. Supposedly, Captain Riggins was aided primarily by John Peterson since several of the militia jumped overboard and swam to shore. Some recent studies have disputed this account. Just like many other centuries-old stories passed on over time, there was another version of the battle that was given to Woodruff Boggs, a former resident of Bricksboro, and recorded in *Maurice River Town*. In this account, Jonathan Dallas had loaded a boat with supplies to be shipped from the area. Somehow, the British heard about the vessel and determined to seize it if they were not paid a certain amount of money. Dallas agreed to do this but changed his mind and decided to defend his ship with the help of the militia, who barricaded themselves aboard the boat. They attacked the British when they attempted to board. Many were killed and buried on the banks of the river. John Ogden, 100 years later, supposedly dug up brass buttons and shoe buckles that had belonged to the British soldiers. A recent archeology study on the skirmish on the Lower Maurice River, conducted by Hunter Research for the National Park Service, did not find archeological evidence of this battle.

Another interesting event that took place in 1797 was a court case recorded in *History of the Counties of Gloucester, Salem and Cumberland*, written by Thomas Cushing and Charles Sheppard in 1883. According to them, on February 28, 1797, John Patterson, an Irishman, murdered Capt. Andrew Conrow and attempted to kill two others of his crew, badly wounding them on their vessel on the Maurice River between Dorchester and Leesburg. Reportedly, a cabin boy escaped up the rigging and thus saved his own life. This same boy became the chief witness in a trial against Patterson. During the trial, which was held in a Presbyterian church in an unspecified local town, Patterson became frenzied with anger and attempted to choke the witness to death. He was then convicted and sentenced to be hanged, but hanged himself the next morning with a silk handkerchief on the upper hinge of the cell door. Cushing and Sheppard wrote that Patterson cheated the gallows of the most deserving victim who ever faced them in the county.

The town of Port Elizabeth experienced rapid growth from 1799 to the early 1800s. Its busiest years were likely from 1825 to the late 1800s. It was well known for its glass industry and as a significant port. It gradually declined with the expansion of the railroad, the advent of the automobile, the use of alternative fuel sources, and the development of rival industries in the area. The surrounding villages and towns gained prominence in the early 1800s. Dorchester and Leesburg became known for shipbuilding. In 1849, the East Point Lighthouse was constructed largely due to the efforts of Joshua Brick, a prominent local citizen, who persistently promoted the need for a lighthouse at the mouth of the Maurice River. The contract for its construction was ultimately awarded to Nathan and Samuel Middleton. It is the second oldest lighthouse in the state.

By the 1850s, the Maurice River Cove was well known for the cultivation of oysters. There were as many as 500 sailing vessels in the oyster business at the time. People referred to the boats as having hearts of oak, and the boats were so numerous that the view from the river was described as a forest of masts. Once the railroad was extended to the Port Norris area in the 1870s and later to the Maurice River in the 1880s, the oyster business rapidly expanded. Many oystermen and commercial fishermen were guided by the beam of the East Point Lighthouse.

According to *Biographical, Genealogical and Descriptive History of the First Congressional District of New Jersey*, published in 1900, several prominent citizens up to that time were from Maurice River Township. William Ogden was born in Port Elizabeth in 1838. In 1682, his ancestors came from England with William Penn in the ship *Welcome*. His father, Samuel Ogden, operated a store in Port Elizabeth for several years and died in 1862. William Ogden was a member of the Society of Friends and was well respected. It seems that the early inhabitants in this part of New Jersey were of sturdy stock. In defiance of wild animals and vast forests, they established homes for themselves in the wilderness. They changed the landscape from unbroken forest into houses and cultivated fields and towns. George Hampton, while not born in the township, was well known in the county as an attorney. He served as sheriff of Cumberland County and was a judge of the common pleas court. He married Mary Ann Errickson, a daughter of Thomas and Anna Buck Westcott Errickson, of Leesburg. Another reputable individual, J. Alfred Bodine was born in Port Elizabeth in 1831. Though he did not stay in the area, he went on to become president of the Bodine Glass Company in Williamstown. He likely learned the glass trade locally. Randall Marshall, the paternal grandfather of Dr. Joseph C. Marshall, who practiced medicine in Tuckahoe, was born in 1771 and reportedly was involved with the Port Elizabeth Glassworks. He was a pioneer in that business in southern New Jersey and also owned and operated a tannery at Port Elizabeth.

Residents of Maurice River Township were patriots who willingly joined the ranks of Union soldiers who fought in the Civil War. Four young soldiers from the township had the distinction of being the first Union soldiers to enter the Confederate capital of Richmond, Virginia. Unfortunately, they did not invade the city in glory but were taken there as prisoners while fighting in Virginia. At that time, there were five battles during seven days led by Robert E. Lee and George B. McClellan. It was during the Battle of Gaines's Mill that Benjamin, Richard, William, and John Mitchell were captured. Benjamin was wounded during the battle and died two weeks later in a Confederate prison. His body was not returned home.

Continuing with the tradition of patriotism in the region, the residents also played an important role in World War II. Not only did many of the young men in the area serve as soldiers, but the Delaware Bay Shipbuilding Company built many vessels for the US government and the Navy that served in the war efforts.

Shipbuilding was booming in Leesburg and Dorchester in the early 1900s. Today, the *A.J. Meerwald*, the official tall ship of the state of New Jersey, does public sails from the region. In 1928, *A.J. Meerwald* was built as an oyster schooner at the Dorchester shipyard, which was then owned by Charles H. Stowman & Sons.

In the 1930s, some oystermen made a lot of money during Prohibition by rumrunning on Delaware Bay. It is said that the captains would disguise their boats by stringing a series of letters on the name board on the side of the vessel so that it could not be easily identified by the Coast Guard if spotted. It was a booming time at Thompsons Beach in the 1930s and 1940s as well. There were over 100 homes, stores, boat rental establishments, and a boardwalk there. Folks from surrounding towns would join the beach residents on Friday evening at Captain Klein's place for music and refreshments. East Point Beach thrived in that period as well. Capt. Harry Badger's speakeasy was a happening place on Friday and Saturday evenings.

A great flood in 1950 virtually destroyed Thompsons and Moores Beaches. In fact, 13 people from Maurice River Township died in that horrific event, which struck unexpectedly on November 25, 1950. There was a group of young boys in an Explorers group who were staying that weekend at the lighthouse. They watched houses from Thompsons Beach float by on the bay.

There are tremendous efforts under way today to save the lighthouse. Friends of East Point Lighthouse are making great strides through a grant to restore the lighthouse to its original beauty. They are also working with the US Army Corps of Engineers to protect the surrounding beach and meadows from the drastic erosion that is occurring in the area.

The township today has several remaining businesses including Bailey's Seafood, A Girl's Place Bait Shop, Dorchester Shipyard Inc., Yanks Marine, Allen Steel, Whibco Inc., George's Pizzeria, the Citgo station, Lillian's Produce, Maurice River Diner, Barnacle Bill's, Southern State

Correctional Facility and Bayside Prison, and the marinas, including Boat World, Anchor, Haase's, and Popeyes. The Maurice River is the home of the *A.J. Meerwald* and its port at Bivalve.

The area is a secret place of hidden beauty that is well worth visiting. In this space is silence, peace, and magnificent scenery. In the stillness, it is possible to slow down, relax, and return to an earlier time when life was simpler and times were slower.

One
Port Elizabeth

Port Elizabeth was once an important town in the early history of the state of New Jersey. According to township records, it came into prominence shortly after 1778. Prior to that, there were only a few scattered dwellings from early settlers in an area of vast woodlands along Manumuskin Creek. Due to innovative early residents, the development of natural resources, and some decisions made by the state government, the area rapidly developed into an industrial hub. At that time, the state assembly legalized diking corporations, and a bridge and dam were built across the Manumuskin Creek. The dam caused meadowlands to dry out, which could then be used for farming, and the bridge opened the area to commerce. Structures were also built along the riverbanks downstream for shipping. It eventually became an important port location where goods were shipped to major cities.

The owner of most of the land in the area was Elizabeth Clark Bodly, originally from Salem. She was a Quaker whose remains are buried in the Friends Burial Grounds on Route 47 in Port Elizabeth. She laid out and sold lots in 1785, and the town quickly sprung up. Hotels were built in the late 1700s and early 1800s to accommodate the traffic and visitors to the village.

A glass factory was built by James Lee around 1799. It became the Eagle Glassworks factories and the third glass-manufacturing business in the state. Due to the abundant sand and silica in the region, the glass industry went on to become a major employer and source of revenue. Abundant lumber from the pinelands was shipped for building and for fuel for businesses and homes in the cities.

Port Elizabeth Methodist Church was built in 1827 to replace the county's first Methodist church, built in 1786. The present-day library was built by Dr. Benjamin Fisler, who also built the church and several other structures in town.

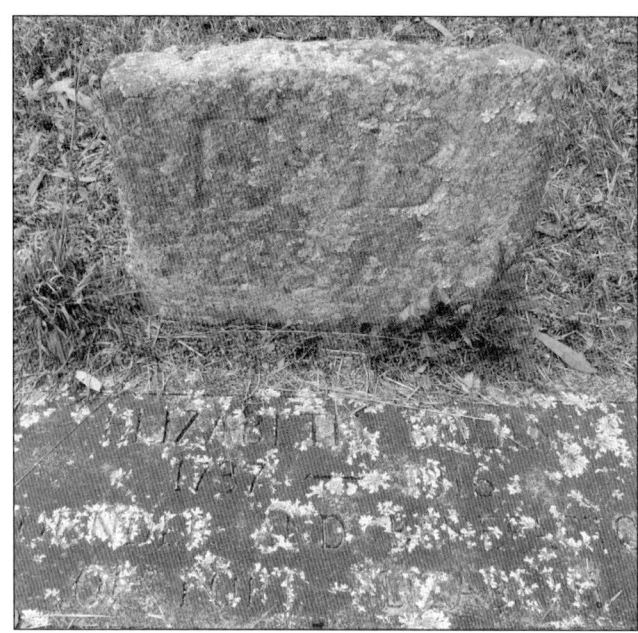

Elizabeth Bodly was a Quaker who was given the lands that became the town of Port Elizabeth. After 1778, the area came into prominence as an industrial center and, later, one of the state's federally designated ports. Bodly laid out and sold lots in 1785, and the area quickly developed. She is buried in the Friends Burial Grounds on Route 47 in Port Elizabeth. Her original tombstone includes only the initials EB, because it was considered vain to use a person's full name. The marker on the ground was added later. Elizabeth Bodly was born in 1737 and died in 1816. (Courtesy of the Robert Legg family collection.)

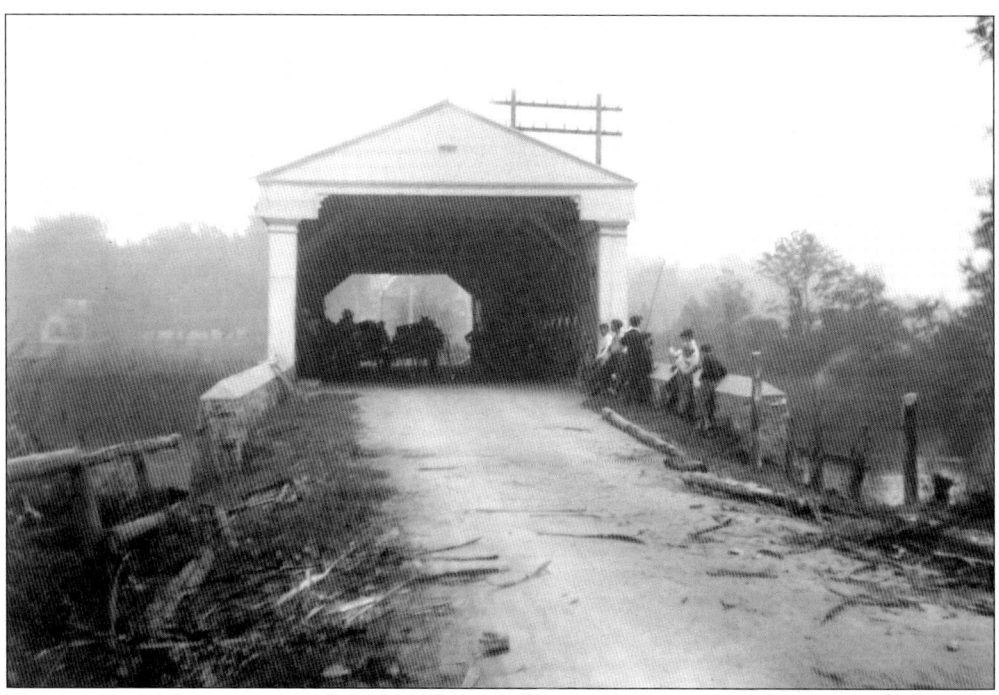

This picture of the covered bridge over Manumuskin Creek in Port Elizabeth was taken before 1908. When the highway was just a dirt path, it was well used by horses and buggies and then by early automobiles. (Courtesy of the Maurice River Township Heritage Society.)

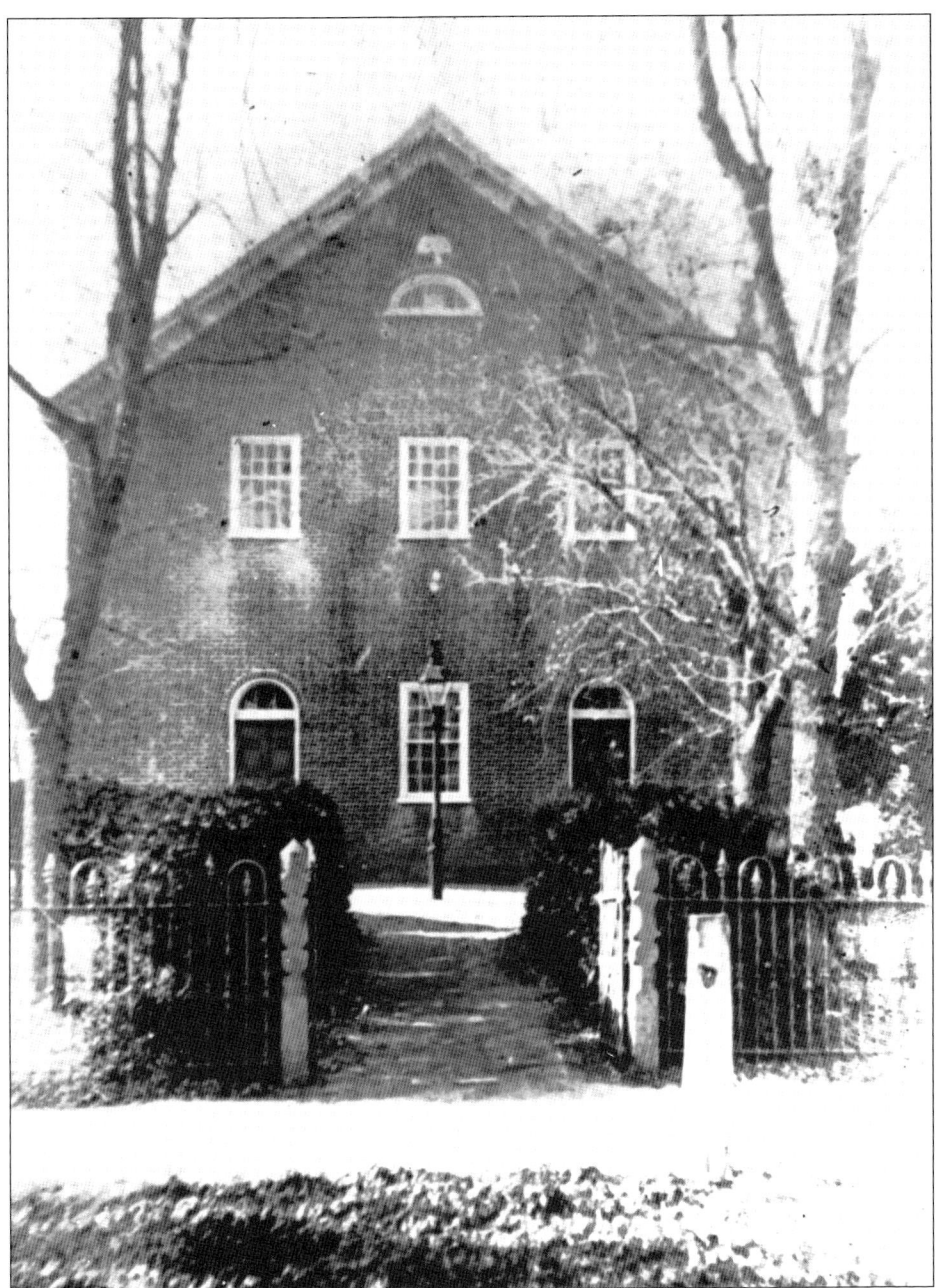

The Port Elizabeth Methodist Church congregation was founded in 1778. It was a time when the American colonies were asserting their independence and turning toward the church, especially the Methodist Church. There were many traveling evangelists at the time, and Benjamin Abbott was one of them. He was a wild character until he had a conversion experience at the age of 40. He helped to establish the Methodist faith in Port Elizabeth and many other parts of New Jersey. Initially, meetings were held outdoors or in homes depending on the weather. The first church was built on land bought from Elizabeth Bodly. The first house of worship was a wooden building. The brick church pictured here was constructed between 1827 and 1830 and still stands today. (Courtesy of E. Kellet and the Maurice River Township Heritage Society.)

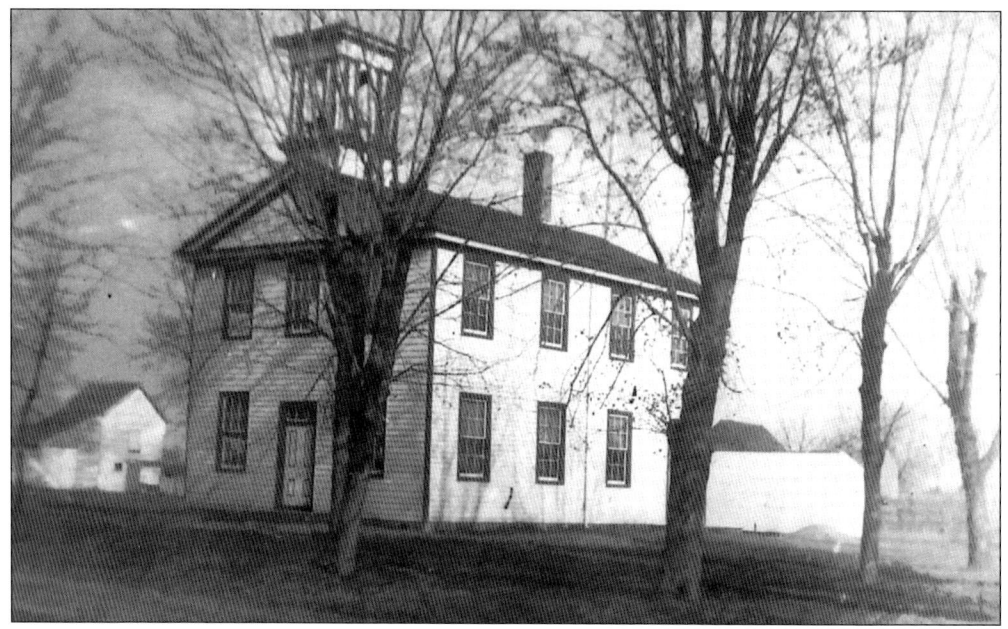

This is a picture of the Port Elizabeth School. It is not known when the first school was established, but it is believed that there was a schoolhouse at Board Landing on Manumuskin Creek near the Eagle Glassworks prior to March 1783. In *A History of Port Elizabeth*, F.W. Bowen writes that it was mentioned on a deed at that time. Later, Elizabeth Bodly deeded land for a one-story schoolhouse in 1798. A second story was added in 1810 so that it could be used as a Masonic lodge. (Courtesy of E. Kellet and the Maurice River Township Heritage Society.)

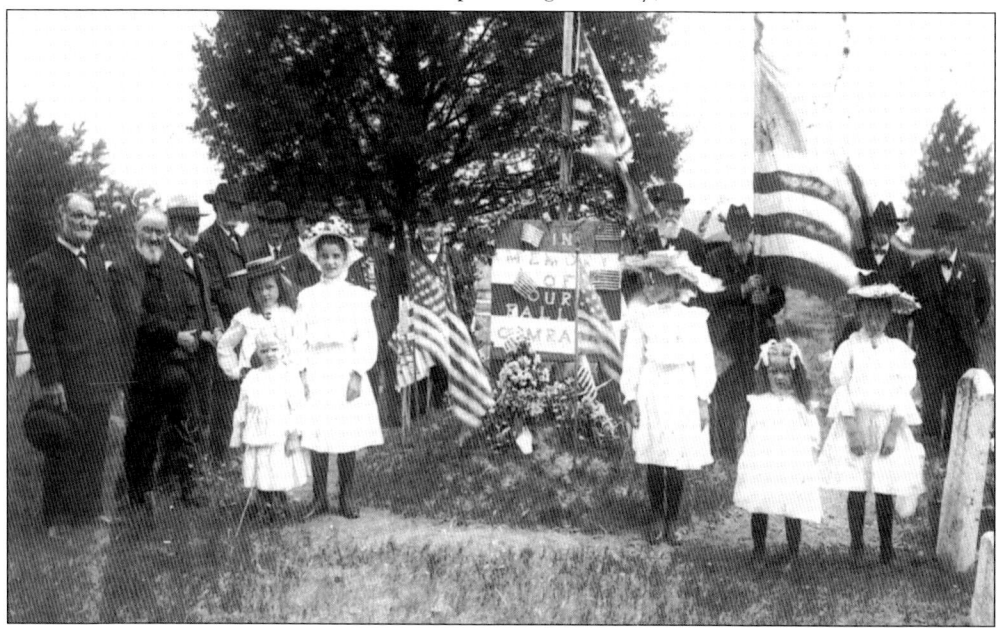

This is the Port Elizabeth Methodist Church Cemetery on the Fourth of July in 1906. The second man on the left is Benajah Peters Thompson Jr. The little girl standing in front of him is his daughter Helen, who was six years old. (Courtesy of E. Kellet and the Maurice River Township Heritage Society.)

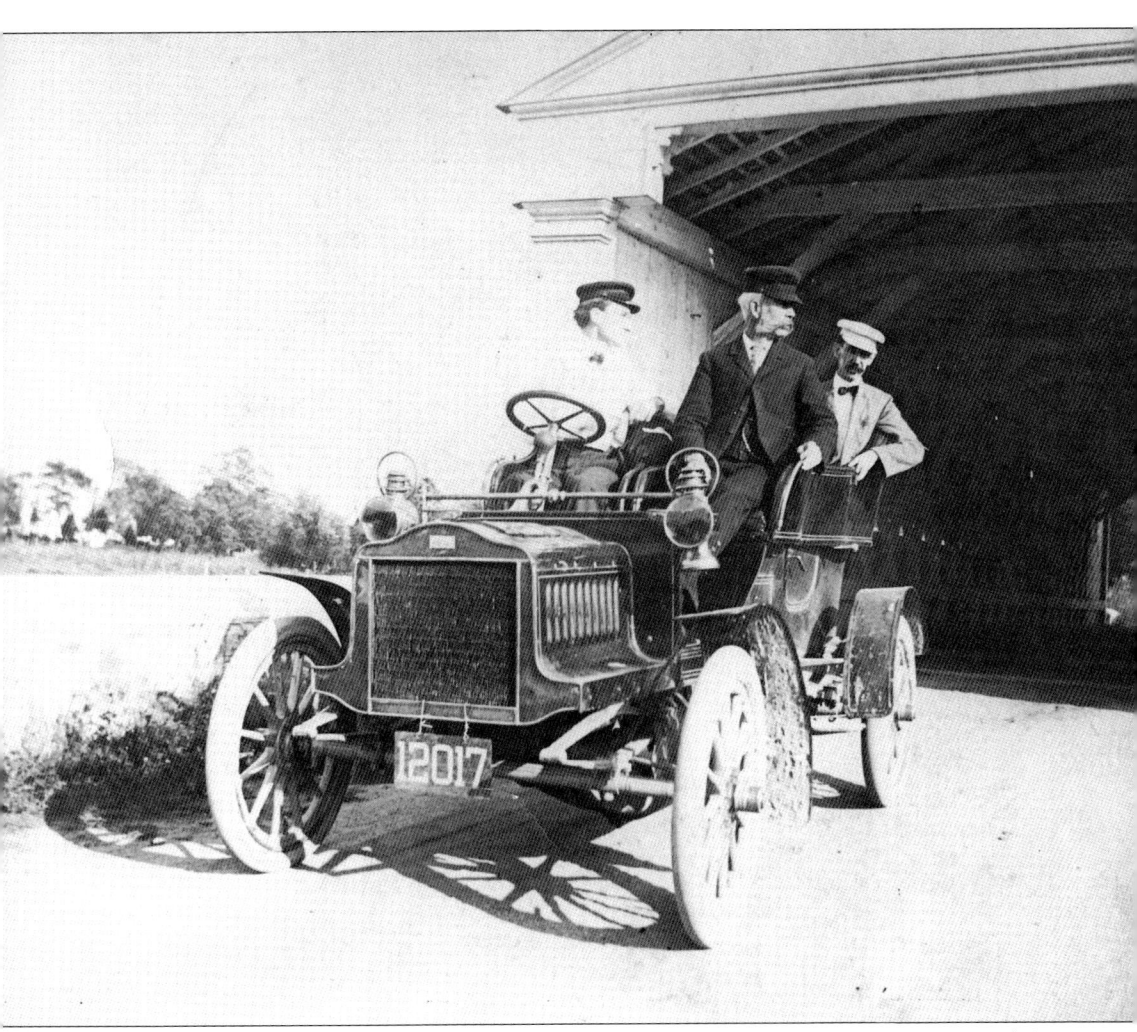

This c. 1907 photograph shows the covered bridge in Port Elizabeth along with an early automobile and its three well-dressed passengers. There is a glimpse of homes across Manumuskin Creek. (Courtesy of Vic Ballato.)

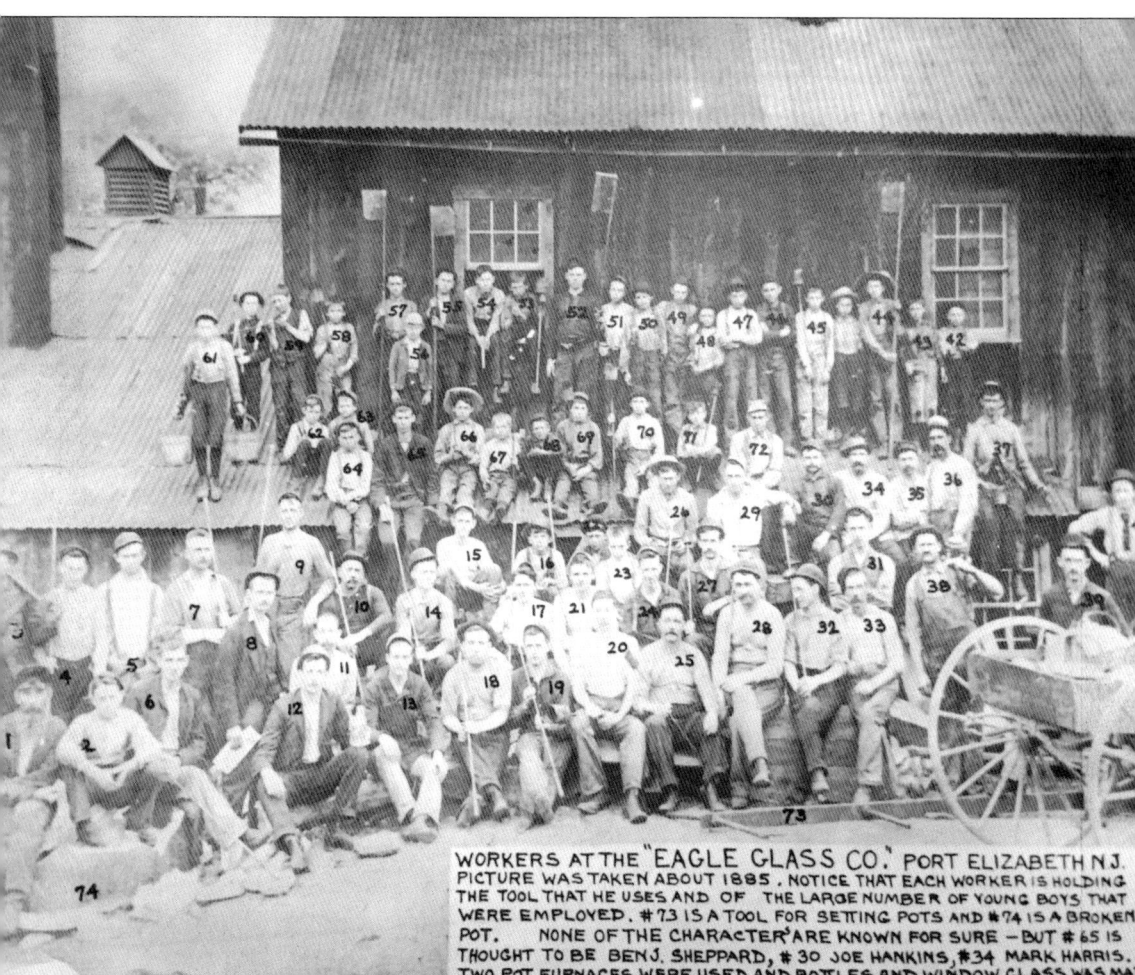

WORKERS AT THE "EAGLE GLASS CO." PORT ELIZABETH N.J. PICTURE WAS TAKEN ABOUT 1885. NOTICE THAT EACH WORKER IS HOLDING THE TOOL THAT HE USES AND OF THE LARGE NUMBER OF YOUNG BOYS THAT WERE EMPLOYED. #73 IS A TOOL FOR SETTING POTS AND #74 IS A BROKEN POT. NONE OF THE CHARACTERS ARE KNOWN FOR SURE — BUT #65 IS THOUGHT TO BE BEN J. SHEPPARD, #30 JOE HANKINS, #34 MARK HARRIS. TWO POT FURNACES WERE USED AND BOTTLES AND WINDOW GLASS WAS MA

The Eagle Glass Company factories were built and established by James Lee around 1799. It was considered one of the largest producers of window glass made by the cylinder method in the state at the time. This picture had a notation on it that stated that it was taken around 1885. However, in *Maurice River Town*, Herbert Vanaman noted that this facility was idle after 1884. Each worker is holding some type of tool that he used in his job. Note the large number of young boys who were employed at the time. While not certain, it is believed that No. 65 is Ben J. Sheppard, No. 30 is Joseph Hankins, and No. 34 is Mark Harris, all local men. Two pot furnaces were used at this facility, and bottles and window glass were made at the time. (Courtesy of the Maurice River Township Heritage Society.)

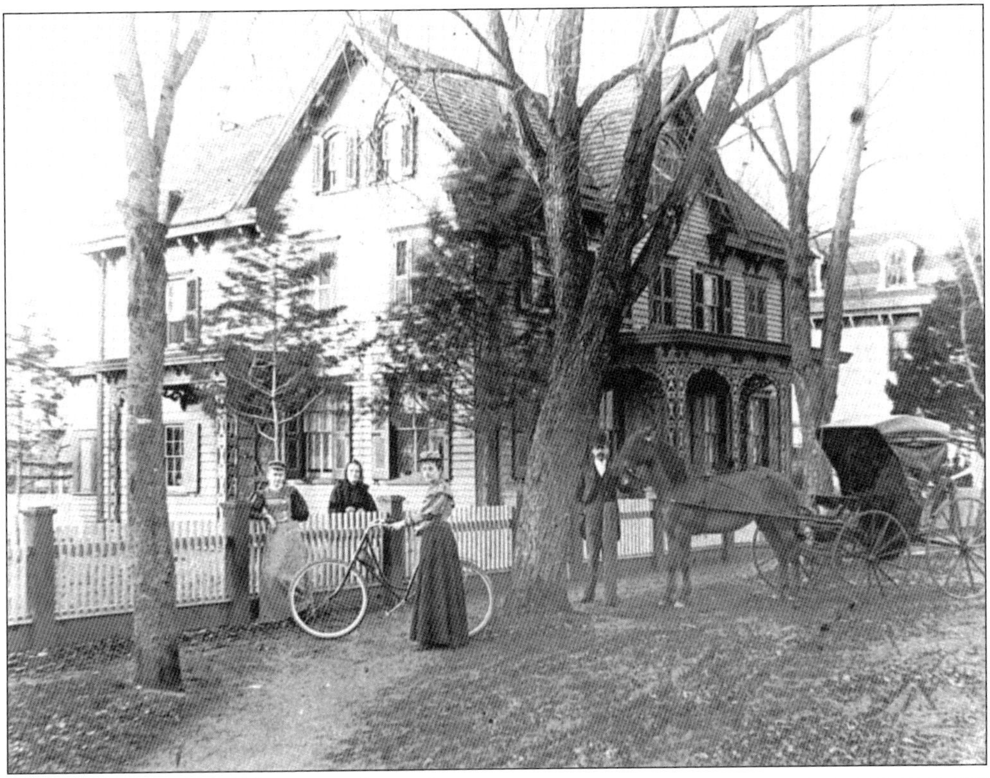

The C.B. Ogden family home was located on Quaker Street in Port Elizabeth. In this photograph is a well-dressed, well-to-do family standing in front of their large Victorian-style home. Their modes of transportation in the late 1800s included a bicycle and a horse-drawn carriage. (Courtesy of E. Kellet and the Maurice River Township Heritage Society.)

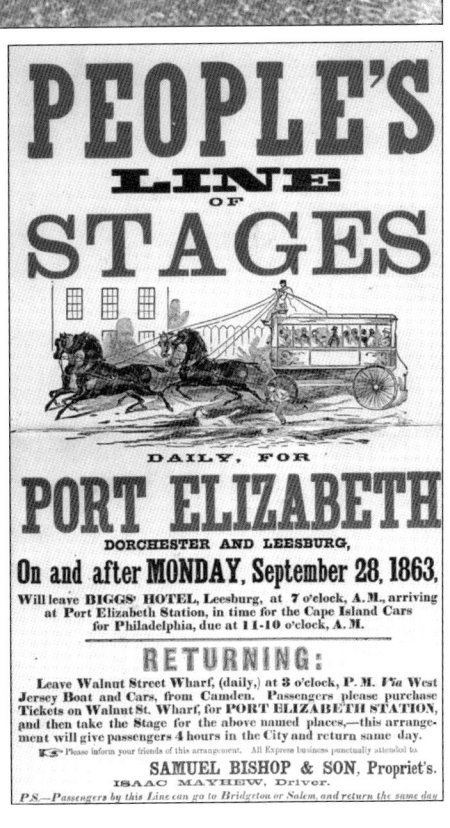

This People's Line poster advertises the schedule for stagecoach transportation after September 28, 1863. Patrons of the Biggs Hotel on the corner of Main and Broad Streets in Leesburg could catch a stagecoach for Port Elizabeth at 7:00 a.m. The driver at the time was Isaac Mayhew. (Courtesy of Drew Tomlin.)

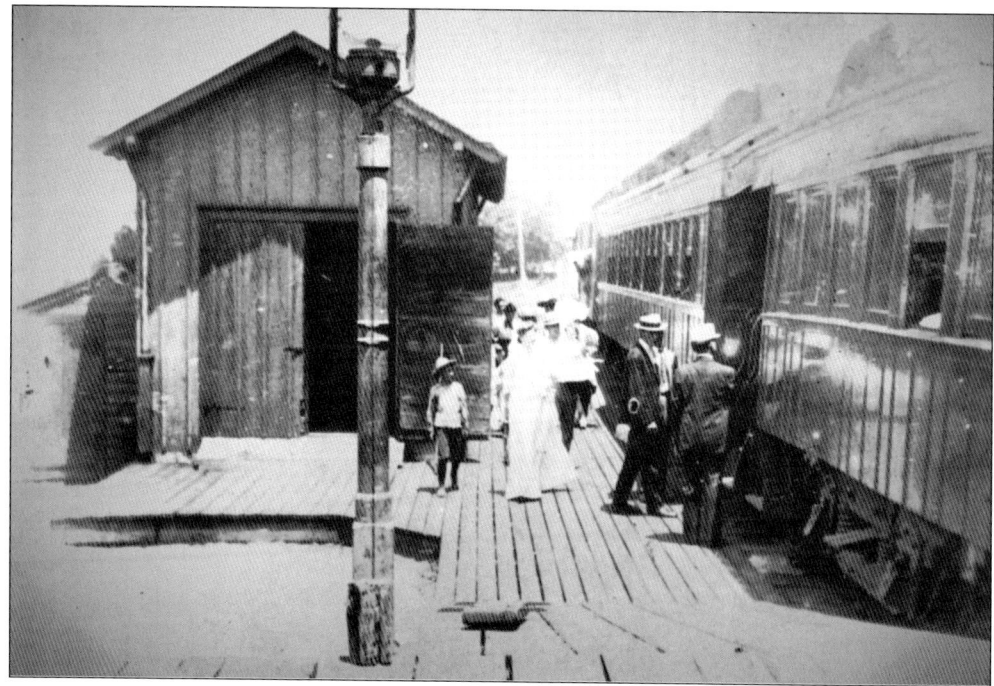

This is a view of the West Jersey Railroad station in Port Elizabeth. The men and women are well dressed, with the men wearing suits and hats and the women in long, flowing dresses. A young child can be seen on the left in what was probably play clothes and a hat. During the height of the railroad business in the late 1800s and early 1900s, there was good service with four trains in and out of the various stations that dotted the villages. (Courtesy of the Maurice River Township Heritage Society.)

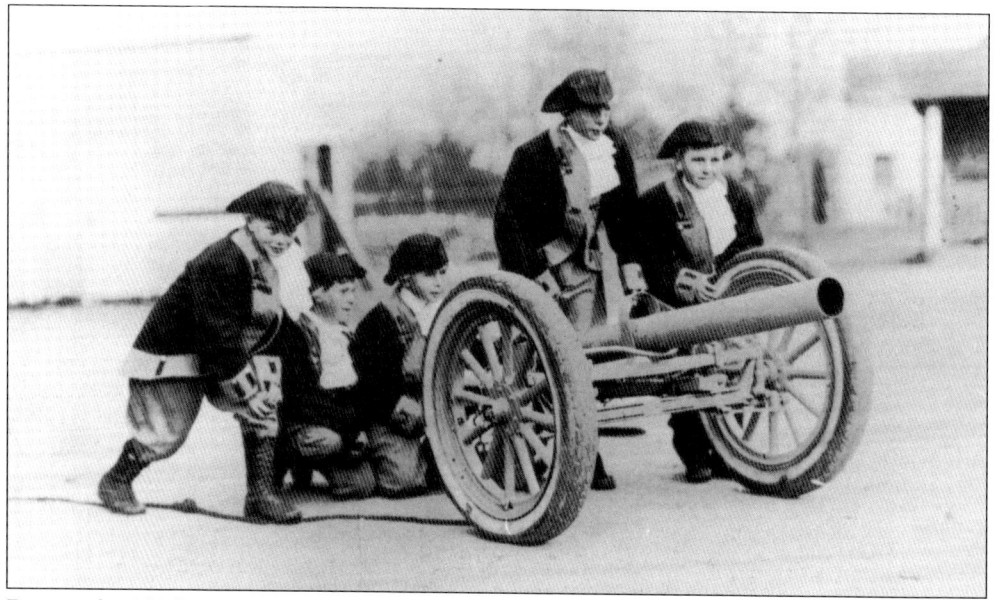

During the 150th anniversary celebration of the founding of Port Elizabeth in 1935, these five young boys dressed in Revolutionary War uniforms and manned a "cannon." (Courtesy of E. Kellet and the Maurice River Township Heritage Society.)

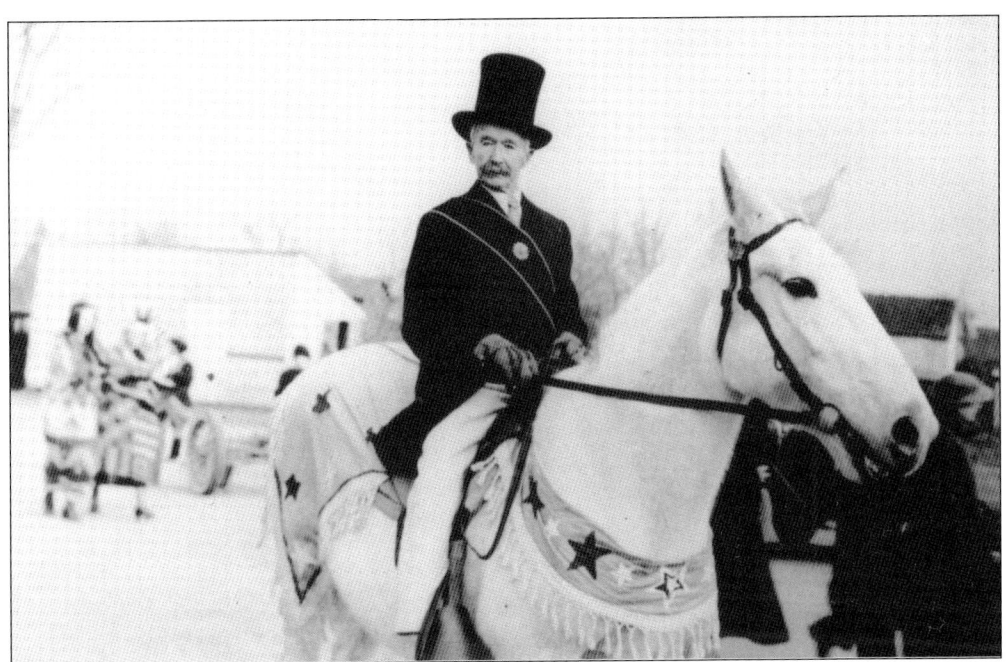

This regal-looking gentleman, wearing a top hat, sits astride his beautiful horse in the parade in Port Elizabeth to celebrate the town's 150th anniversary in 1935. (Courtesy of the Maurice River Township Heritage Society.)

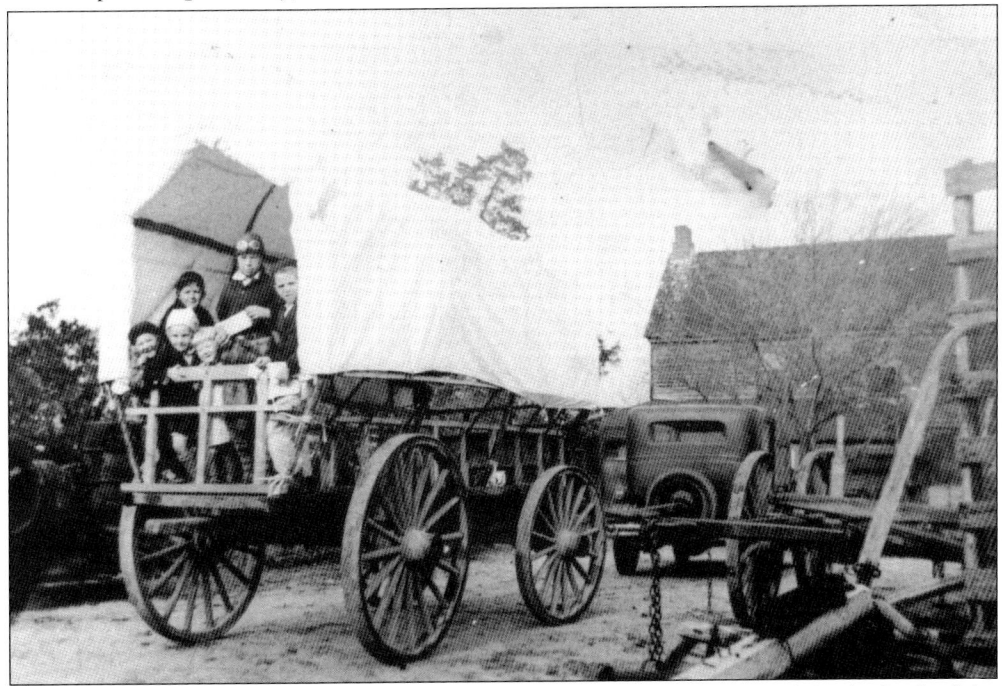

This covered wagon was part of Port Elizabeth's anniversary parade in 1935. In the back of the wagon are Edith Beebe Reeves and Elmer and Naomi Chard with other family members. Note that this wagon is being pulled by an automobile instead of a team of horses. (Courtesy of E. Kellet and the Maurice River Township Heritage Society.)

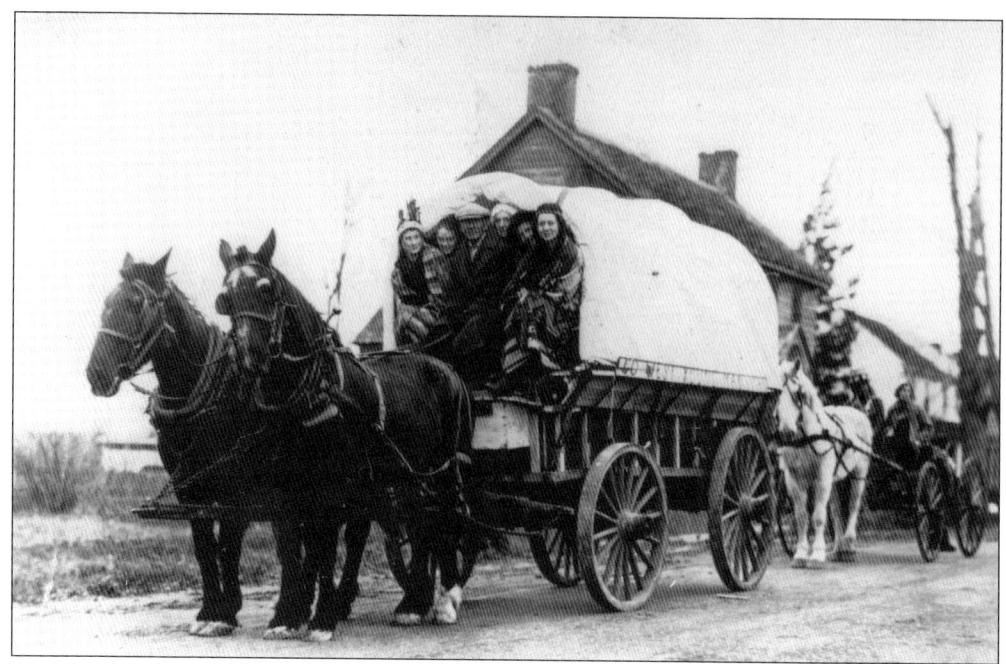

This is another covered wagon featured in the 150th anniversary celebration of Port Elizabeth. It appears as if most of the townspeople took part in this parade. Note the elegant wooden homes in the background. This type of parade took place on the 100th and 150th anniversaries of the town. (Courtesy of E. Kellet and the Maurice River Township Heritage Society.)

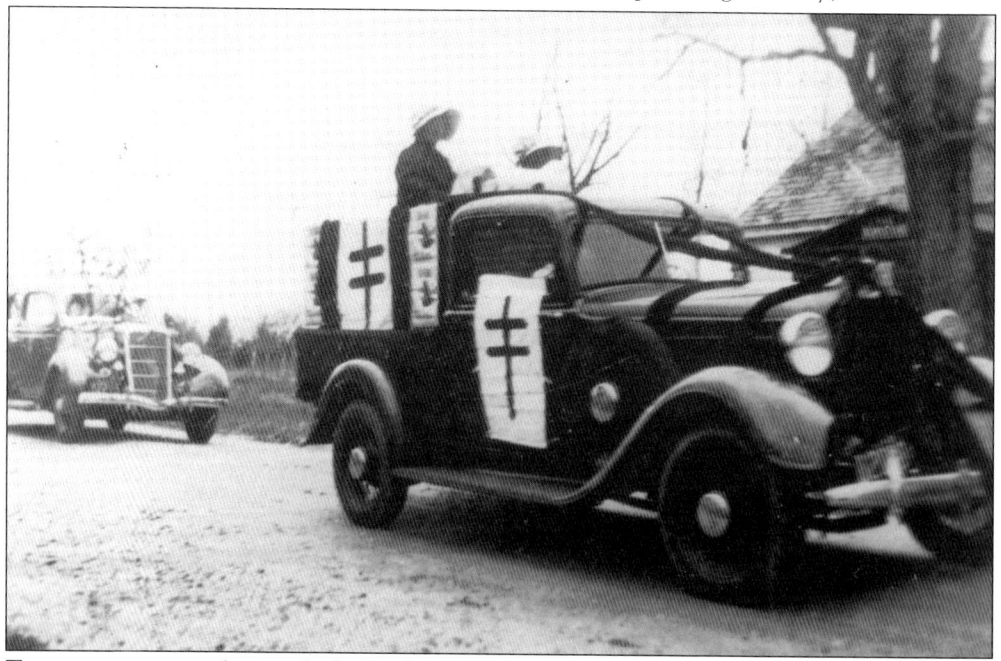

Two women are standing in the back of a vintage truck in Port Elizabeth's anniversary parade in 1935. The symbol on the side of the truck is believed to be the Cross of Lorraine, a Freemason symbol. It was a time of great celebration recognizing Port Elizabeth's role in history and commerce. (Courtesy of the Maurice River Township Heritage Society.)

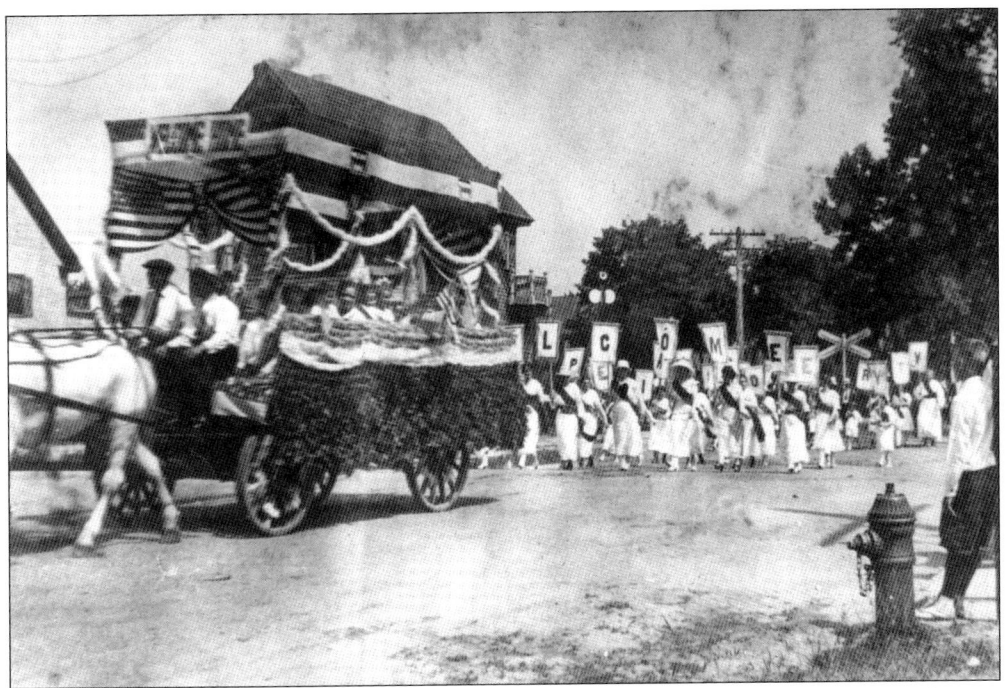

In this photograph of the 150th anniversary parade of Port Elizabeth, a group of ladies is following an early version of a float; note the "Welcome Home" sign on the horse-drawn wagon. The women walking are holding letters that spell "Welcome." (Courtesy of E. Kellet and the Maurice River Township Heritage Society.)

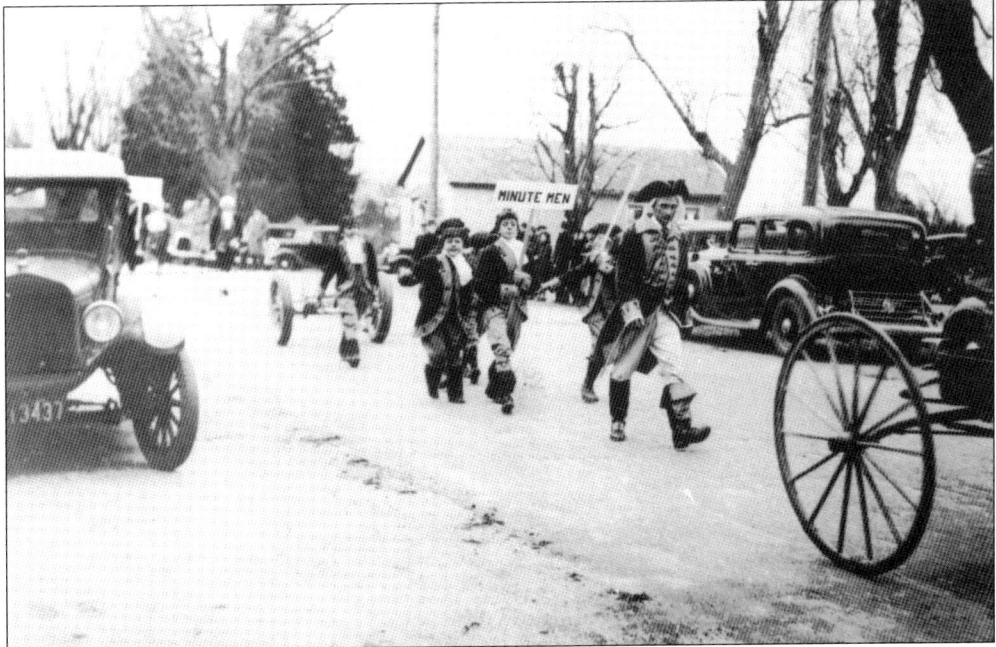

Pictured partaking in the 150th anniversary of Port Elizabeth in 1935 are young boys dressed in Revolutionary War uniforms, marching and carrying a "Minute Men" sign. (Courtesy of E. Kellet and the Maurice River Township Heritage Society.)

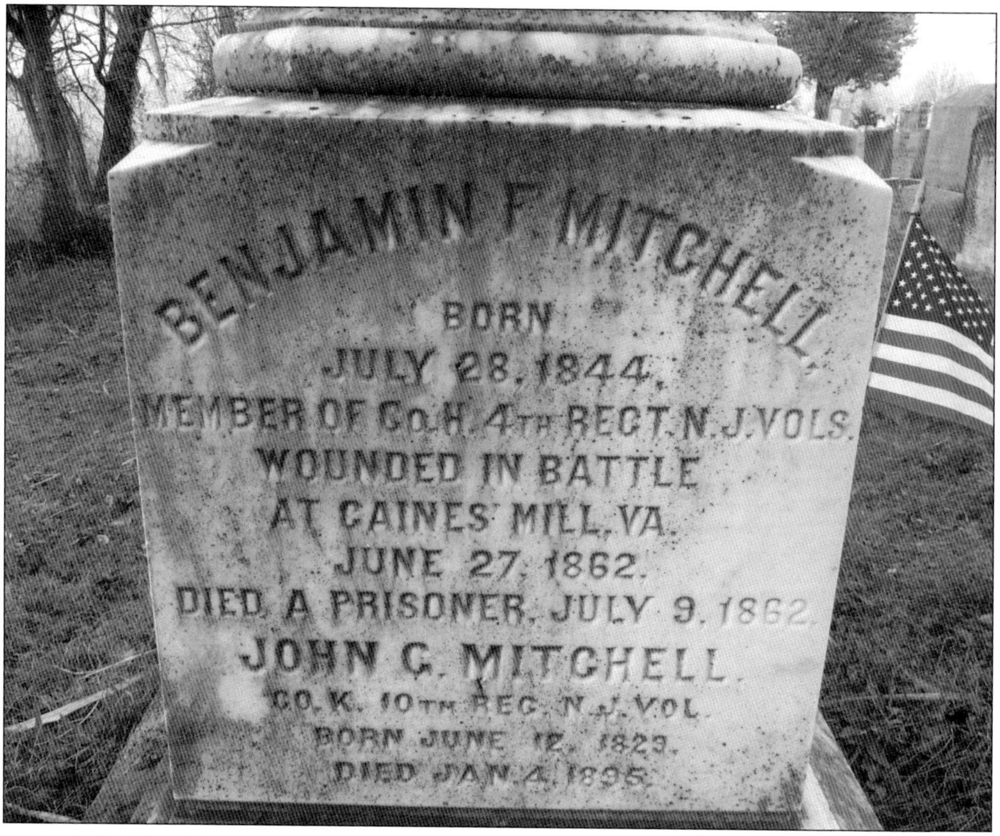

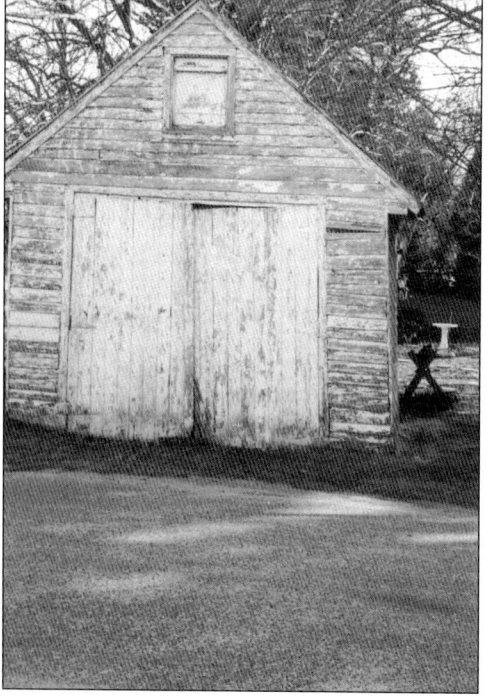

Benjamin Mitchell was one of four young men from Maurice River Township who fought in the Civil War. He was wounded in the Battle of Gaines's Mill and died two weeks later in a Confederate prison in Virginia. There is a memorial in the cemetery at Port Elizabeth Methodist Cemetery honoring him and three other Mitchells: William, Richard, and John. (Author's collection.)

The Casket House is located at the corner of Stable Lane and Second Street. Second Street is now known as Port Elizabeth–Cumberland Road. This building was where caskets were built and stored until needed. (Courtesy of the Maurice River Township Heritage Society.)

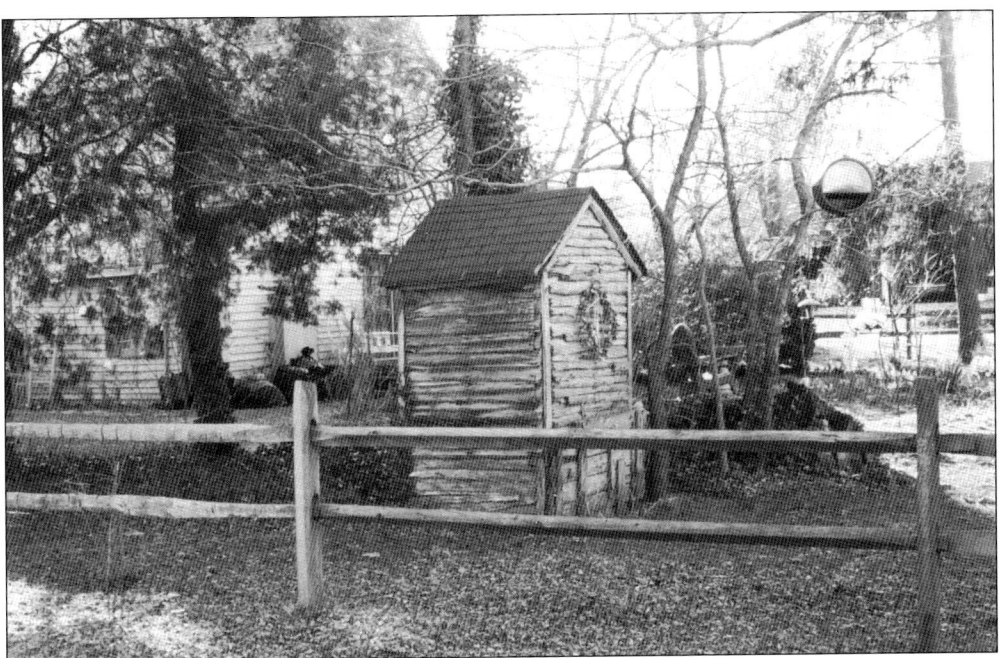

The Casket House in Port Elizabeth was once an active place of business and a well-known landmark. Seen here is the old outhouse, which was located behind the building. People of the early 1900s did not have the advantage of indoor plumbing. (Courtesy of the Maurice River Township Heritage Society.)

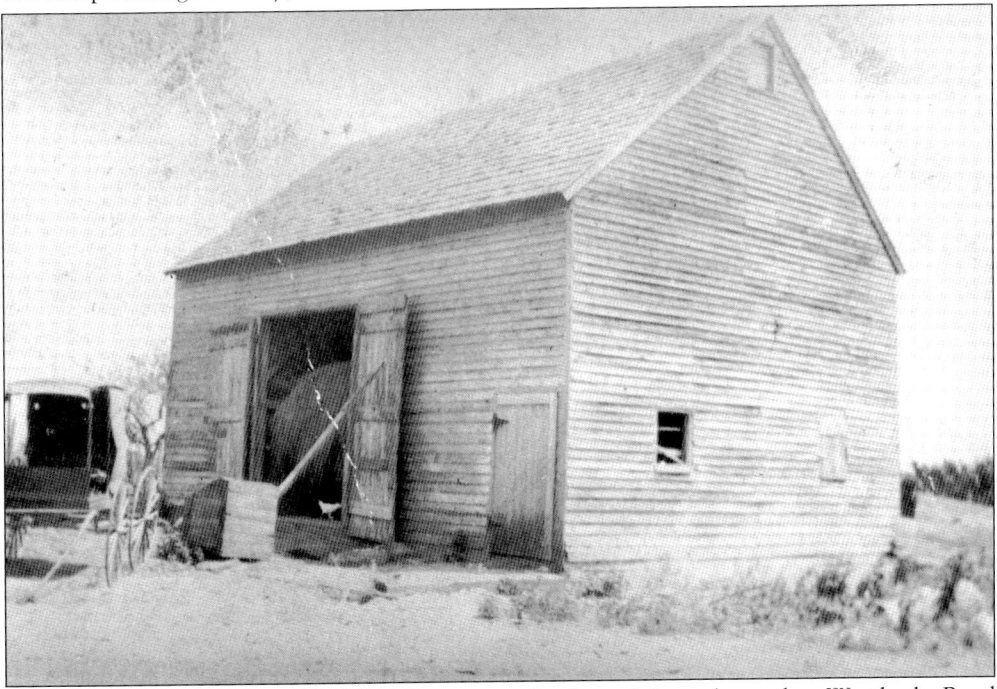

The Bennett barn was an old building that was made of wood. It was located on Weatherby Road in Port Elizabeth. It has since been torn down. (Courtesy of E. Kellet and the Maurice River Township Heritage Society.)

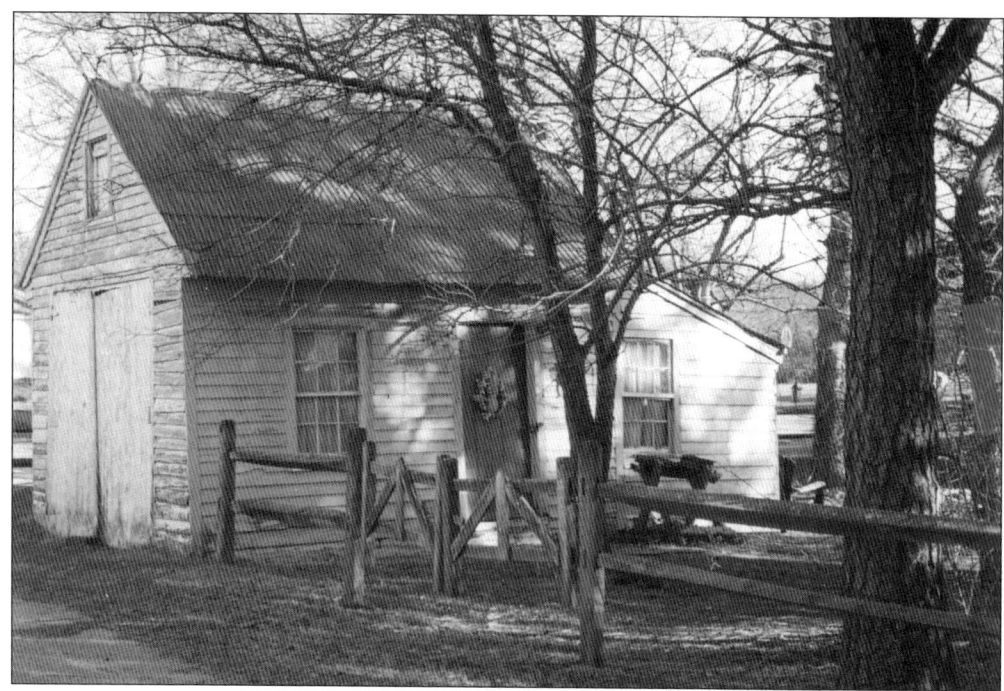

This photograph, taken from the Port Elizabeth–Cumberland Road (formerly Second Street), shows the former Casket House. While the building seems small by today's standards, it stored many caskets in the early 1900s. (Courtesy of the Maurice River Township Heritage Society.)

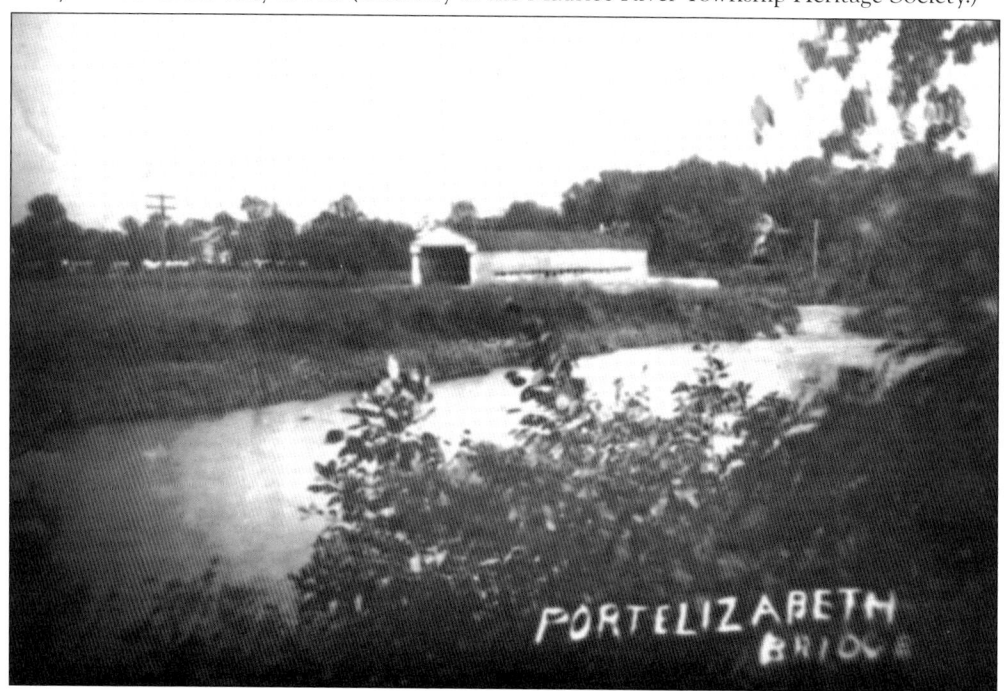

This real-photo postcard shows the length and size of the Port Elizabeth Bridge. Manumuskin Creek is in the foreground. Homes in the booming town of Port Elizabeth can be seen in the background. (Courtesy of Vic Ballato.)

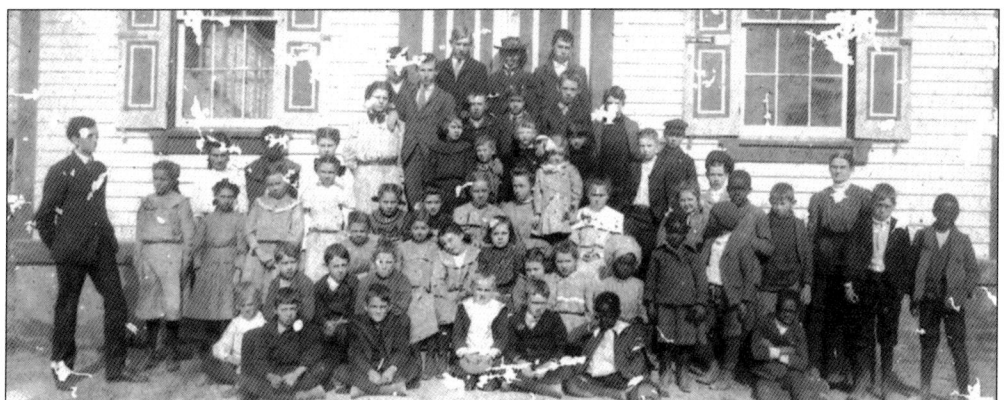

In 1906, children attended the two-story Port Elizabeth School. This group of children represents a wide range of ages. Note the long dress worn by the schoolteacher on the right. (Courtesy of E. Kellet and the Maurice River Township Heritage Society.)

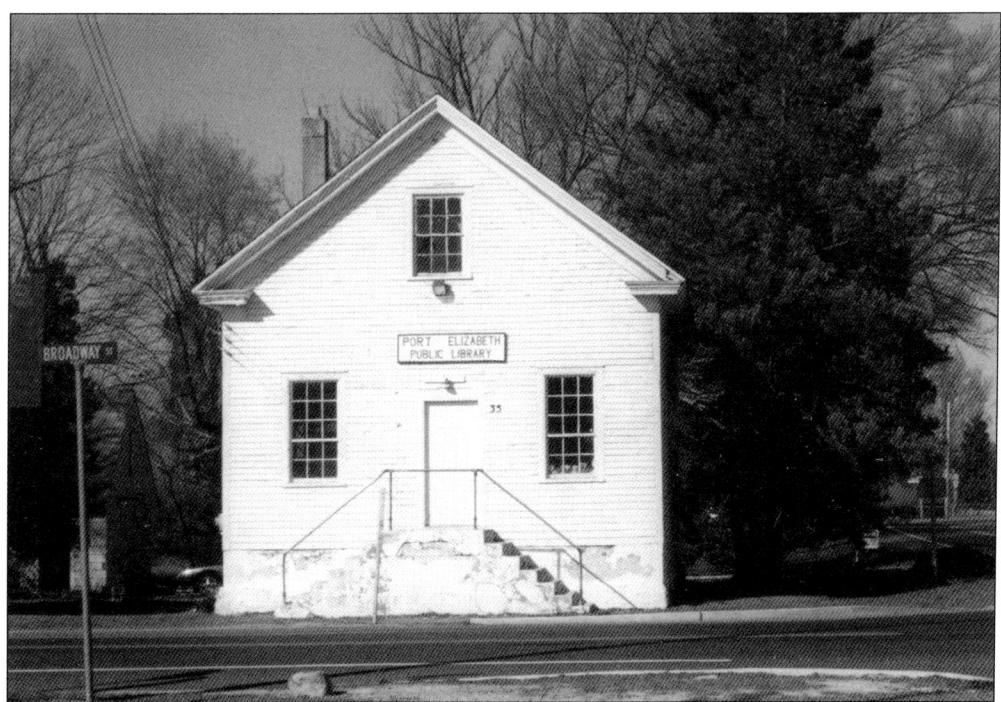

The Port Elizabeth Public Library is a local landmark. Dr. Benjamin Fisler constructed the building in 1810 to be his store, and around that same time, he built his office across the street. The building is currently leased and is being restored by the Maurice River Township Heritage Society. (Courtesy of E. Kellet and the Maurice River Township Heritage Society.)

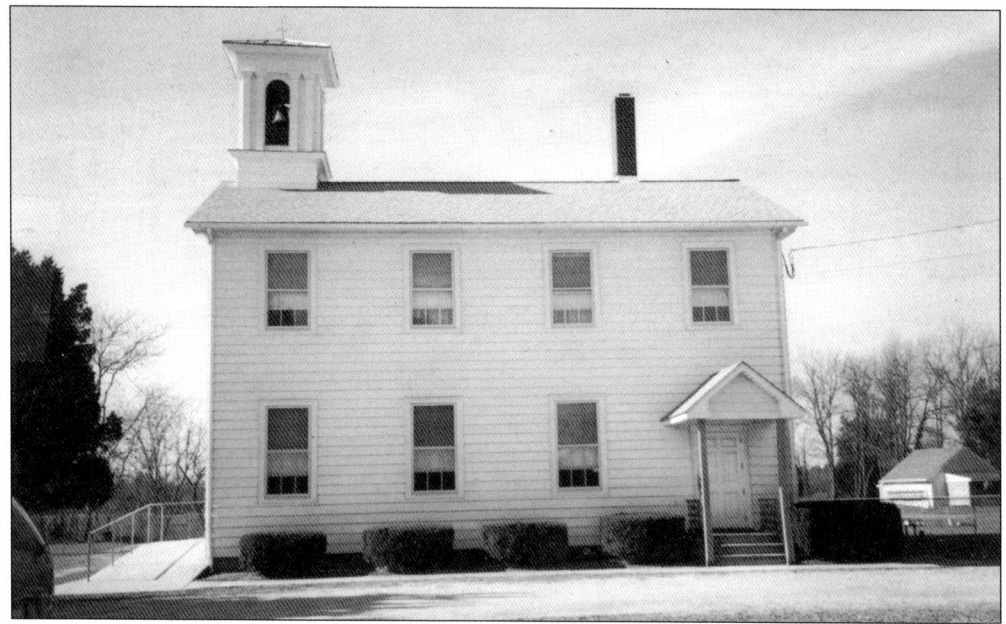

The Port Elizabeth School was built in 1854. When a new school was built in the 1950s, this one was moved alongside the Methodist church and named John Boggs Hall. John Boggs bought and donated the building to the church about 1952. The building now houses Sunday school. (Courtesy of E. Kellet and the Maurice River Township Heritage Society.)

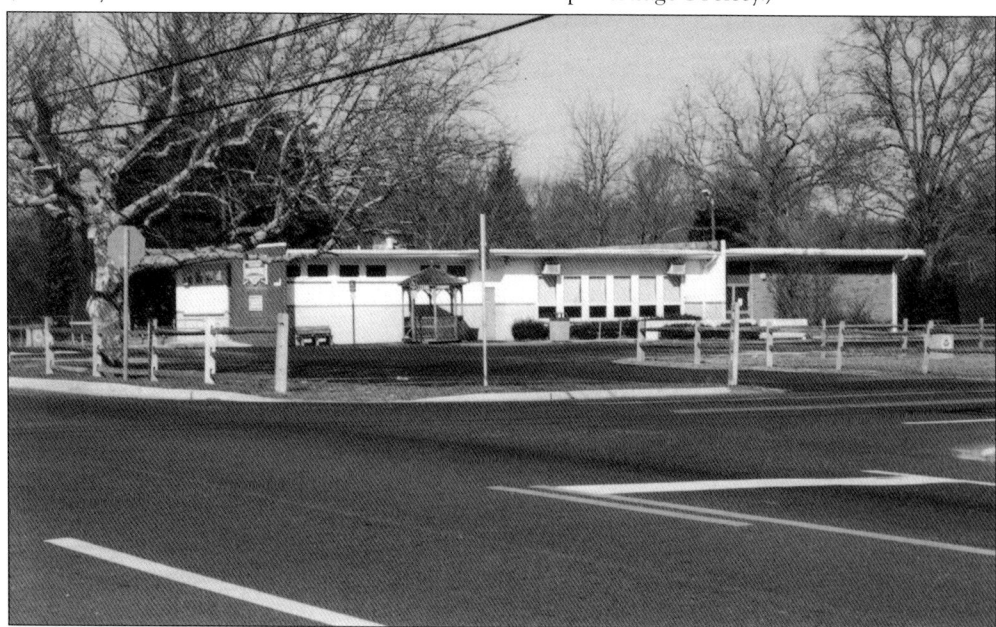

This is the school building that replaced the old Port Elizabeth School. It is located off Route 47. Port Elizabeth was celebrated at one time as one of the most important educational centers in the country. Port Elizabeth Academy, founded by prominent early settlers including Joshua Brick, Dr. Benjamin Fisler, and Thomas Lee, was called the most elaborate school in South Jersey. It was in operation until 1810, according to *Forgotten Towns of Southern New Jersey* by Henry Carlton Beck. (Courtesy of the Maurice River Township Heritage Society.)

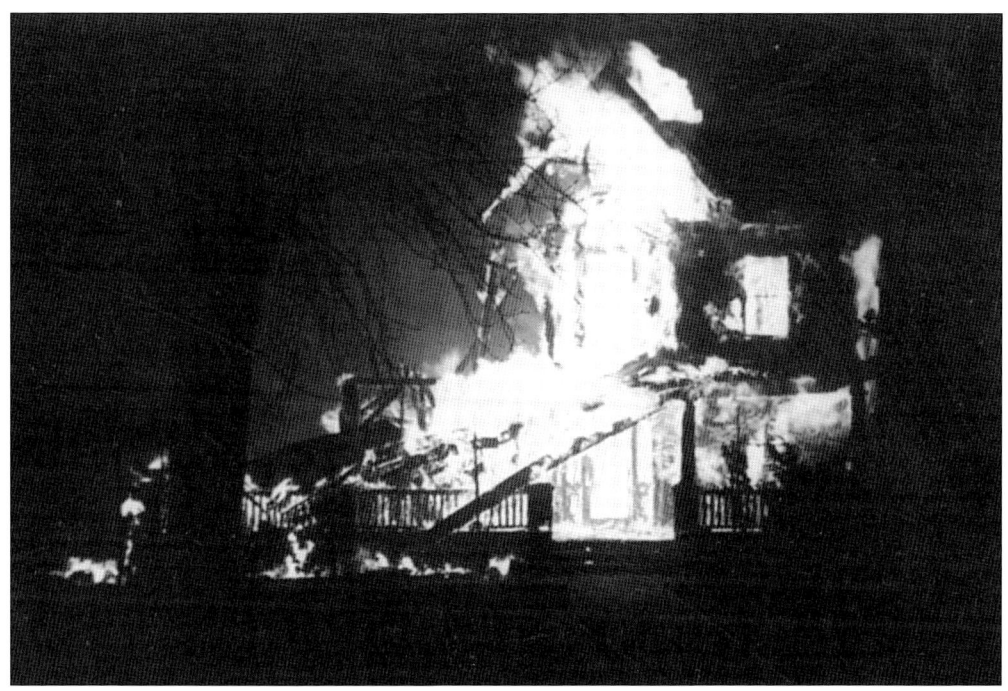

The Port Elizabeth Hotel is seen on fire in 1942. The hotel was also the home of the Heisler family. The old wooden buildings were essentially tinderboxes if they caught fire. The hotel was not rebuilt. (Both, courtesy of Drew Tomlin.)

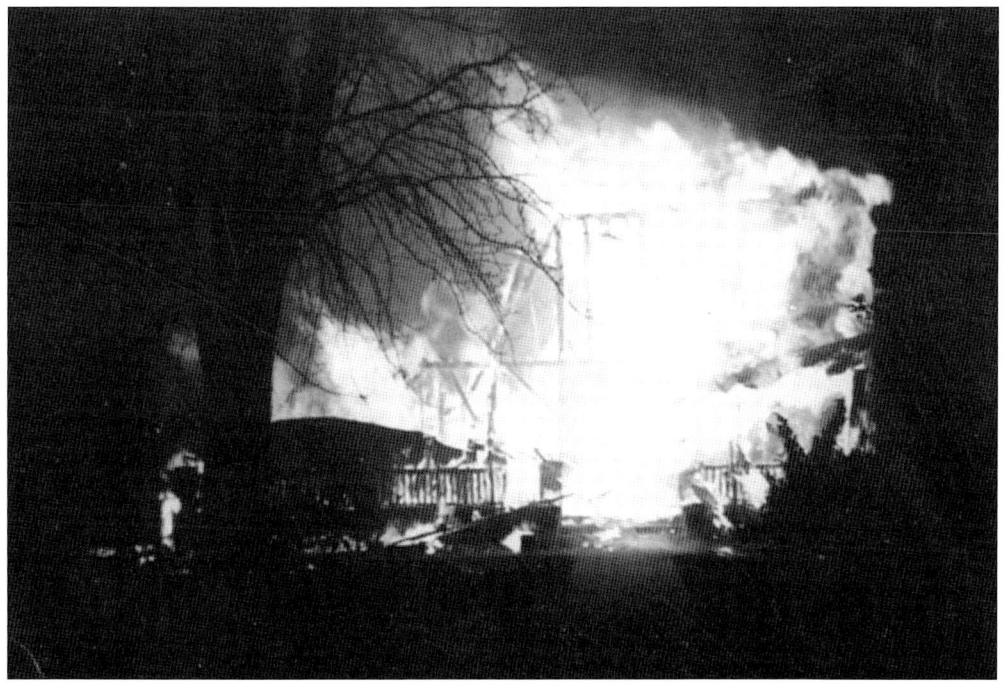

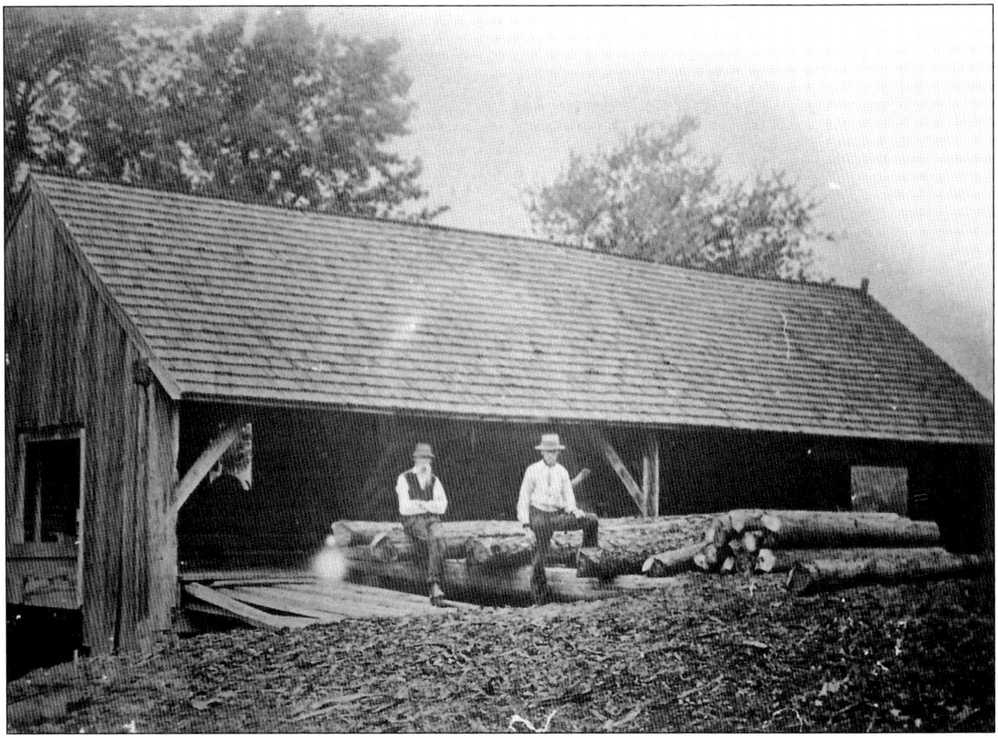

Seen here is Reeves Sawmill in Port Elizabeth. During its heyday in the early 1800s, Port Elizabeth shipped lumber from its ample pine barrens to large cities within and outside the state. Prior to the advent of coal for heating buildings, wood was used as fuel. (Courtesy of Drew Tomlin.)

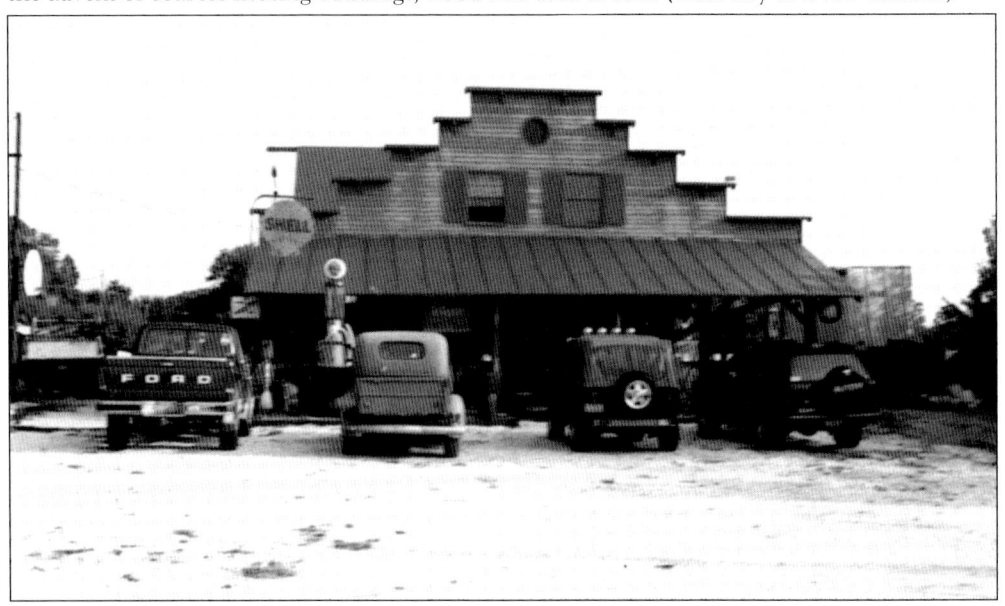

South Jersey Pickup Truck Company is located by the Port Elizabeth Bridge on Route 47. It has been in operation since 1989 and is owned by Vic Ballato. It is a well-known business in the region. Ballato and his family came to the area when they purchased a cottage at Thompsons Beach in 1975. (Courtesy of Vic Ballato.)

Two

Dorchester

Dorchester is a quaint village along the Maurice River. It is located about three miles south of the town of Port Elizabeth off Route 47. In records from the township's 1998 bicentennial, it is noted that in the year 1799, Peter Reeve bought the land that Dorchester now occupies from the West Jersey proprietors and divided portions and sold lots to individuals. In *Cumberland County New Jersey: 265 Years of History*, Charles Harrison reports that only three homes were located there at the time of the purchase.

Like its neighboring town of Leesburg, this place attracted men who were skilled craftsmen in the boatbuilding industry. In fact, shipbuilding was Dorchester's main industry for over a century. Methodist church records from the neighboring town of Leesburg recorded steamboats on the river between the two villages in 1879. One of the steamboats, named *Sarah K. Taggart*, offered river excursions for area residents in 1880. Another steamer, *Jersey Blue*, took an excursion to the bay town of Fortesque that same year. Based on church documents, quite a few locals took that trip. A famous oyster vessel, the *A.J. Meerwald*, was built in 1928 at the Dorchester shipyard, which was then owned by Charles H. Stowman & Sons. This vessel was fully restored, thanks to the efforts of several persistent individuals, and is located at its current home port on the other side of the river at Bayshore Center at Bivalve.

Another landmark in town is the Dorchester Methodist Church, built in 1856 close to the river. It once had a very tall steeple that had to be replaced after it was struck by lightning in 1911. In 1905, there was a hotel in town on the corner of High and Main Streets known as Sickler's Hotel. J.R. Sickler was the proprietor of the facility. It was a popular location that catered to stagecoach and river travelers. In the 1800s and early 1900s, there was a variety of stores and services in Dorchester including Compton's General Store, the Dorchester shipyard of Charles H. Stowman & Sons, and a blacksmith livery.

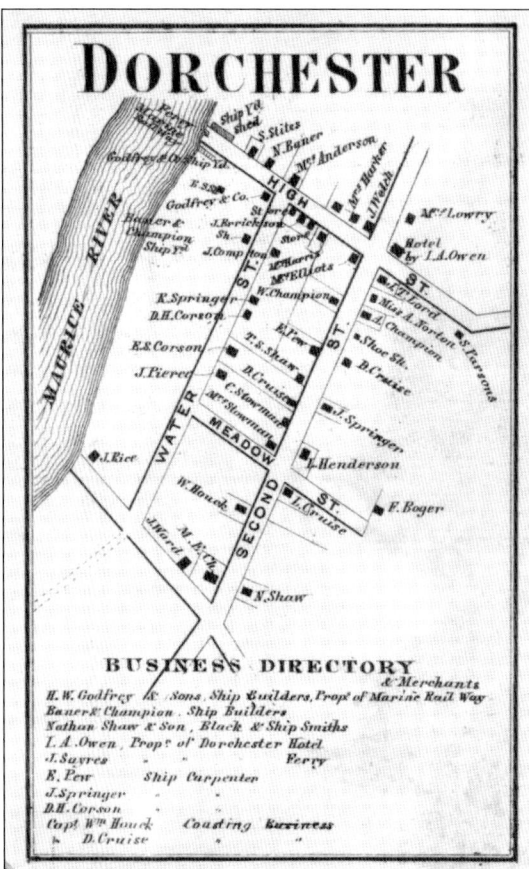

This is a business directory for the town of Dorchester in 1862. There were several businesses in addition to the shipbuilders, which were quite active. Some of these local businesses included a hotel, ferry, and carpentry and blacksmith shops. (Courtesy of Library of Congress.)

This cannonball is believed to have been made in the 1600s. Its egg-like shape, three-inch diameter, and solid metal construction meet the criteria for early Dutch manufacturers. One of the local legends is that this cannonball may have been fired during the battle when the Dutch ship *Prince Maurice* was burned and sunk by local Indians. (Courtesy of J. Roy Oliver.)

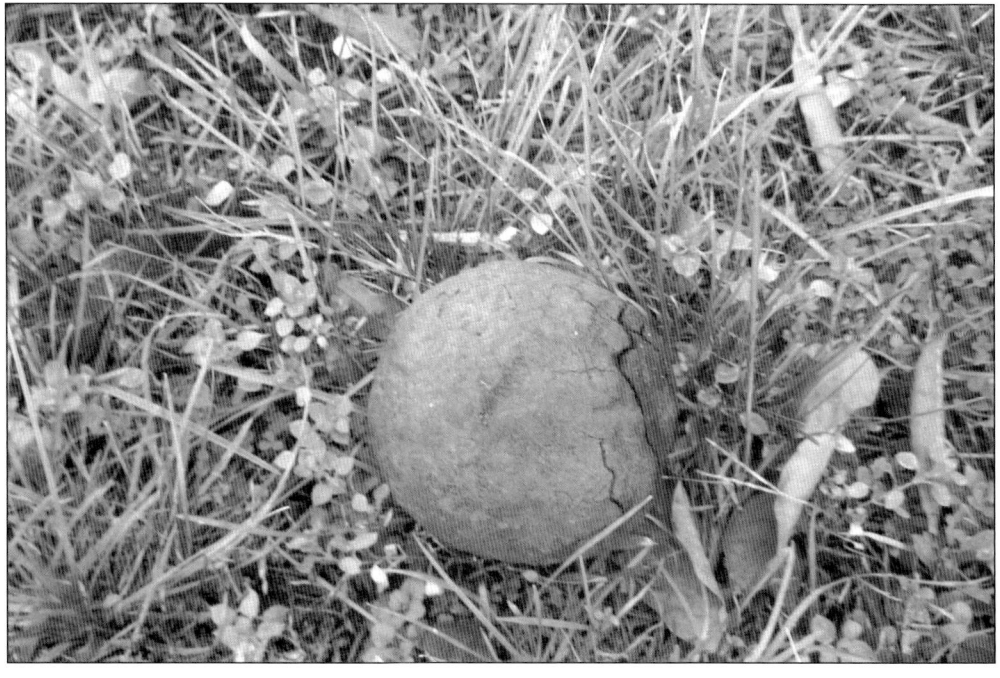

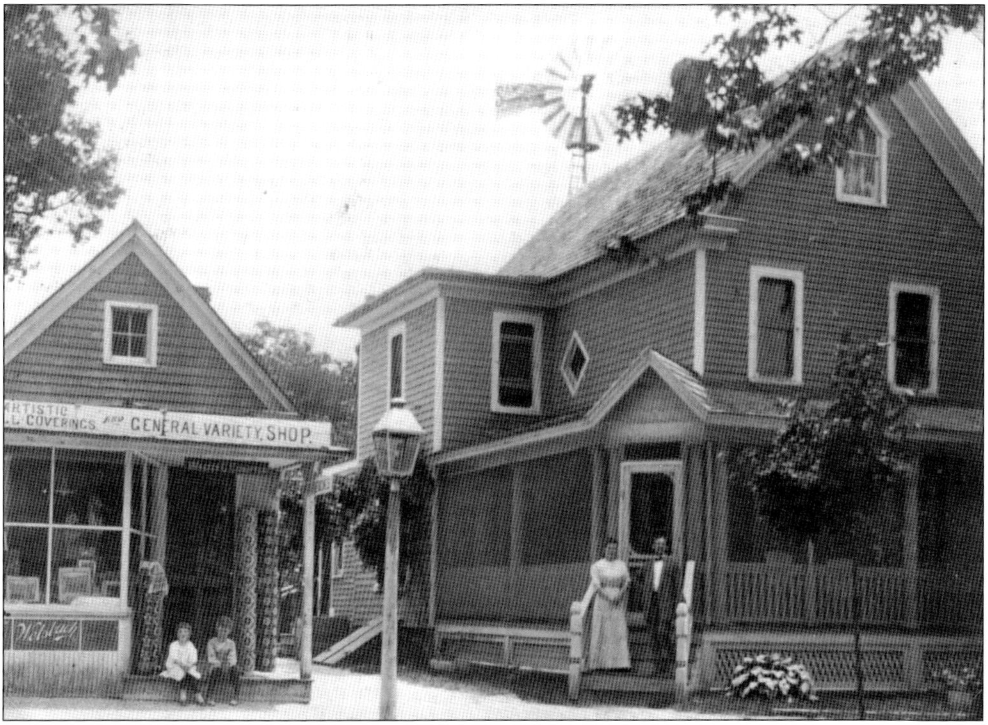

Pictured more than 100 years ago are Walter and Anna Compton's Dorchester home and store. The Comptons sold wall coverings, carpets, and a variety of other household goods. Note the rolled-up rugs on the front porch of the General Variety Shop, and the American flags in the front window display. The two children are Carrie Compton Sooy and Walton Stowman. Behind the Comptons' home is a windmill. After the store closed, it became a post office, and in the 1960s, the building was moved to the village of Smithville. (Courtesy of Bob Legg.)

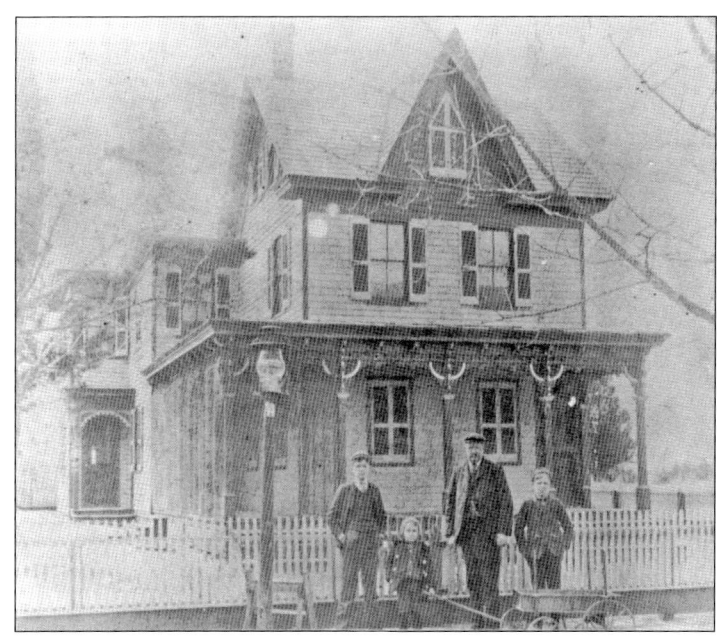

This is the former home of Capt. Lewis Steelman, the father of George, Leslie, Harry, and Bessie (Dubois). The older man in the photograph is Captain Steelman. His three sons are believed to be pictured with him. Note the wagon. The home is located on Church Street in Dorchester. Later, it was the home of Melvin and Kathryn Davis, and was then occupied by the Bruce Haley family. (Courtesy of Bob Legg.)

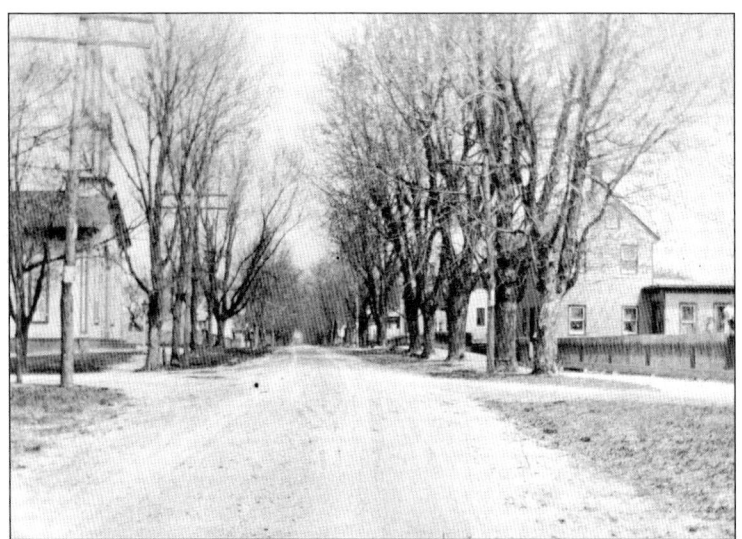

This photograph of Main Street in Dorchester looking north was taken before 1911. The house on the right was owned by Edwin Compton and was a funeral home at the time. The road was simply a well-worn dirt path. The Dorchester Methodist Church is on the left with its tall, pre–lightning strike steeple. (Courtesy of Bob Legg.)

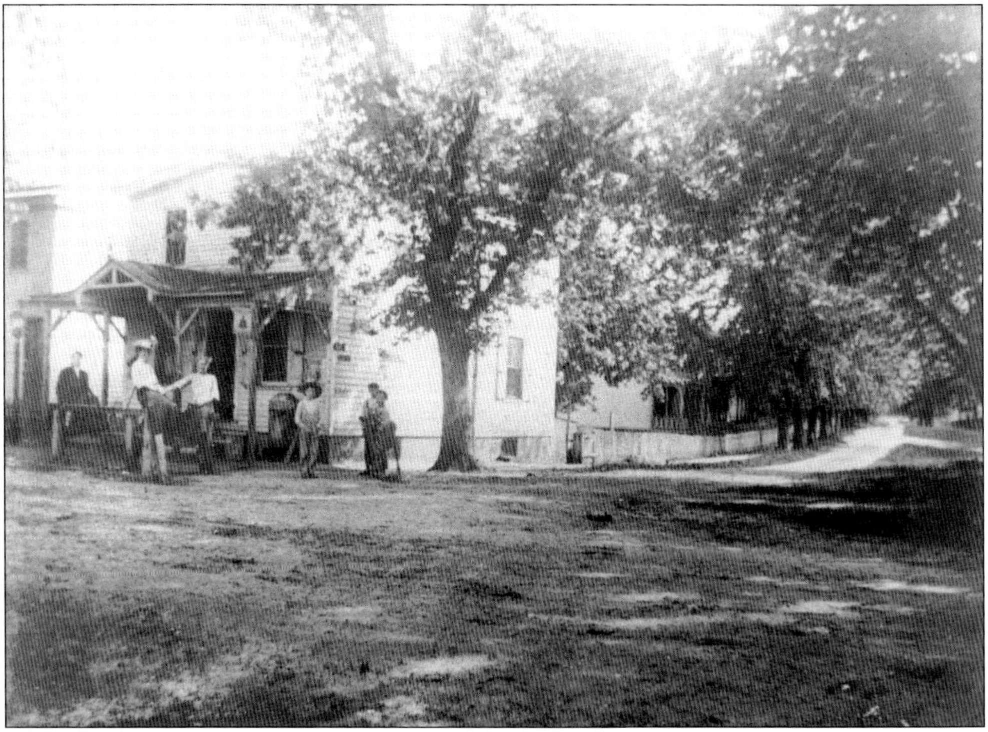

On the corner of Carlisle and Front Streets was a structure that, at the time of this photograph, was someone's home. In the late 1800s, it became a store that serviced the oystermen. Pictured are three adults on the front porch, one of them a stylish woman sitting on the rail. Three young lads also wanted to be a part of the photographic moment. Today, this home stands unoccupied, across the street from the home of the author's nephew Ronald Flynn. (Courtesy of Bob Legg.)

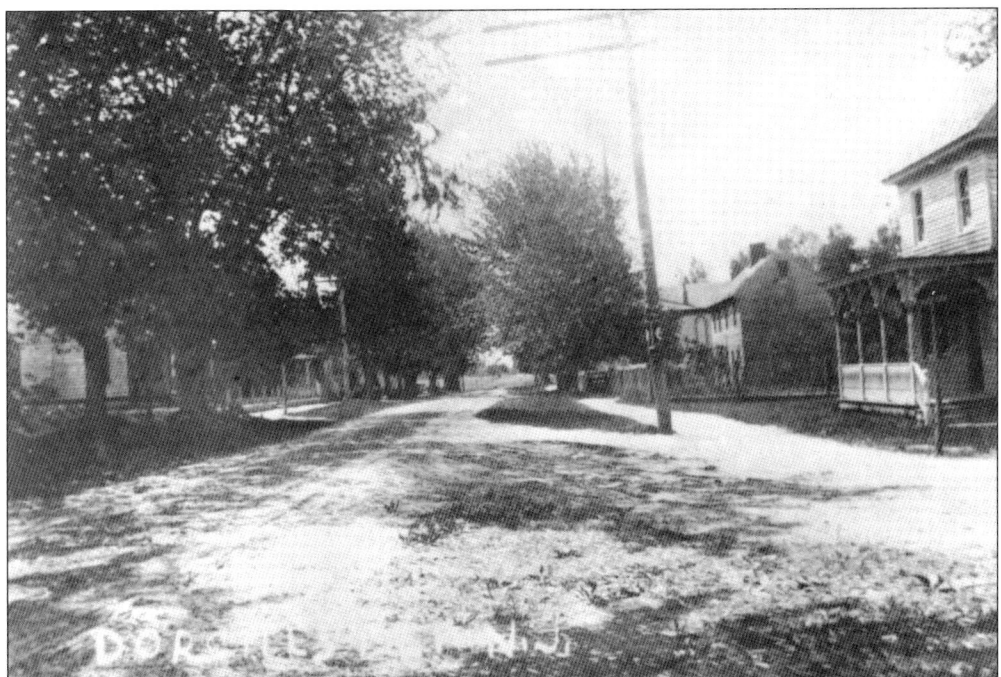

In 1906, this was Main Street in Dorchester looking south. When the photograph was taken, the first house on the right was owned by George Stowman, and the second on the right belonged to the William Jackson family. The houses on the left belonged to, from near to far, Lucius Cruise Walter C. Compton, George Shaw, Francis Pew, and Edwin Compton. (Courtesy of Bob Legg.)

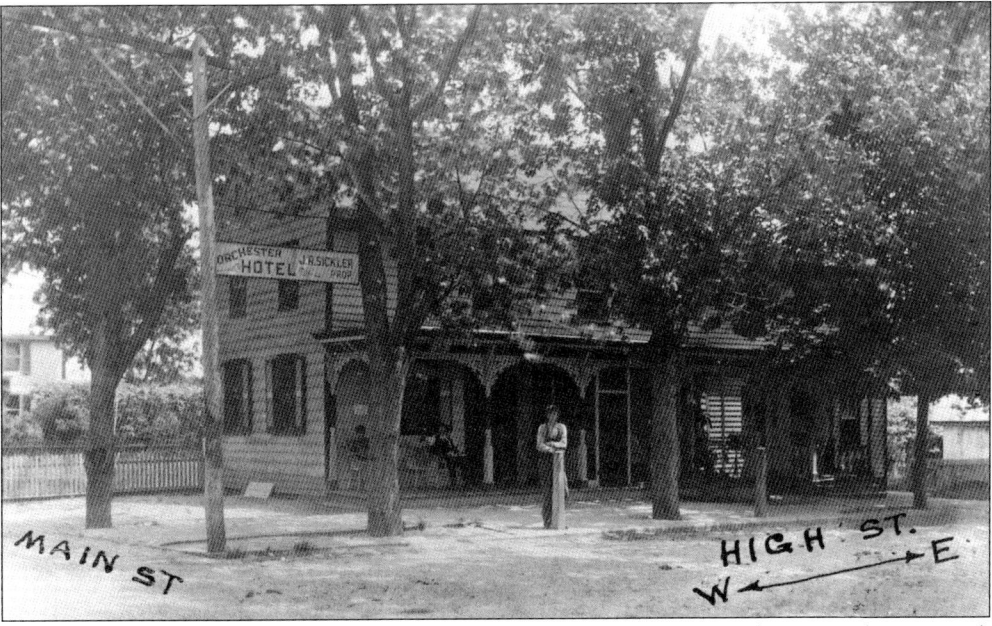

In 1905, Sickler's Hotel sat on the corner of High and Main Streets in Dorchester. In this postcard, the man standing in front of the establishment is suspected to be the proprietor, J.R. Sickler. This was a well-utilized establishment for people traveling through town. (Courtesy of the Maurice River Township Heritage Society.)

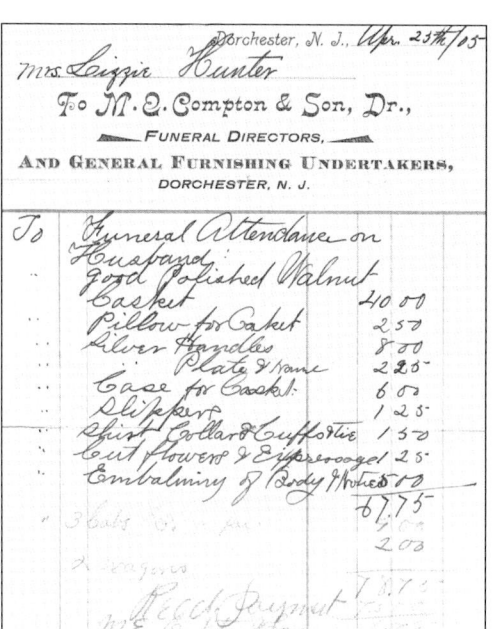

This itemized bill from the Compton funeral home in Dorchester from April 1905 totals less than $80, although that was probably a good deal of money at the time. The cause of death for Lizzie Hunter is not known. (Courtesy of Drew Tomlin.)

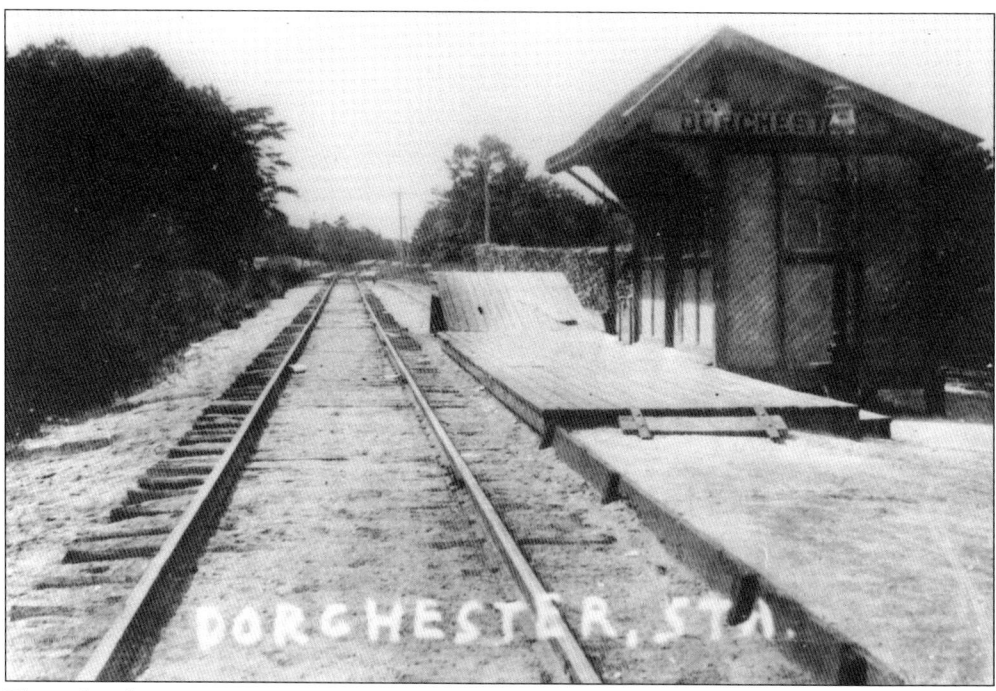

The railroad station was formerly located on High Street. Passenger trains used to come through town. The mail also arrived by train, and the postmaster had to go to the station to pick it up. The Maurice River Railroad was incorporated in 1887 and provided service from Manumuskin Creek to the Maurice River. Before completion, it was incorporated into the West Jersey Railroad, with four round trips per day. The service included passengers and freight when the oyster industry was thriving in the late 1800s. Train service continued into the 1950s in this area with less frequent service. Initially, there were agents at Mauricetown, Heislerville, and Maurice River. Dorchester was unmanned. (Courtesy of Bob Legg.)

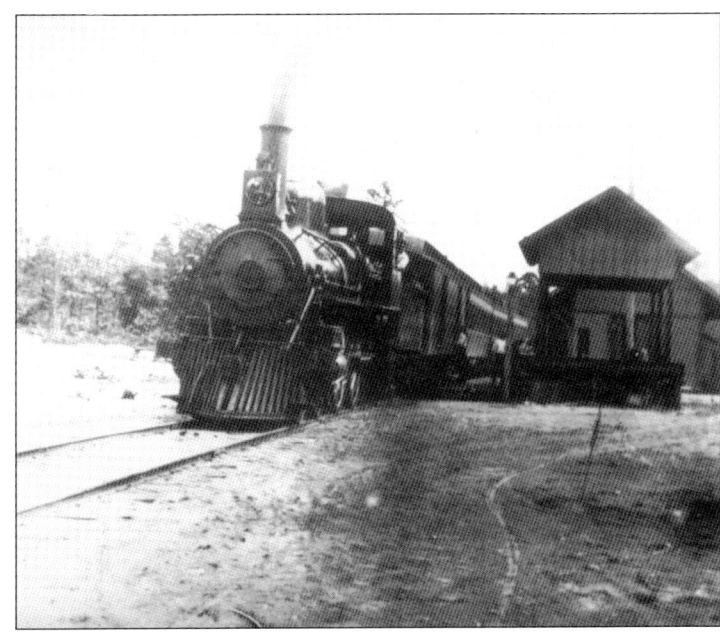

The Mauricetown station was located on the east bank of the Maurice River in Dorchester. This picture was taken in 1906. The trains, powered by steam engines, offered an alternative to horse-and-buggy travel. Local people could venture much farther from home in a shorter length of time. The world of individuals and families greatly expanded when train service began in the late 1800s. (Courtesy of the Maurice River Township Heritage Society.)

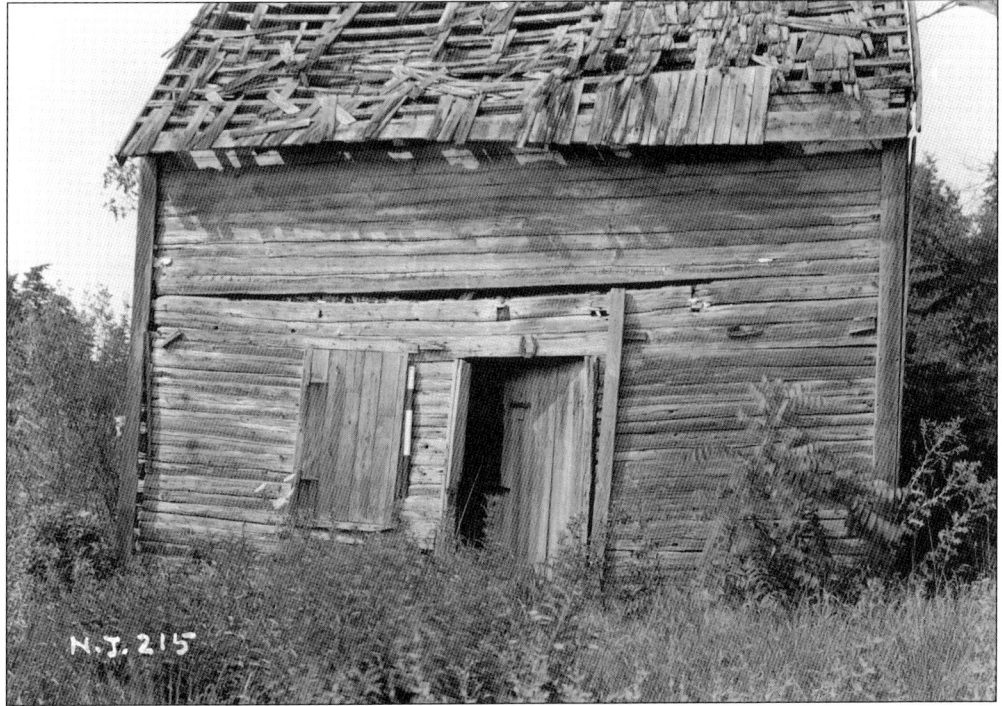

The Reeve-Marshall Log House is on the list of historic homes for New Jersey. It once stood near Dorchester. It was purchased by Peter Reeve from James Marshall in 1798 and changed hands many times. It was sold to Henry Davis Bane at some point in the late 1800s. People may recognize it as Bane's log cabin. His widow sold it to Druzilla Stowman. In 1926, Rebecca Stowman transferred it to S. Sykes and Edmund Mershon. It was taken down and moved to Salem, where it was erected on the lot of the Johnson House. It was used as part of a stockade erected for a Swedish celebration in June 1938. (Courtesy of Library of Congress.)

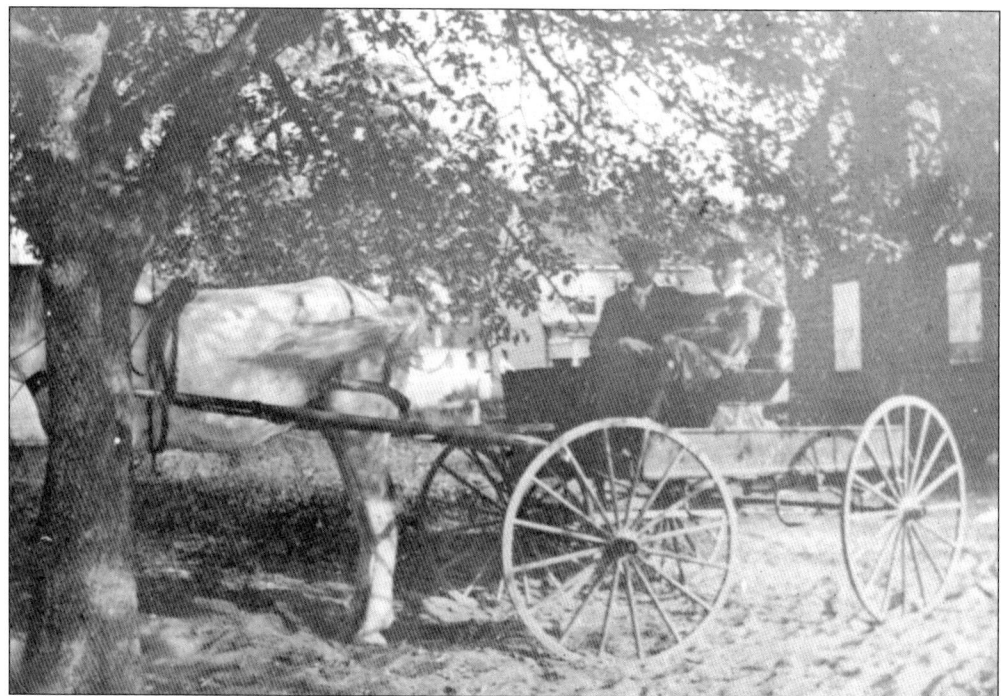

This horse and buggy are sitting in front of what used to be the paint house at Stowman Shipyard. Kathryn Stowman reportedly told Bob Legg's mother, Kathryn, long ago that the people in the photograph are Carlton Smith and Walton Stowman. (Courtesy of Bob Legg.)

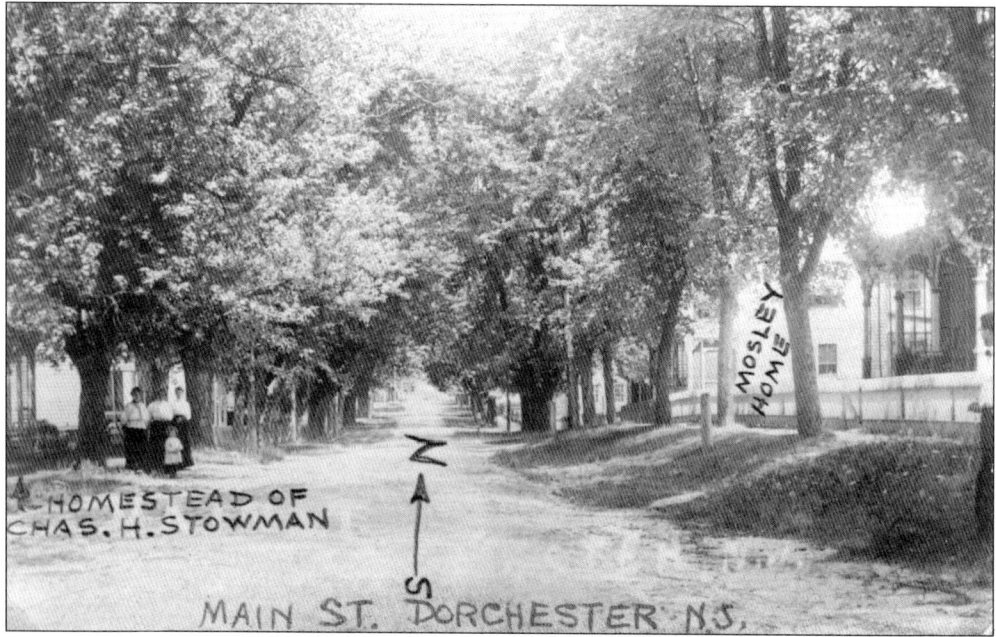

Main Street looking north is seen here. Note the numerous mature trees lining the dirt path. The three women appear to be wearing nearly identical long black skirts and white blouses. They are standing with a small girl in front of the Charles Stowman homestead. Clothing once lacked the variety that modern people enjoy. (Courtesy of the Maurice River Township Heritage Society.)

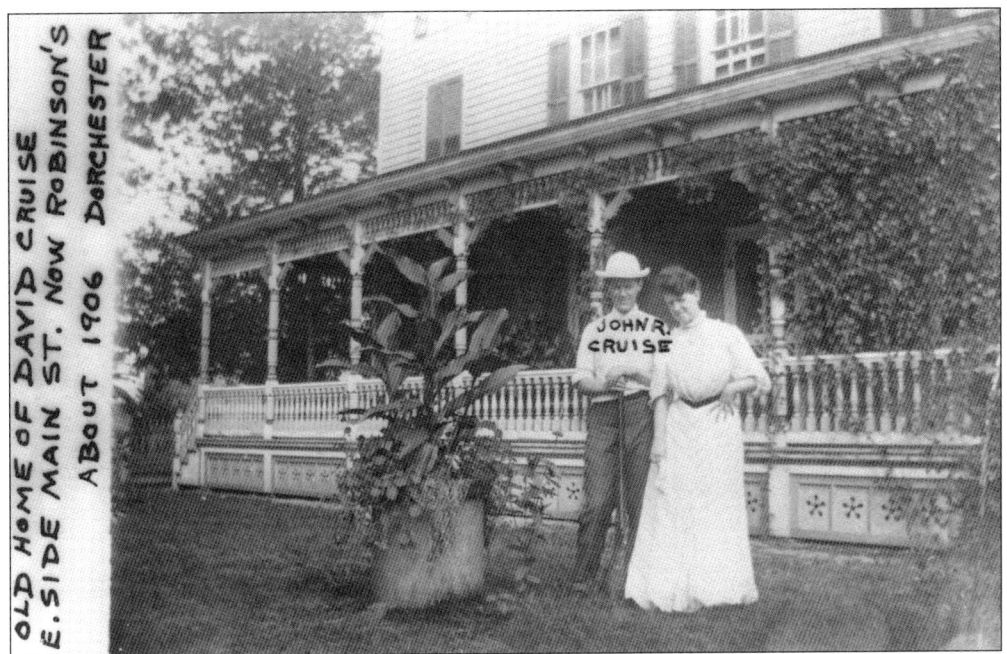

Pictured in 1906 is the home of David Cruise. It was located on the left side of Main Street and south of the railroad tracks coming into town. John R. Cruise and his wife posed for this photograph in front of their beautiful home. Note the detailed wood trim and the grand porch. It is easy to picture the family members sitting on the front porch, sipping lemonade in rocking chairs, and greeting neighbors on summer evenings. (Courtesy of Bob Legg.)

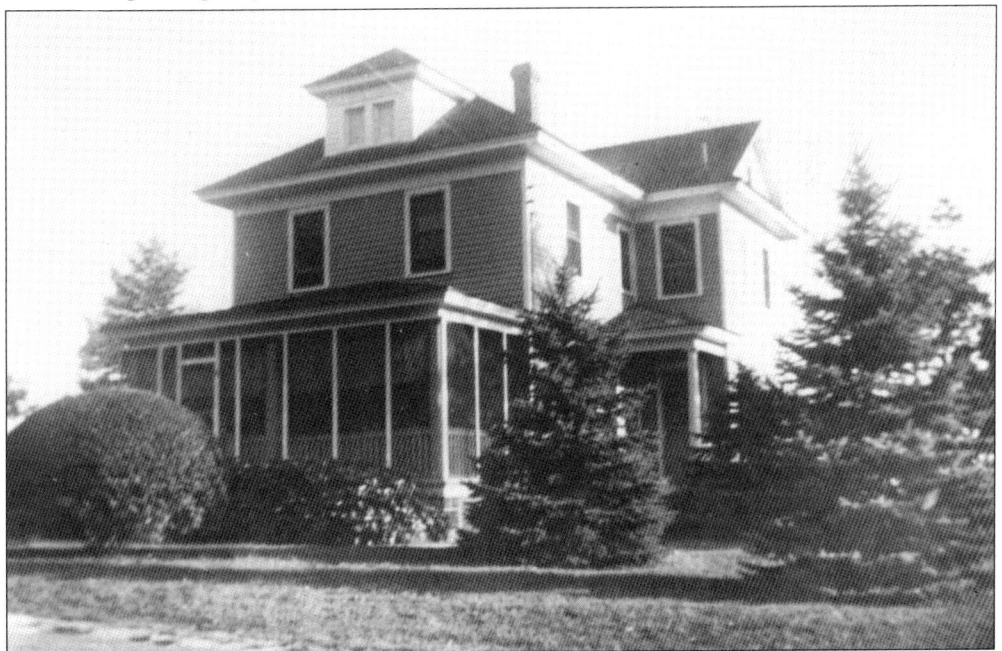

This grand Dorchester home on the corner of Meadow and Front Streets was built in 1915. It was owned by Burrous and Susie H. Shaw, the parents of Florence Champion, Elsie Stafficker, and Miriam Powell. (Courtesy of Bob Legg.)

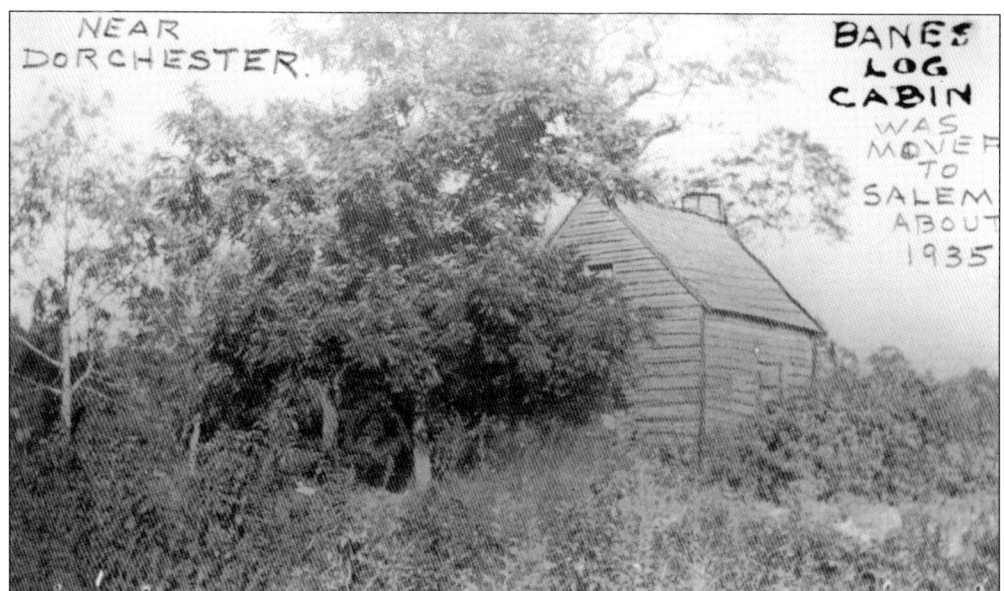

Bane's log cabin was formerly on Delsea Drive, south of the Pine Grove Restaurant on the opposite side of the street. It was dismantled and moved to Salem about 1935. It belonged to the Stowman family. (Courtesy of Bob Legg.)

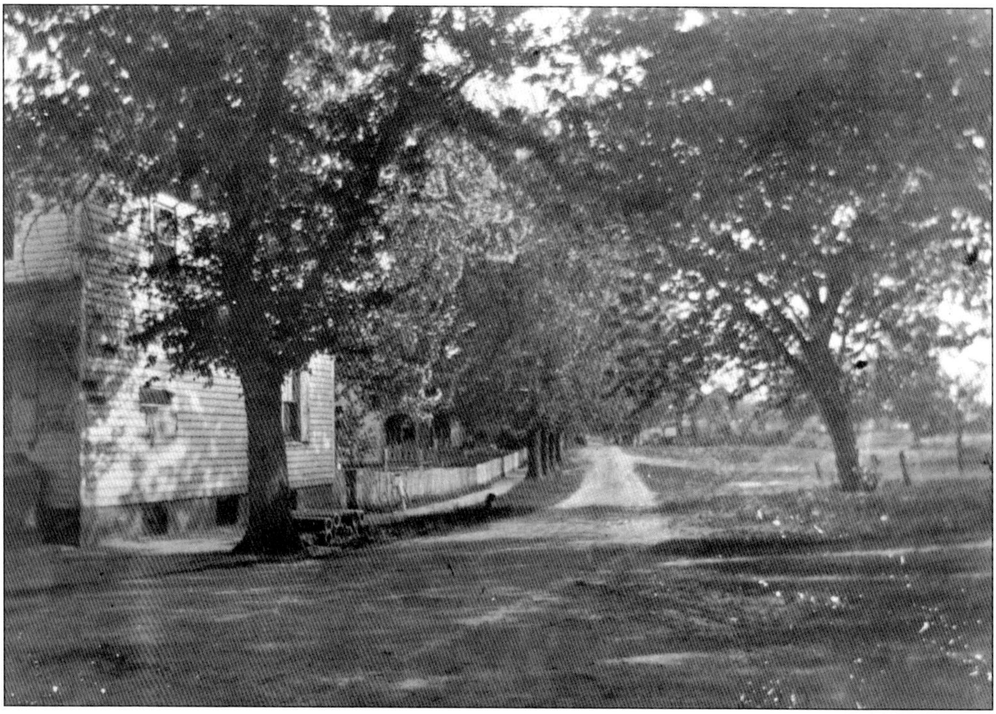

The corner of High and Front Streets facing south is the subject of this c. 1900 photograph taken before any shipyard buildings were added. There was a splendid view of the Maurice River before building started for the shipyard. (Courtesy of Bob Legg.)

Kathryn Stowman Davis is standing next to a car in front of the shipyard office. The building in the background belonged to Champion's Store. (Courtesy of Bob Legg.)

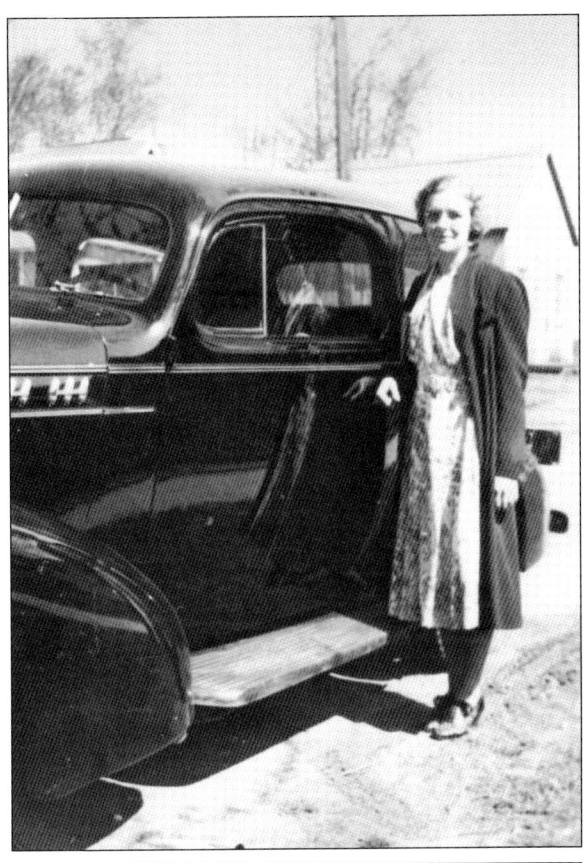

Down by the swimming hole are a bunch of youngsters enjoying the refreshing water on a hot day. This photograph was taken in 1930. From left to right are (first row) Elwood Lowe, Charles "Bud" Sharpless, Virginia Sutton, Gladys Sutton, and Miriam Compton; (second row) Bob Henderson, Charles Stafficker, William Sharpless, Virginia Roe, Margaret Stafficker, Elizabeth DuBois, and Dorothy Compton. (Courtesy of Bob Legg.)

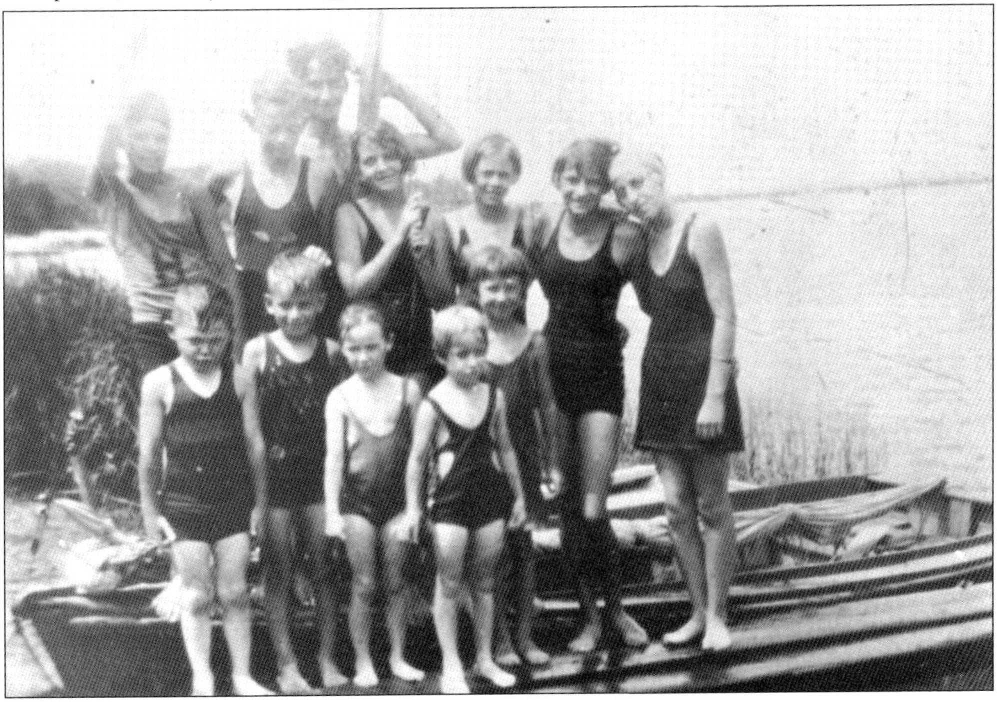

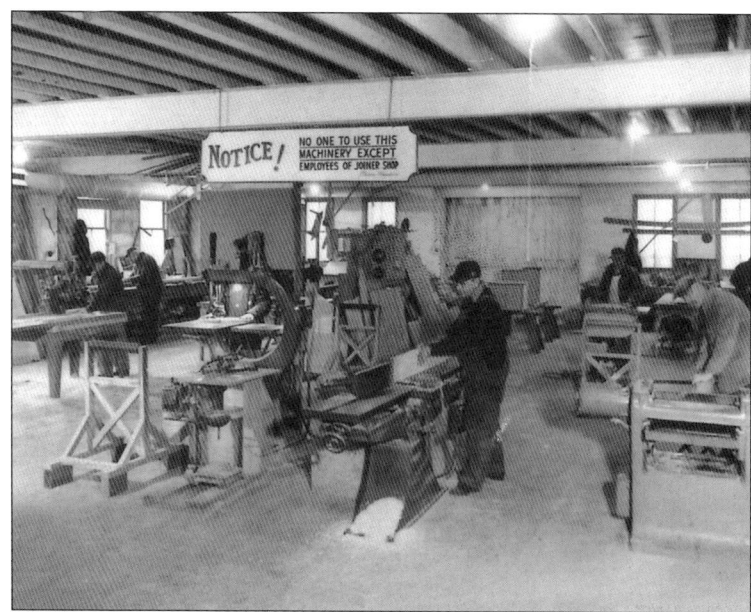

This 1950s picture shows workers in the Dorchester shipyard. Considering workers are wearing hats and coats, it must have been cold in the building. Note how clean and orderly the workshop appears. (Courtesy of the Maurice River Township Heritage Society.)

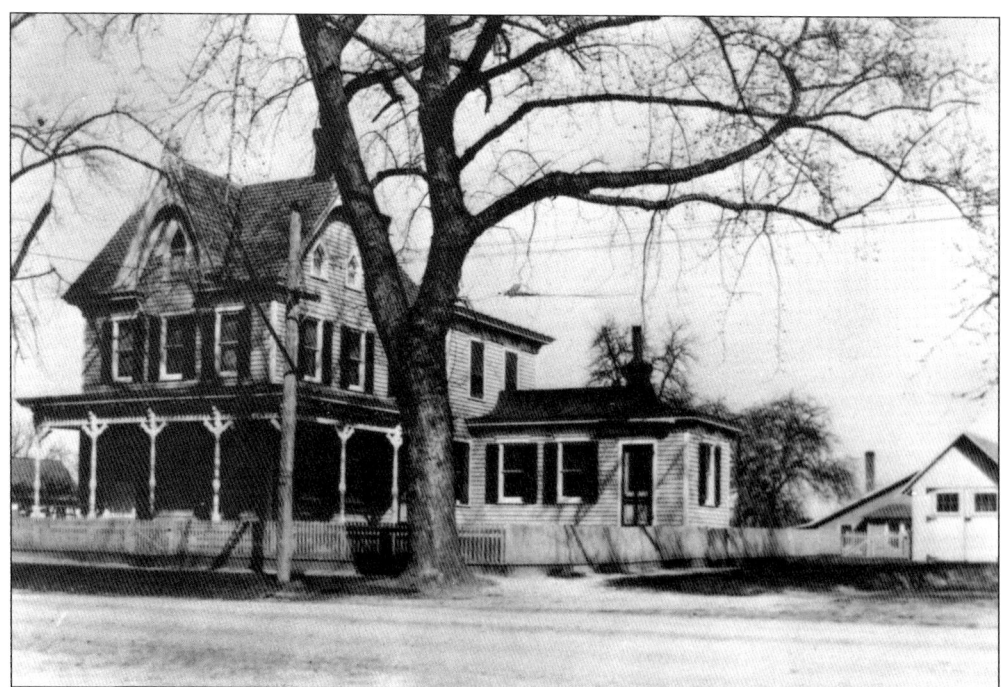

George and Phebe Shaw owned this beautiful home on the corner of Main and Meadow Streets. Note the gingerbread pattern on the peaks of the roof and the picket fence. This was one of the well-kept homes in town. It was lovingly cared for by its owners and always had a fresh coat of paint. Later, the Shaws planted boxwoods out front. (Courtesy of the Legg family collection.)

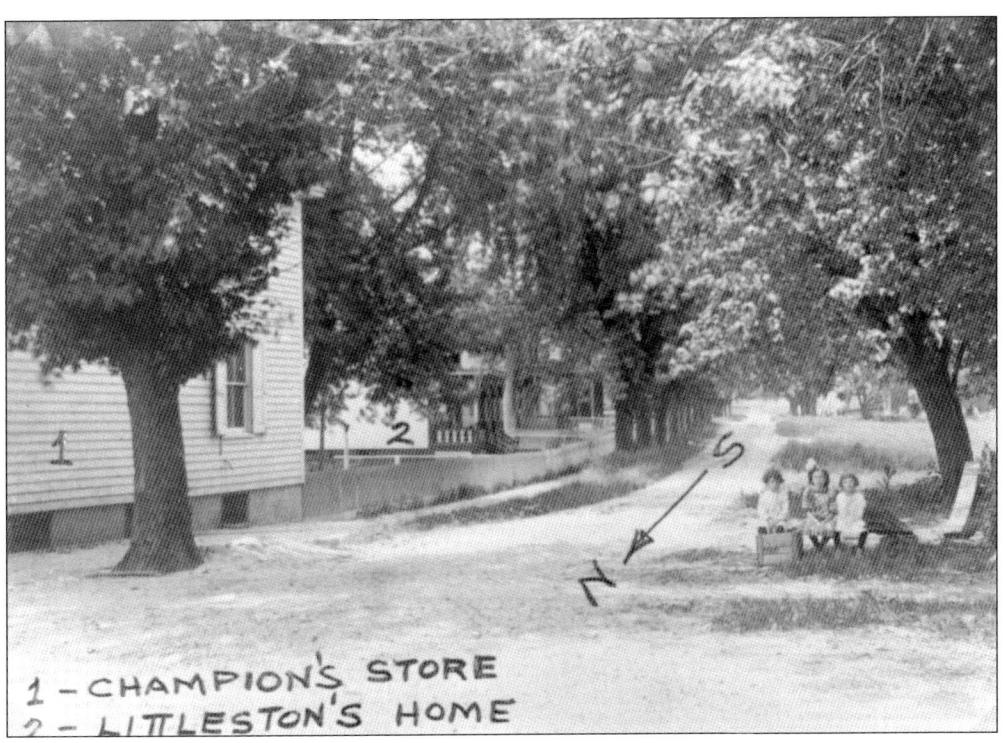

1 – CHAMPION'S STORE
2 – LITTLESTON'S HOME

The Champion family had a general store in Dorchester in the early 1900s. Pictured is the store on the corner with the Littleston family's home beside it. Three little girls are sitting on the bench on the right. (Courtesy of Bob Legg.)

The funeral bill for Lottie Cox on July 9, 1933, had a remaining balance of $38. It was prepared by the Compton Brothers, who served Dorchester and Port Norris. Lottie Cox was Drew Tomlin's great-grandmother. (Courtesy of Drew Tomlin.)

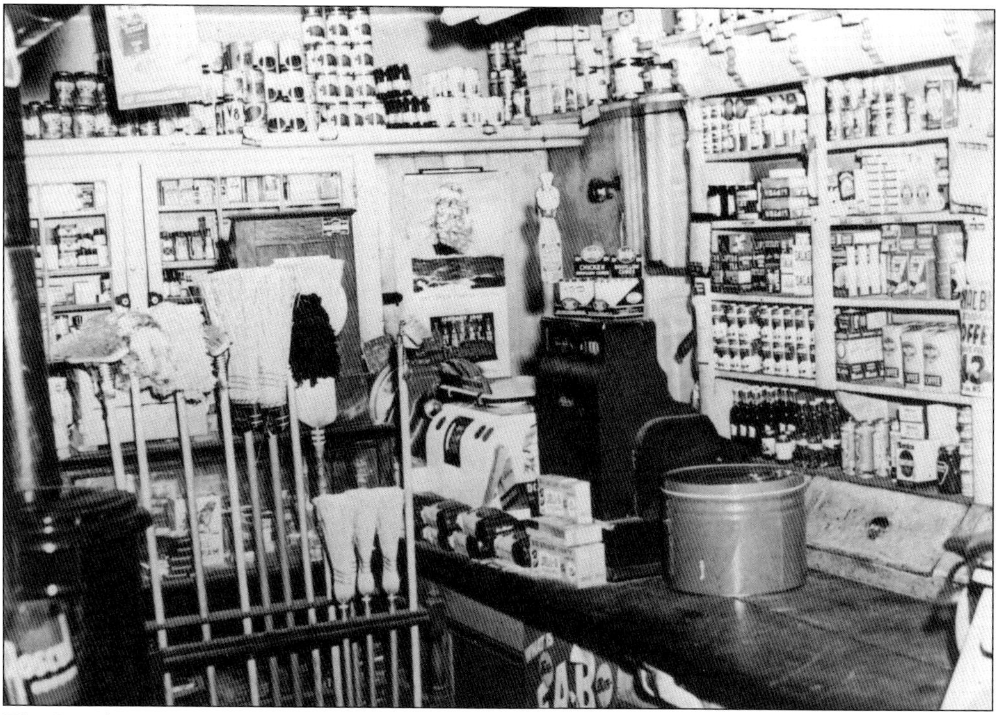

The Dorchester General Store was well stocked in 1949. Note the shelves packed with canned goods, and the brooms on display. The wall calendar proudly displays a sailing vessel. It would have been a convenient place to get household supplies. This store also supplied the oystermen who would go out for a week at a time to dredge for oysters. It was formerly known as Champion's General Store. (Courtesy of Bob Legg.)

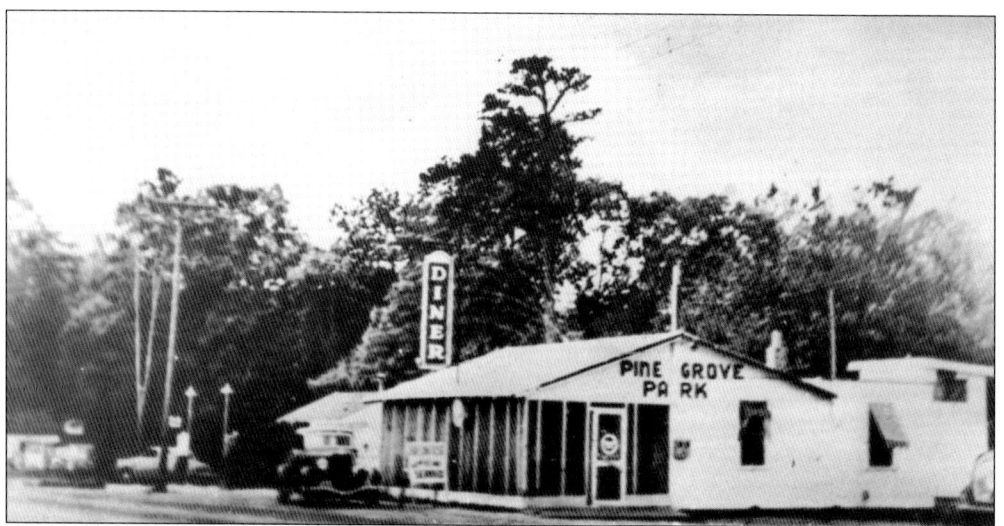

Pine Grove Park restaurant, located on Delsea Drive, was owned by the Rumbold family at the time of this picture in the 1930s. Nora Rumbold ran the restaurant with the help of her children. Other owners included the LaFlash and Daniloff families. In this photograph, the restaurant has an open porch. It was later enclosed, and an addition was added. It is no longer in business. (Courtesy of the Maurice River Township Heritage Society.)

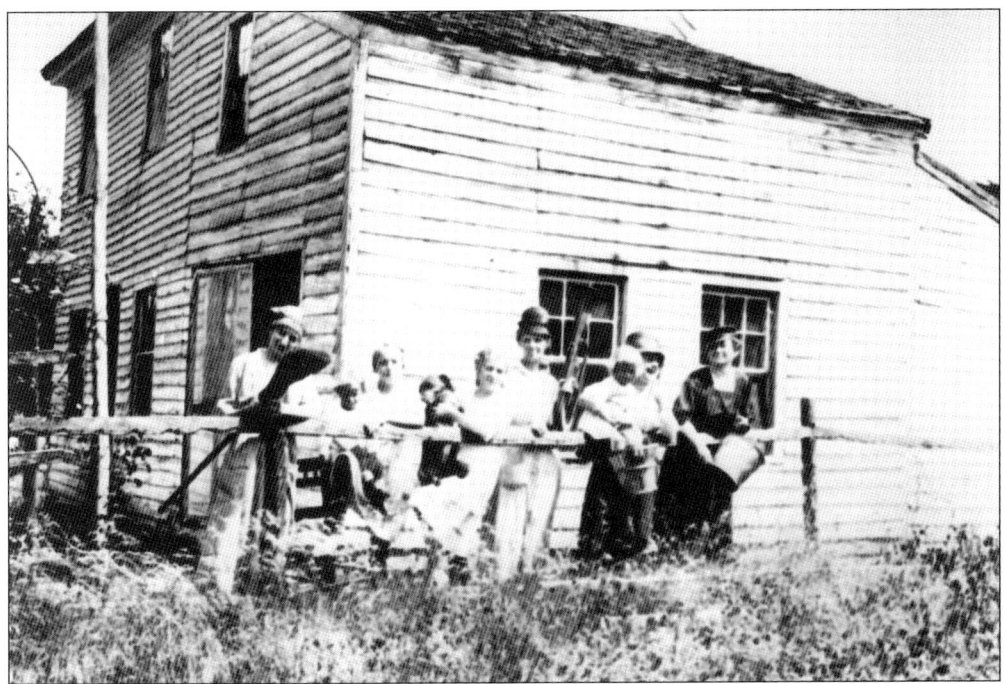

Pictured is a Meadow Street home that was used as a boardinghouse by people who were at the shipyard to have work done on their boats. It was later owned by the Fauver family. After that, it was owned by Charles and Ruth Lee. The last owners were Clarence and Anna Hughes. This house has since been torn down. (Courtesy of Bob Legg.)

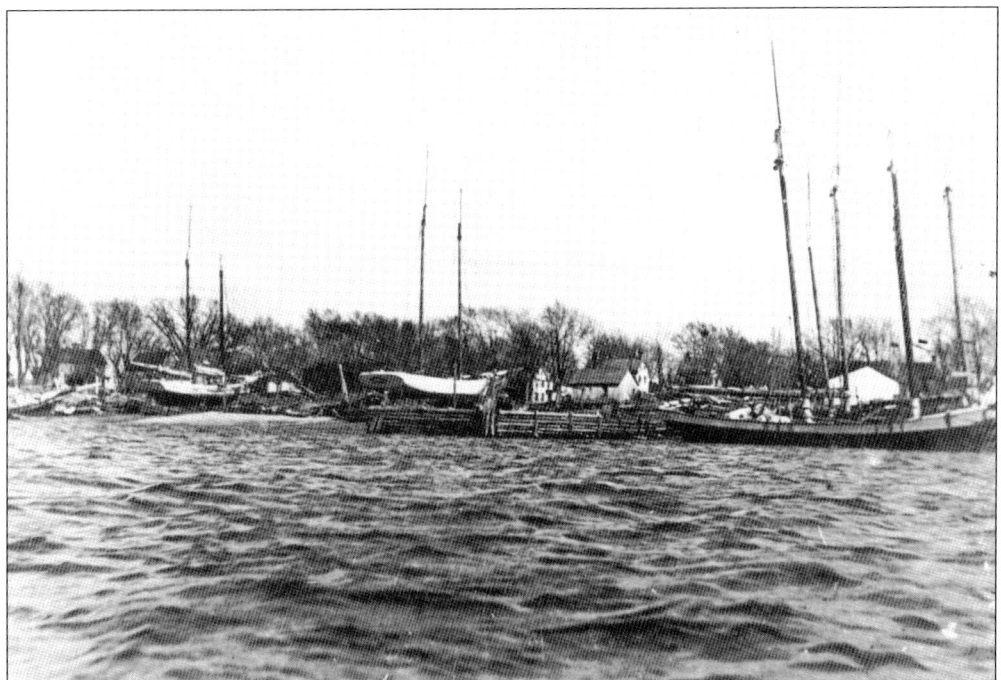

A water view of the Dorchester shipyard is seen here. Note the tall masts. It was a productive time for boatbuilding in the 1930s. (Courtesy of Bob Legg.)

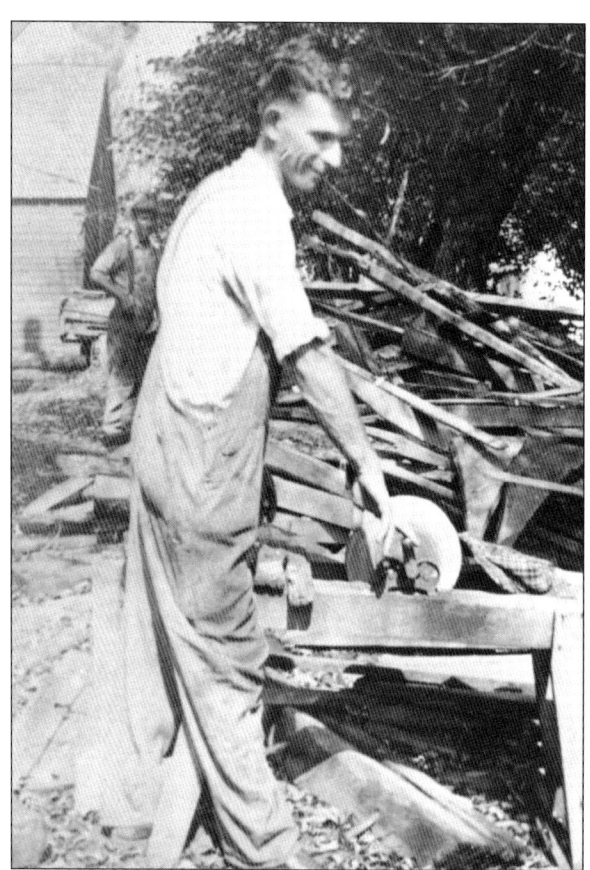

William Stowman is pictured working hard at his shipyard. He was one of the Stowman brothers who owned the shipyard at the time. (Courtesy of Bob Legg.)

This young man on horseback is Charles Stowman. The young girl on the sidewalk is Shirley Grier. The structure in the background was a blacksmith shop owned by Lon Shaw. While she was growing up, Bob Legg's mother spent time watching him work. (Courtesy of Bob Legg.)

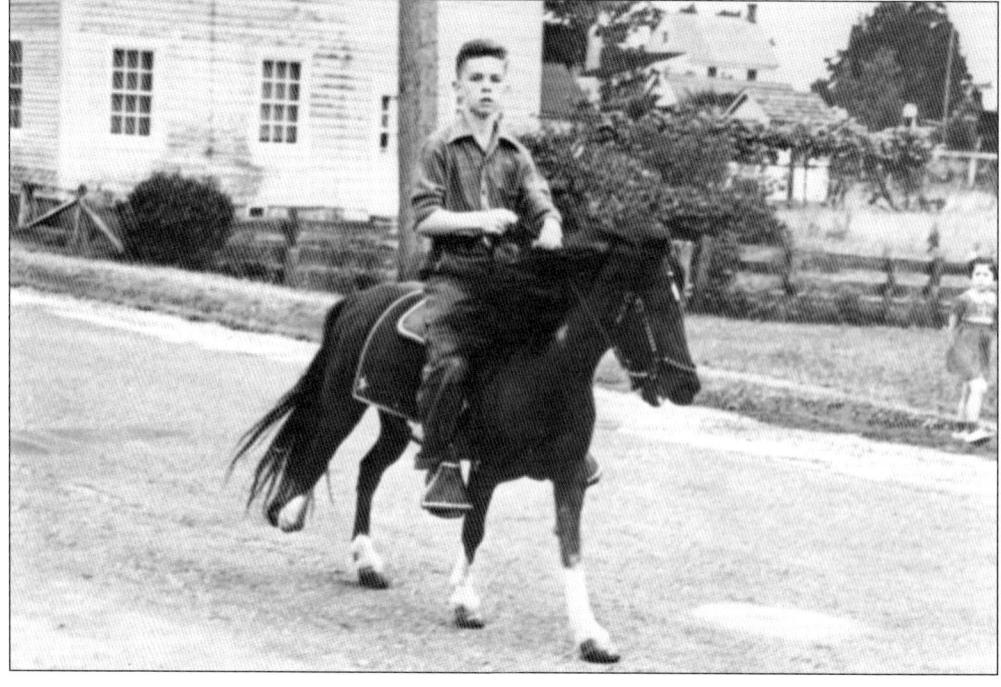

Elma Stowman Polise is seen sitting in her front yard on a summer's day. Across the street was the home of Wilbert Cruise. This picture was taken in the 1960s. The homes are located on Main Street in Dorchester. (Courtesy of Bob Legg.)

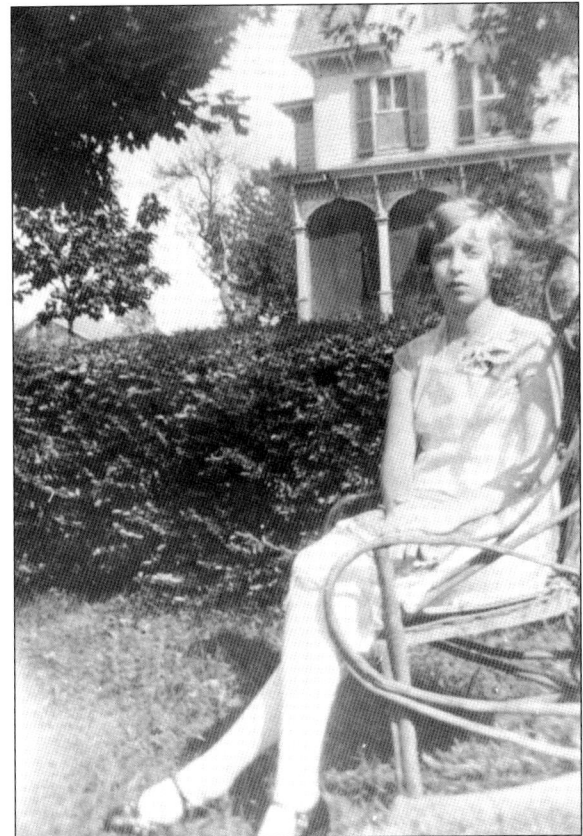

This is a photograph of the former home of Wilbert Cruise on Main Street. Note the gingerbread peaks. After the Cruise family, the Whilden family owned the house. At that time, the porch was no longer there. (Courtesy of the Bob Legg family collection.)

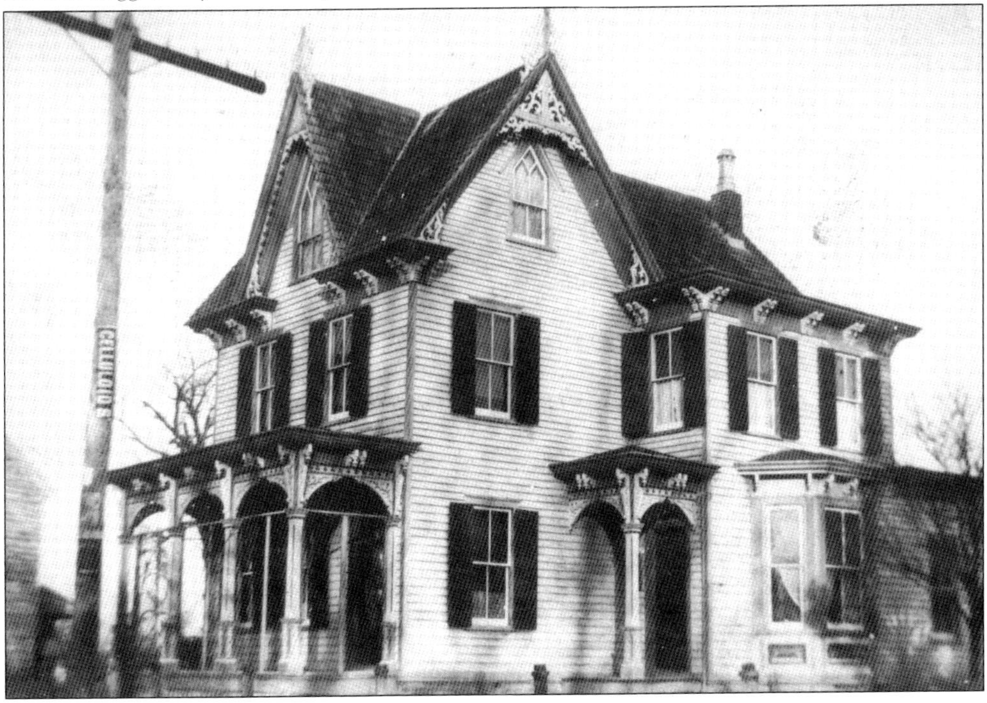

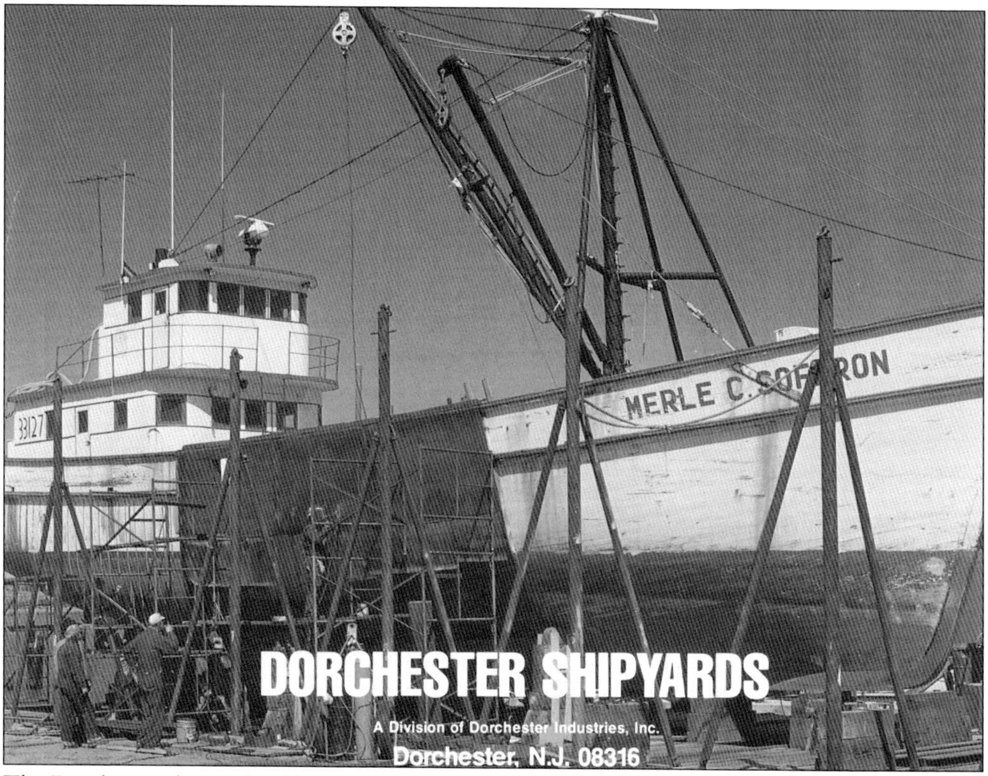

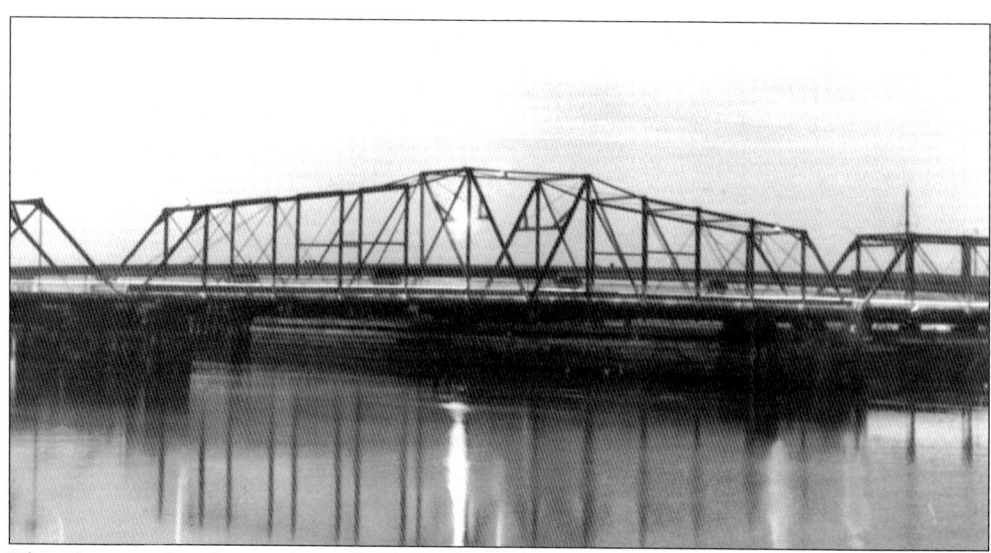

The Dorchester shipyard published this brochure. In the photograph, shipyard workers are making repairs to a vessel. (Courtesy of Drew Tomlin.)

This photograph, taken in the early 1960s, shows the Mauricetown Bridge. The old wooden slats of the bridge made a clickety-clack sound as cars passed over them. The old bridge was replaced in the 1970s with a modern concrete structure. This bridge joins Maurice River Township to Mauricetown in Commercial Township. (Courtesy of Nelson Klein.)

Three

LEESBURG

Leesburg is a rural village situated near the banks of the Maurice River. It was first settled by a small number of Swedish immigrants in the mid-1600s. The Swedes had landed along the banks of Delaware Bay to trade with the Indians there. The land was surveyed by John Worledge and John Budd in 1691, but the town was not officially declared until 1795, when John Lee, a shipwright, founded Leesburg. To this day, the Lee family has descendants in the area. John Lee brought his knowledge and experience of shipbuilding to the area and opened the first shipyard. By doing so, he laid the foundation for the industry of shipbuilding that would make Leesburg and neighboring Dorchester famous for constructing coastal vessels for several decades.

Many of the early residents of Leesburg were devout Christians. The Methodist denomination was prevalent throughout the township. The first Methodist society in the township was organized in Leesburg in 1806. In 1811, the land for the first church was purchased from Joab and Phebee Swain, and the church was constructed in 1812. It still stands today.

In 1849, a wealthy resident by the name of William Carlisle decided to construct a windmill near the river on High Street. This landmark stood until 1927 and was the subject of many photographs. Another famous landmark is the Oakleaf Academy, which was constructed in 1856. It is a two-story, wooden structure that was used as a schoolhouse until June 1958, when it was converted to the Maurice River Municipal Building. It is now utilized as the emergency services building.

Some remnants of the shipbuilding industry are still in place. The Delaware Bay Shipbuilding Company, which is no longer in business, was founded in 1928. It once employed 500 people in five separate businesses. Commissioned by the United States to make vessels during World War II, Delaware Bay Shipbuilding Company was booming. This location once had numerous diked farms that lined the river as far north as Millville. The area is still well known for agriculture.

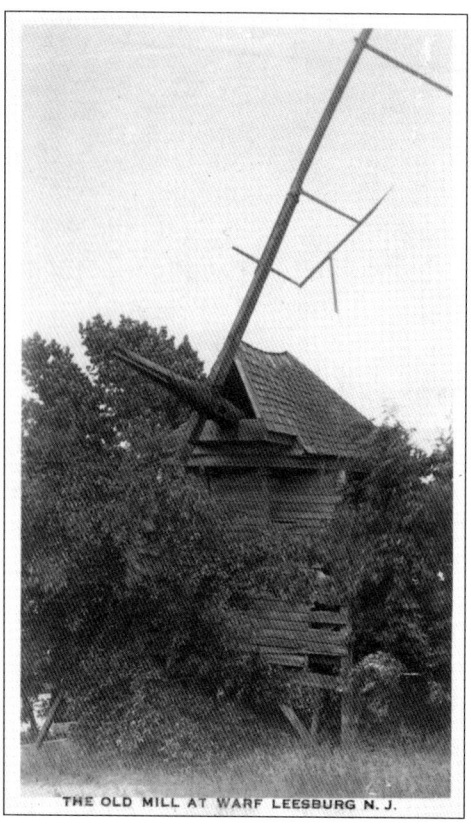

Windmills were popular along the rivers and near the ocean in southern New Jersey in the mid- to late 1800s. The wind was used to power gristmills for grinding grain. In this picture, the windmill has fallen into disrepair. Efforts were made to save the landmark; however, it was demolished in 1927. (Courtesy of the Maurice River Township Heritage Society.)

This is a c. 1920 photograph of the Leesburg Windmill. It was built on a slight hill near the bank of the Maurice River in Leesburg near the blacksmith shop that once thrived in the town. Currently, Allen Steel stands where the windmill once was. (Courtesy of the Bob Legg family collection.)

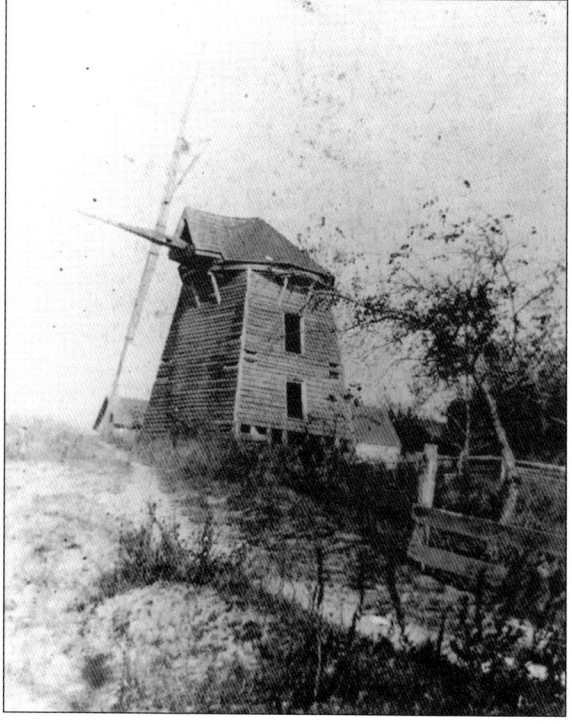

This picture of the windmill in Leesburg was taken in 1906. The structure was built by William Carlisle in 1849. He was an early settler in the area who, according to a 1927 *Camden Evening Courier* article, came to the area from Delaware with 75¢ in his pocket and went on to become one of the wealthiest men in the area. In fact, there is a Dorchester street, Carlisle Place, named after him. (Courtesy of Bob Legg.)

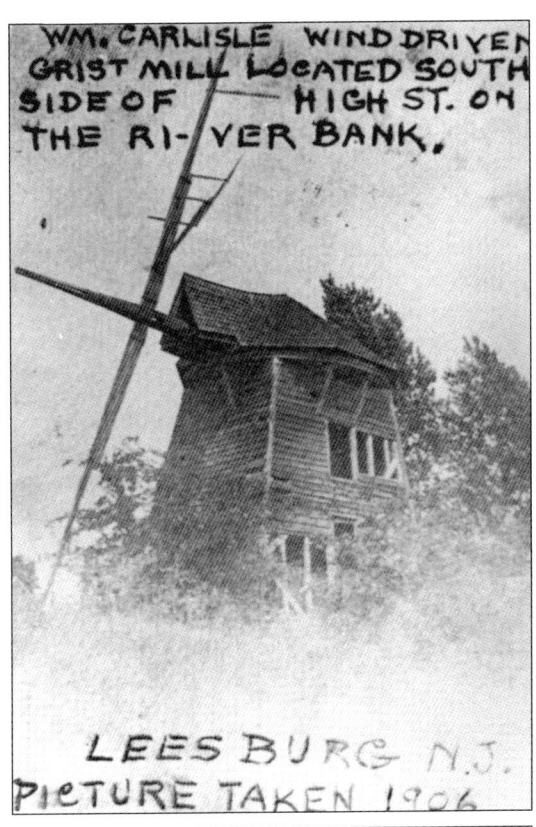

Business owners used horse-drawn buggies to make deliveries in the days before automobiles. In this photograph, Horace Bacon's father stands next to his wagon that advertises Bacon Bros. Bakery. It is easy to imagine the smell of freshly baked bread coming from his basket. Later, the family started Bacon's Market. (Courtesy of Drew Tomlin.)

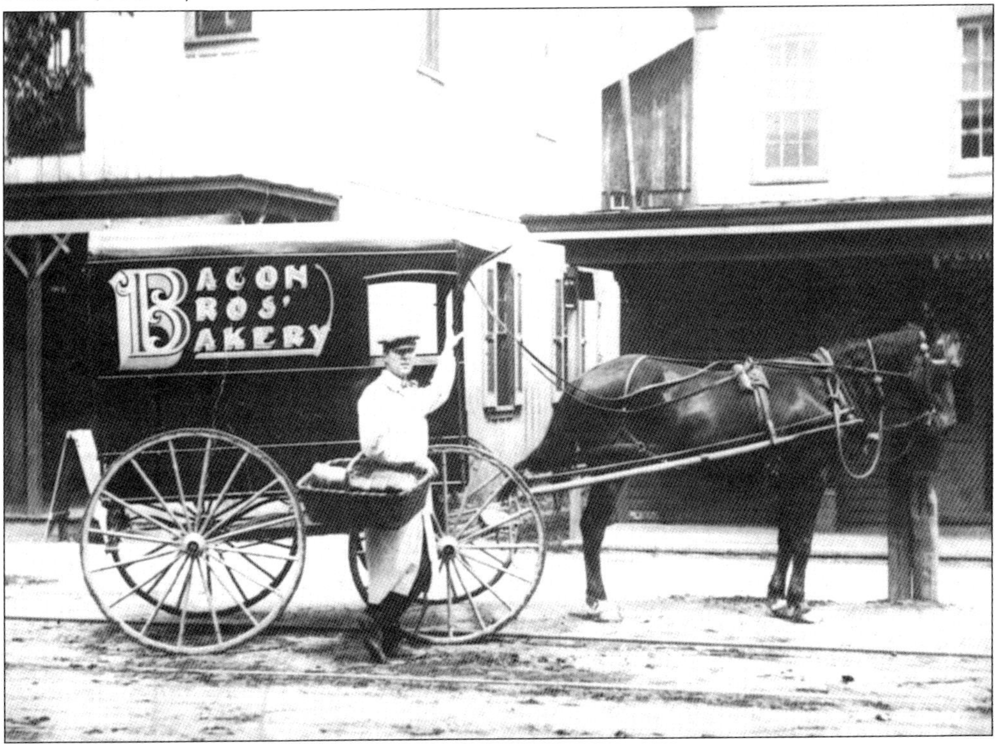

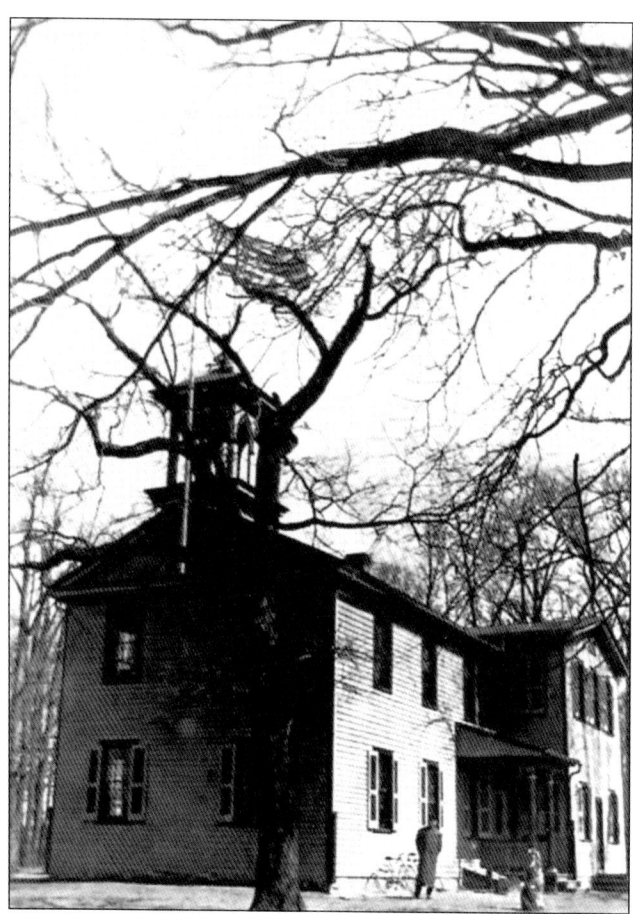

The building of Oakleaf Academy, constructed in 1856, is a local landmark. The two-story, wooden structure was used as a schoolhouse until June 1958, when it was converted to the Maurice River Municipal Building. The author's father attended this school in the 1930s. (Courtesy of the Maurice River Township Heritage Society.)

Sent in 1907, this postcard shows Main Street in Leesburg. Lovely homes line both sides of the tree-lined path. The writing on the postcard was likely made with ink from a fountain pen and ink well. (Courtesy of the Maurice River Township Heritage Society.)

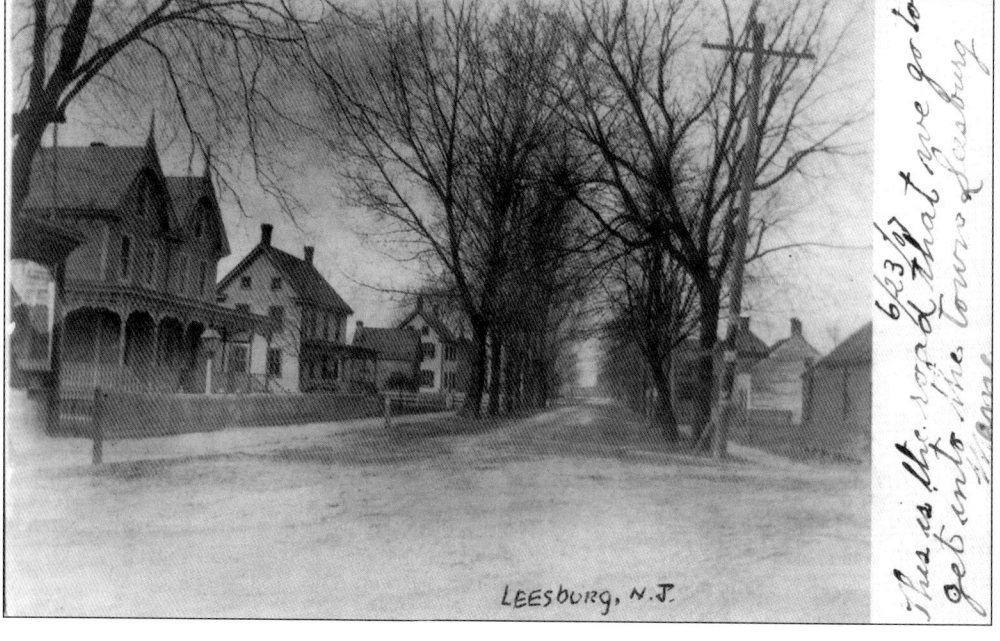

This map of Leesburg in 1896 reveals that the shipyard was owned by Jason Ward at the time. The windmill granary is listed. D.G. Carlisle was the town's physician, and Thomas Biggs owed the Leesburg Hotel. (Courtesy of Library of Congress.)

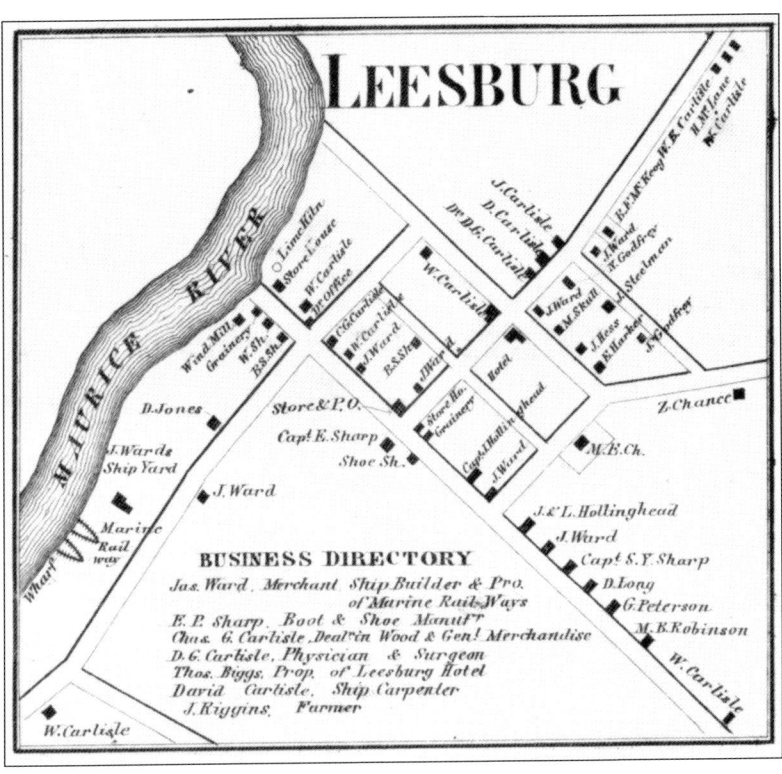

This receipt shows that Barclay Cox, Drew Tomlin's great-grandfather, paid a total of $1.85 in township taxes in 1898. Certainly, people would be glad to receive that bill today. (Courtesy of Drew Tomlin.)

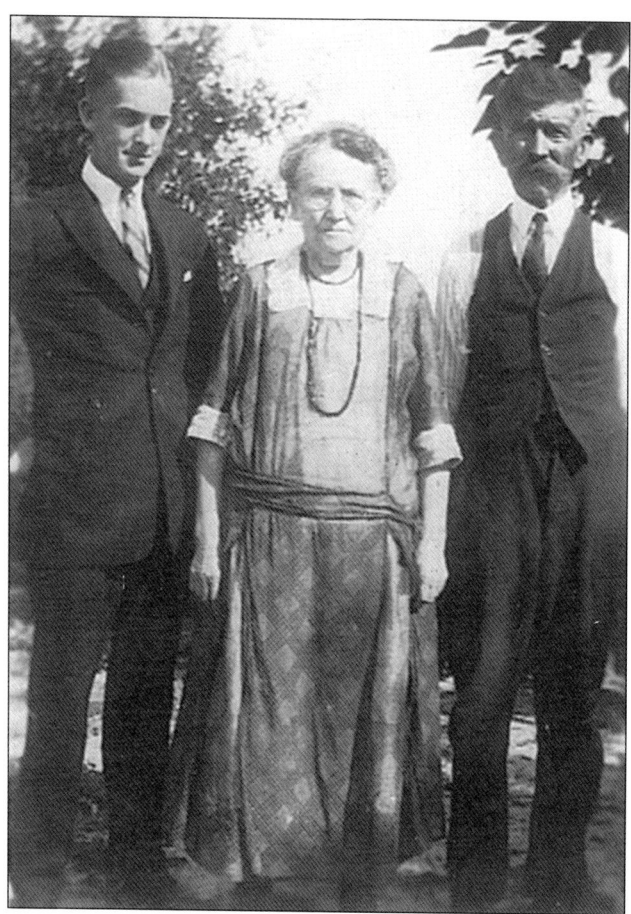

Pictured in Leesburg are, from left to right, John E. Errickson Jr., Phoebe Lee, and John Errickson. Phoebe and John are the author's paternal great-grandparents. This picture was taken around 1915. (Author's collection.)

This burial permit was for an infant named Helen E. Errickson, who died in September 1900 at just six months of age. The cause of death is listed as ileocolitis. The arrangements were handled by Compton funeral home in Dorchester. (Courtesy of Drew Tomlin.)

This is a c. 1917 formal portrait of Lilian and Dalcord Errickson, children of Harold and Ada Errickson. They were raised in Leesburg. (Author's collection.)

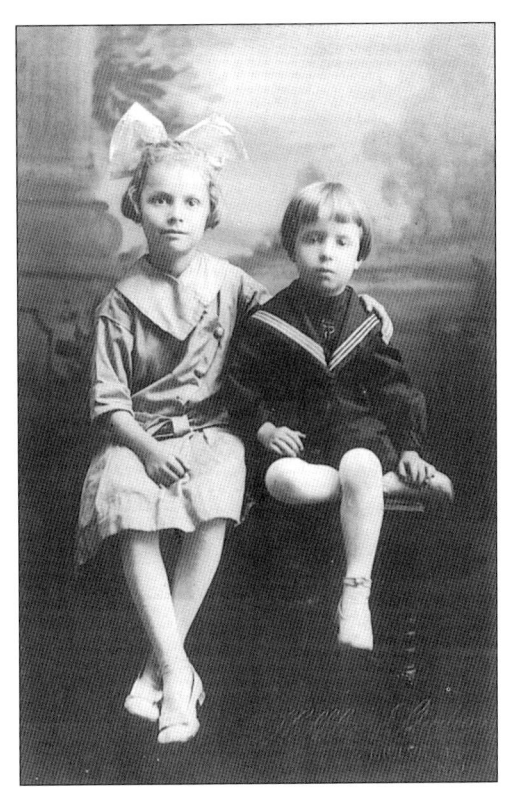

Owned by Wes Shaw, Shaw's Market was a general store and meat market. It stood on the east side of Main Street between Ward Avenue and New Street in Leesburg. It served freshly butchered meat that needed to be cooked and eaten quickly due to the lack of refrigeration at the time. The building was purchased, moved, and preserved in Smithville Village in Goshen Township, where it stands today. Its door has been moved from its original location, which was to the right of the bay window. (Author's collection.)

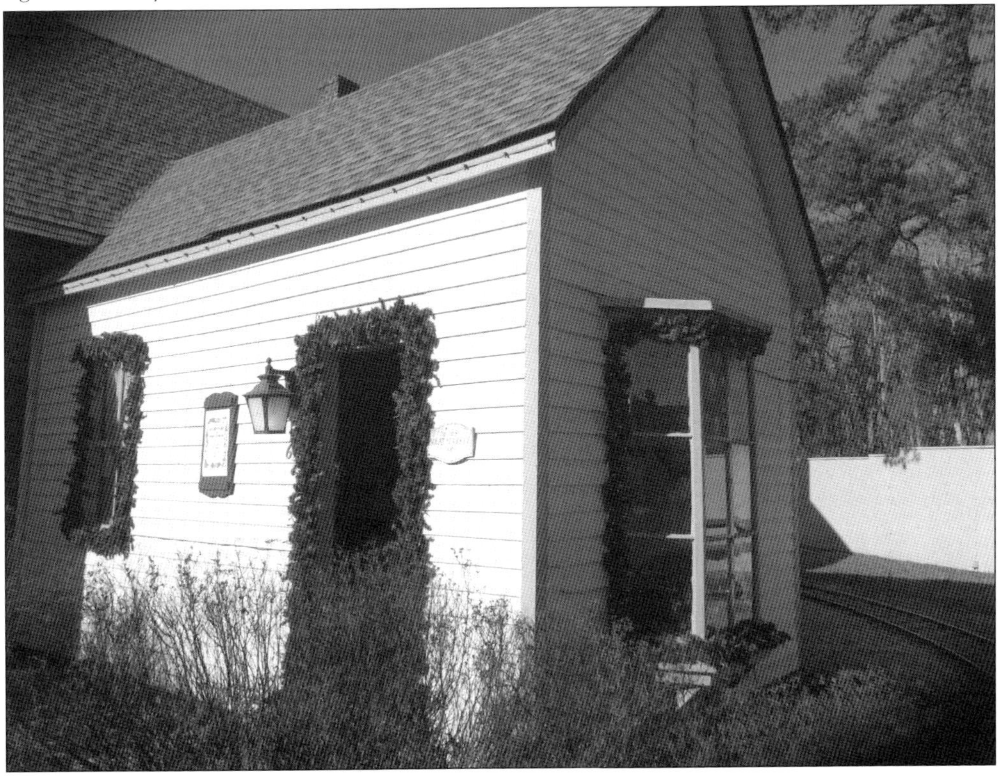

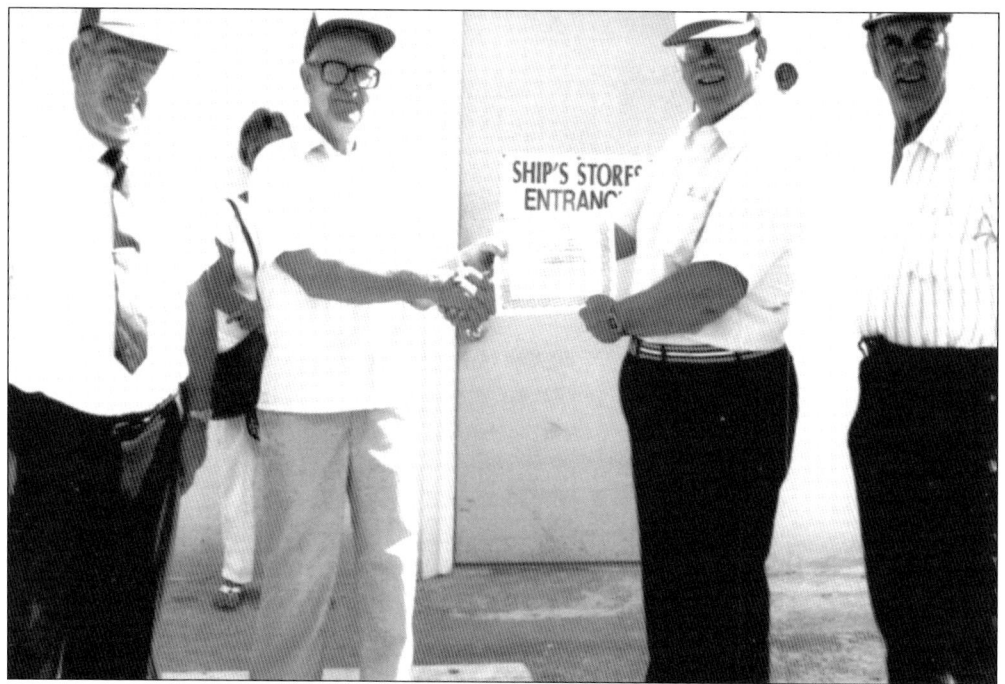

When he bought the corner store at High and Main Streets in Leesburg, Paul Cox Jr. was honored with a ceremony. From left to right are John Feltes, William Trout, Paul Cox Jr., and Ezra Cox. (Courtesy of Mary Hagemann.)

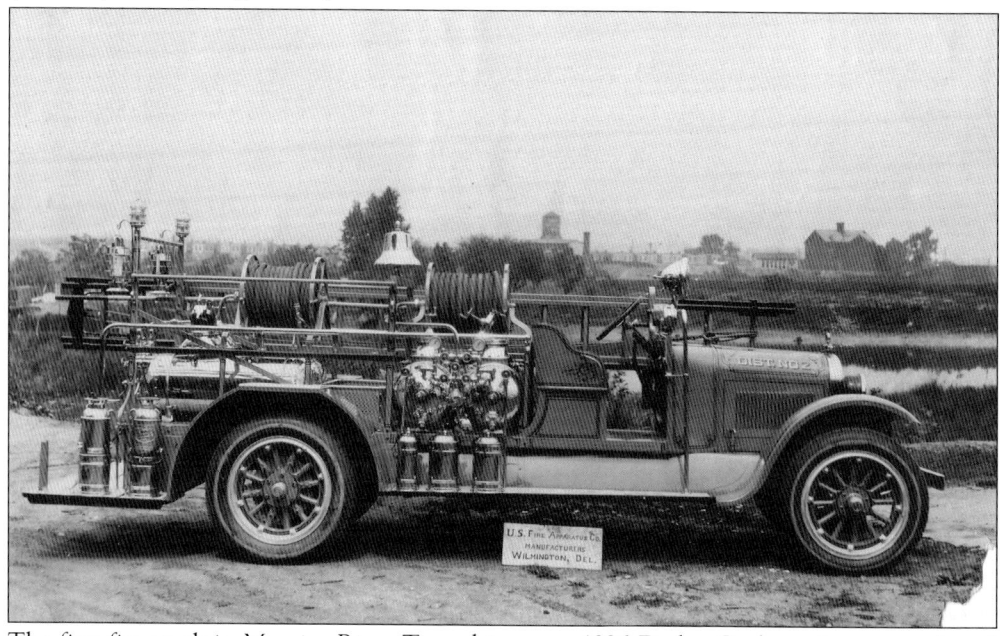

The first fire truck in Maurice River Township was a 1926 Dodge Graham. It was purchased for $4,000 when Dodge Motor Company bought out Graham Brothers Trucks, and was built in Wilmington, Delaware. It was referred to as a chemical engine because it featured a large soda-acid fire extinguisher. It served the township until it was replaced by the Diamond T fire truck in 1942. (Courtesy of Drew Tomlin and Paul Cox.)

Ada Bishop, pictured here, was married to Harold Errickson, and they lived in Leesburg on Main Street. Ada is Lilian Errickson's mother and the author's paternal great-grandmother. (Author's collection.)

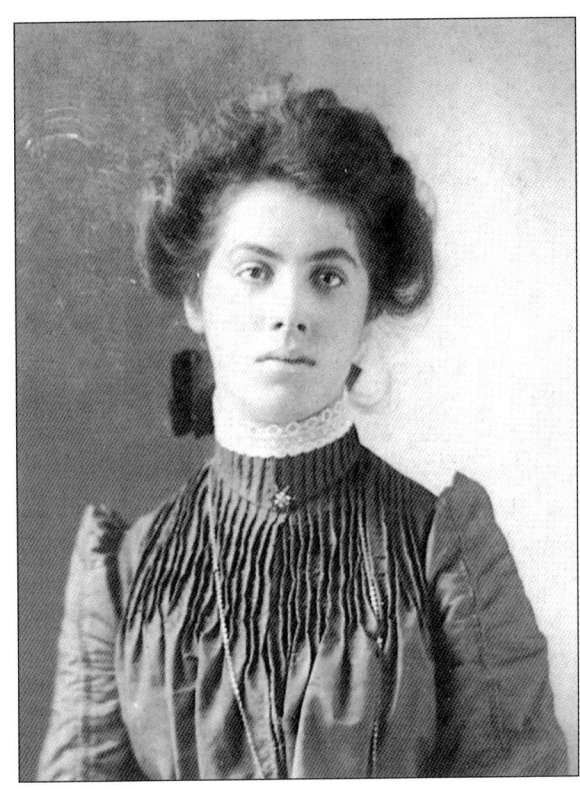

In 1919, the annual tax paid by Barclay Cox to tax collector LeRoy Champion for the year was $12.52. (Courtesy of Drew Tomlin.)

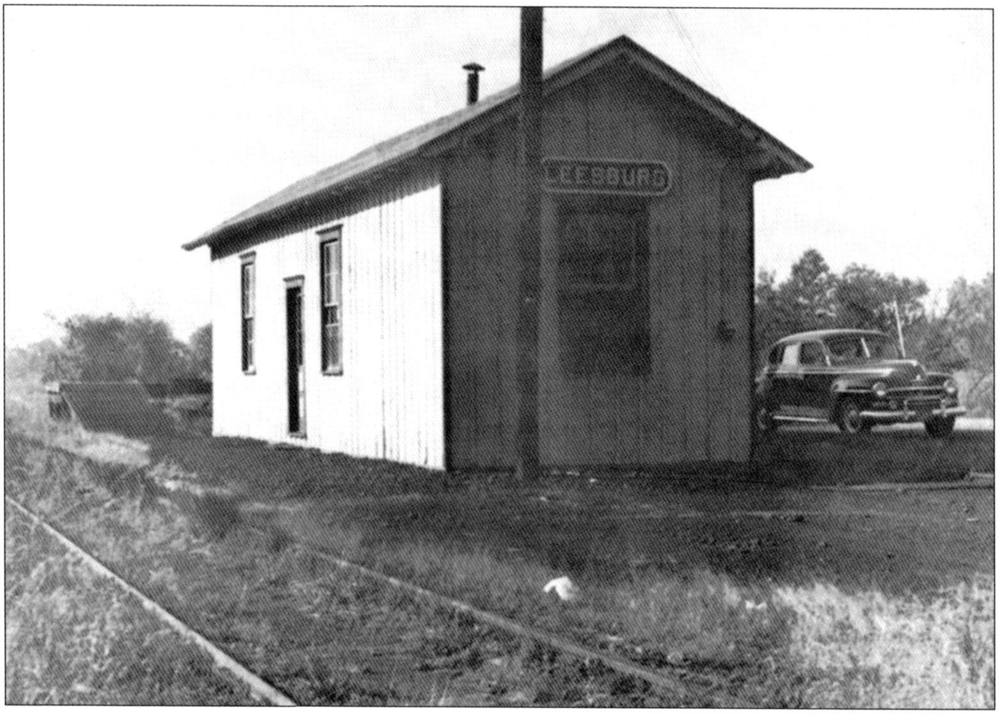

The Leesburg railroad station was a busy place for passengers and freight in the early 1900s, when there were still several trains in and out of town each day. Students from town had to take the train to Millville for their senior year of high school. (Courtesy of Drew Tomlin.)

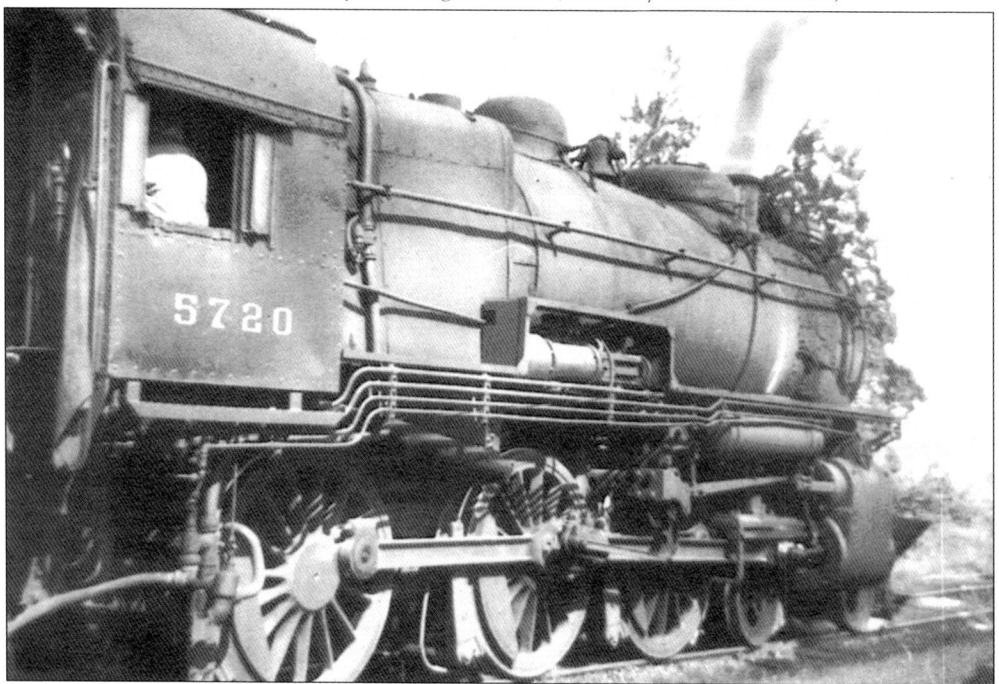

As a young girl, Mary Hagemann loved to snap pictures. She took this photograph in 1959 of the last steam locomotive to ever come through town. (Courtesy of the Hagemann collection.)

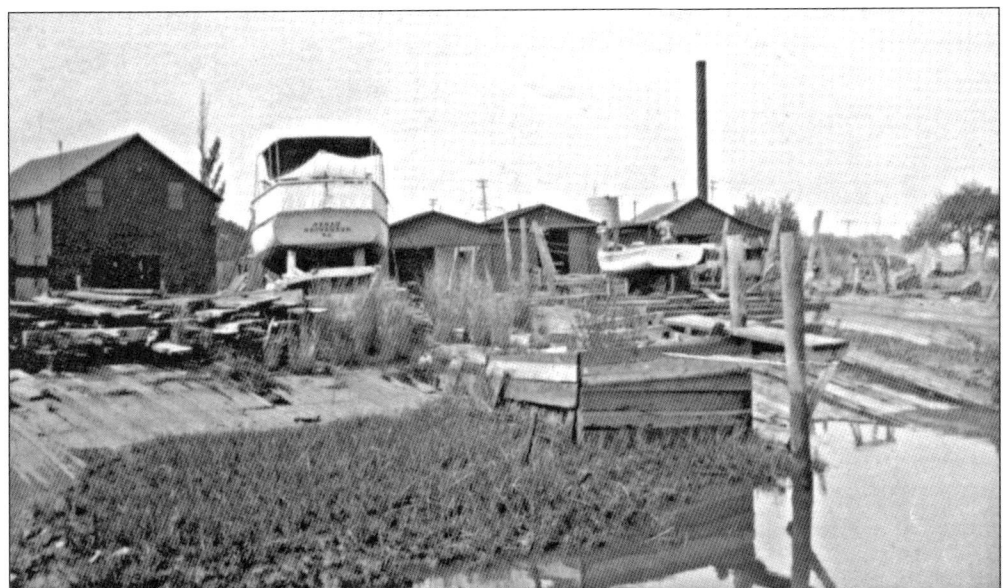

The Delaware Bay Shipbuilding Company in Leesburg was a successful and thriving enterprise in the 1930s and 1940s. This company built many vessels for the government during World War II, including the minesweepers *Fearless* and *Paramount*. Delaware Bay Shipbuilding Company is no longer in business, but its buildings still stand near the water on River Road. (Courtesy of Mary Hagemann, Paul Cox, and Drew Tomlin.)

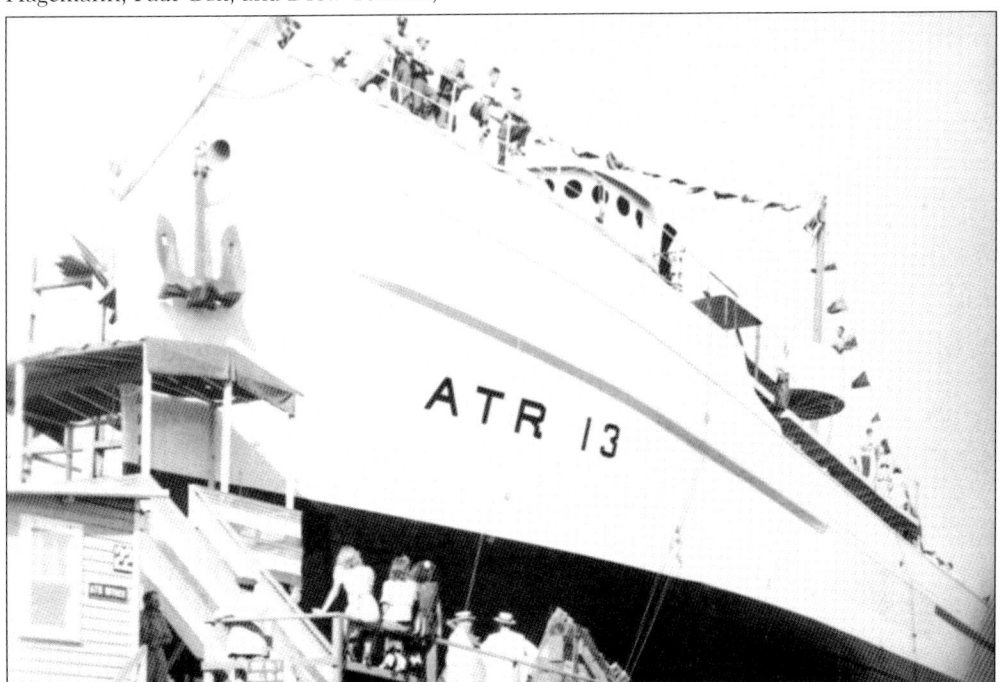

The Delaware Bay Shipbuilding Company, known as Del Bay by the locals, was a happening place in the 1940s. This photograph, taken on August 13, 1943, shows a launching ceremony for a large vessel labeled ATR-13. Many launching events occurred during this decade. (Courtesy of Mary Hagemann.)

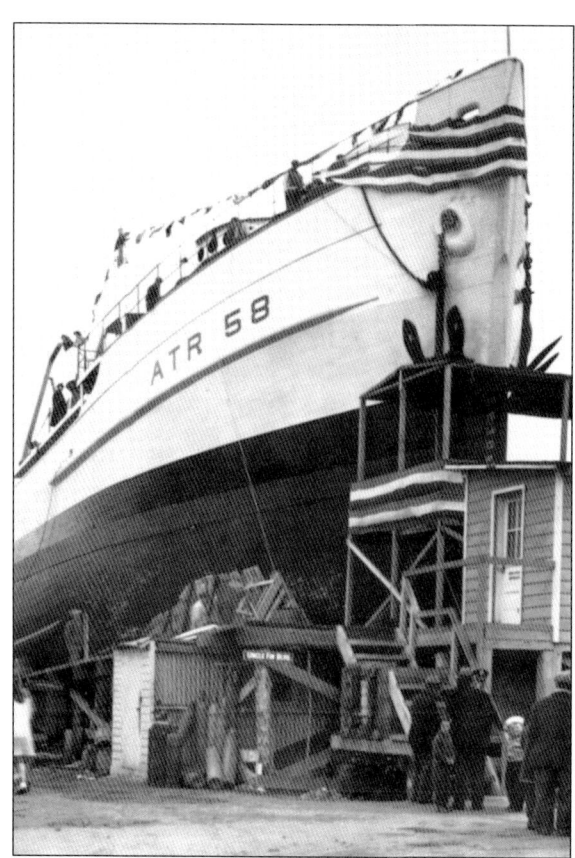

At left, ship ATR-58 is about to be launched at the Delaware Bay Shipbuilding Company on April 23, 1944. Below, a crowd is gathered at the launch of PC-648 in the early 1940s. Ship launchings happened on a regular basis here during World War II. (Both, courtesy of Mary Hagemann)

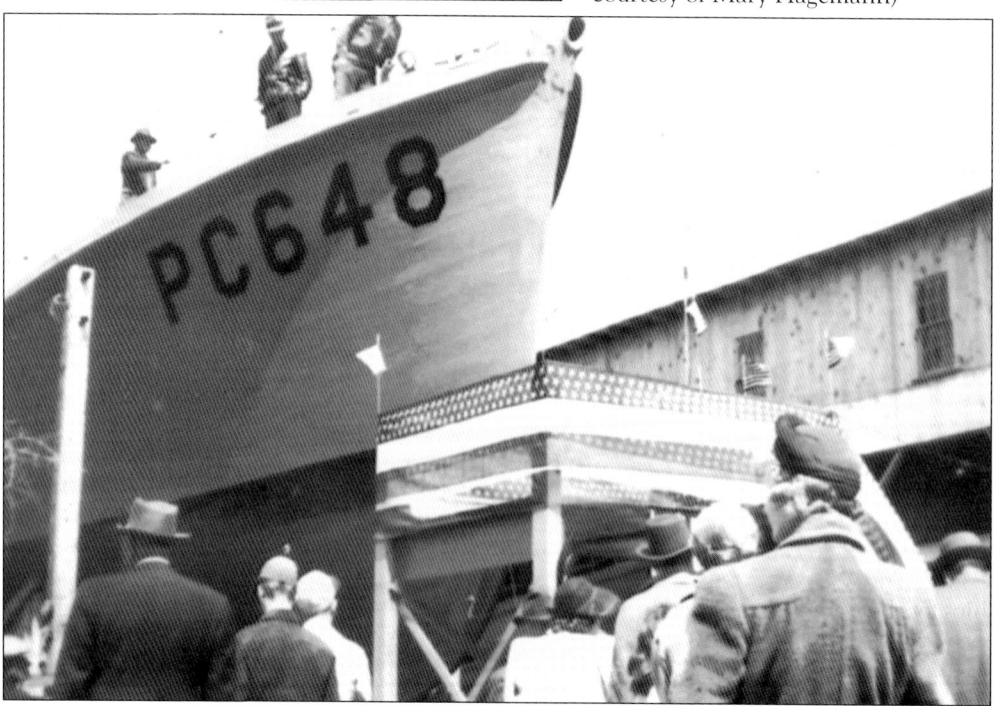

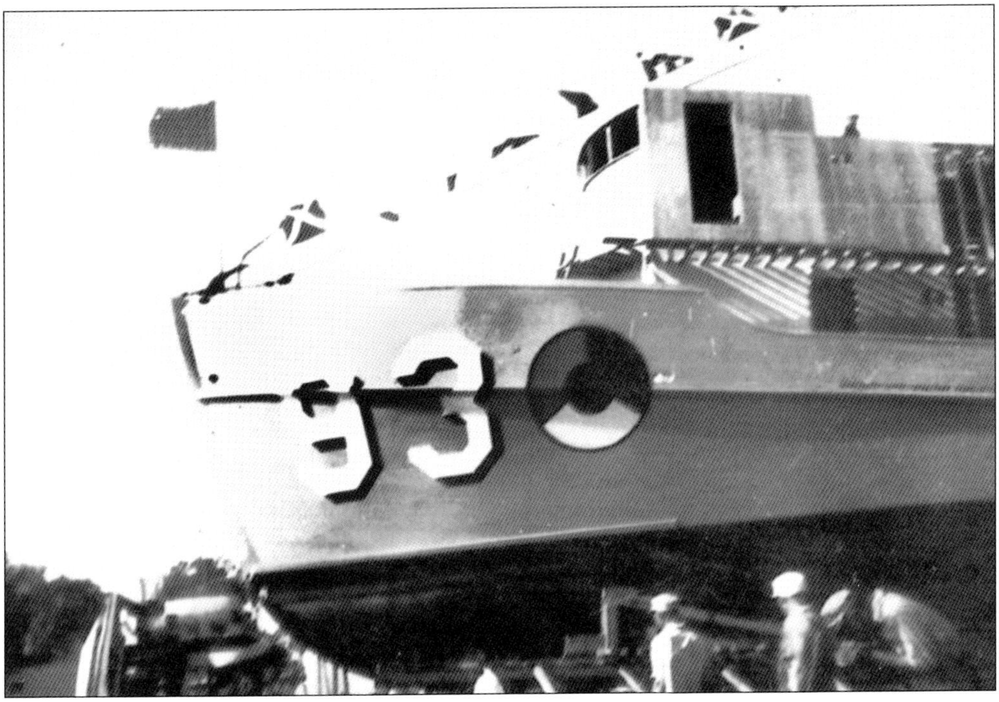

Numbered 93, this ship is pictured at Del Bay during World War II. Note the shipyard workers near the boat preparing for launch. During the war, several hundred people were employed at the shipyard to help build ships for the Navy. Prior to the start of the war, there was already a contract to construct two 97-foot minesweepers, the *Fearless* and the *Paramount*. The war started before they were completed. (Courtesy of Mary Hagemann and Paul Cox.)

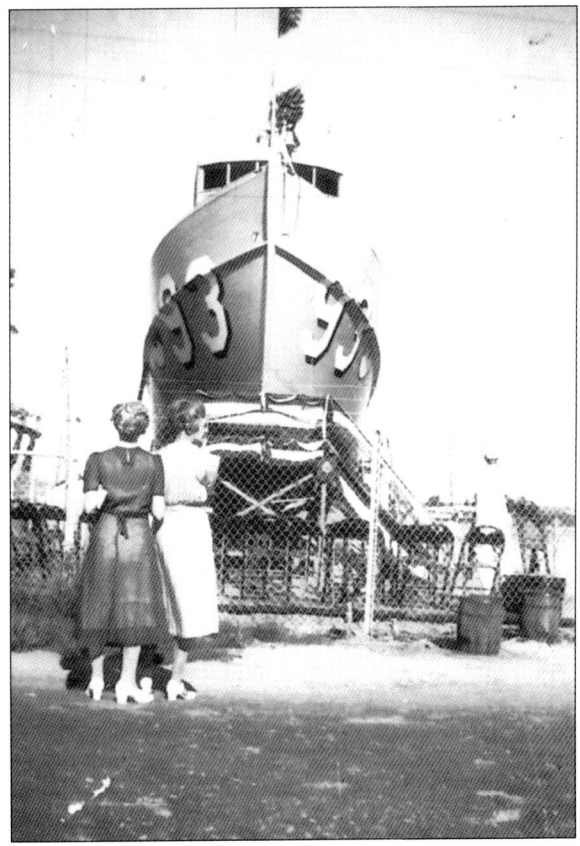

Two stylish women are admiring a newly built ship at Delaware Bay Shipyard in Leesburg. The shipyard was a frequent gathering place for area residents because so many of them had friends or family who worked there. The company produced several significant ships for the war effort, and with each vessel launching, there was always a festive atmosphere. (Courtesy of Mary Hagemann.)

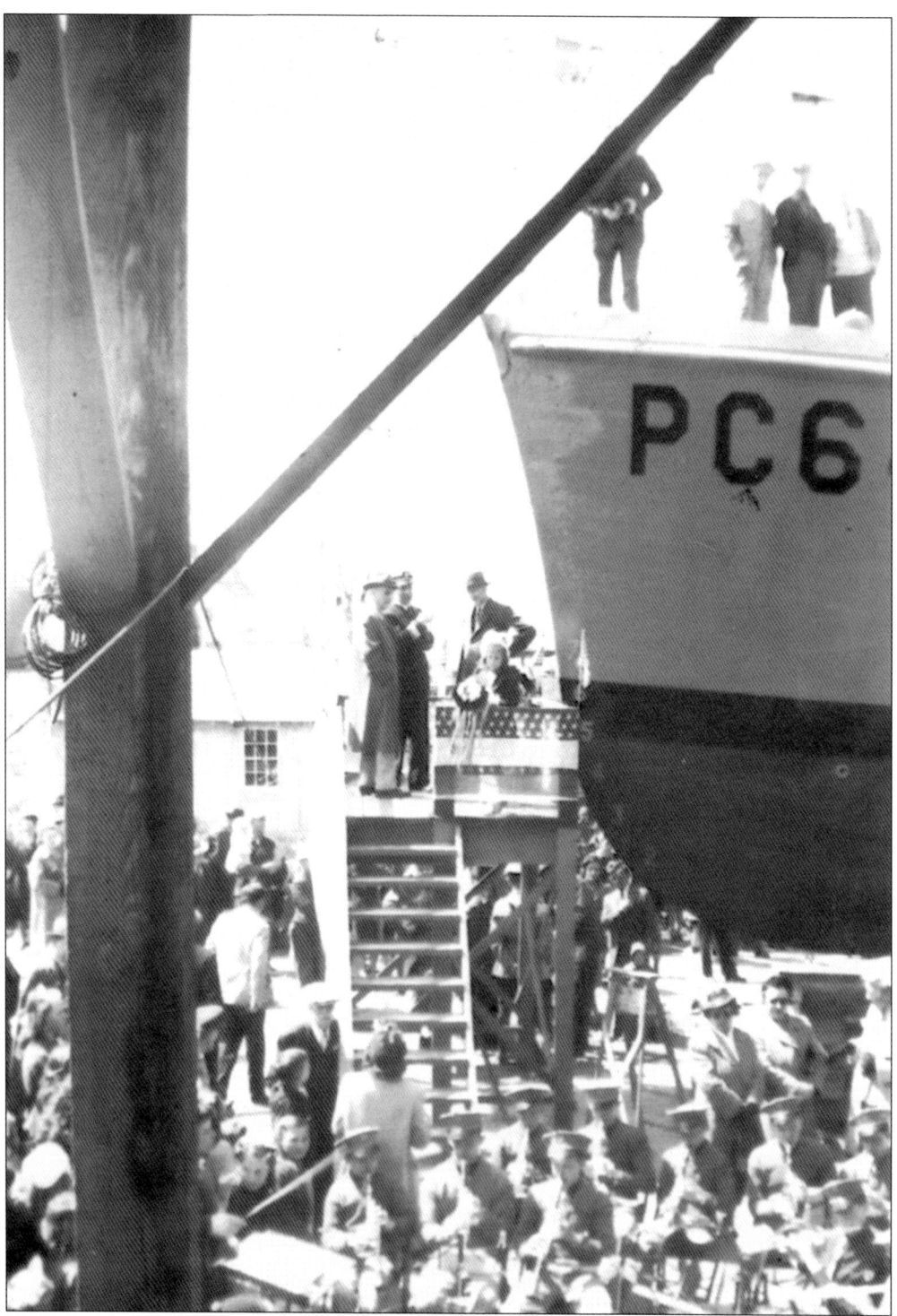

Here, PC-648 is being christened at Del Bay in Leesburg. The ship launchings were attended by dignitaries and most of the people living in the surrounding towns. There were great celebrations with music and food. (Courtesy of Paul Cox and Mary Hagemann.)

At the boat launchings during World War II, there were often bands to provide music and entertainment. The band members dressed in light-brown uniforms that looked very professional. (Courtesy of Mary Hagemann.)

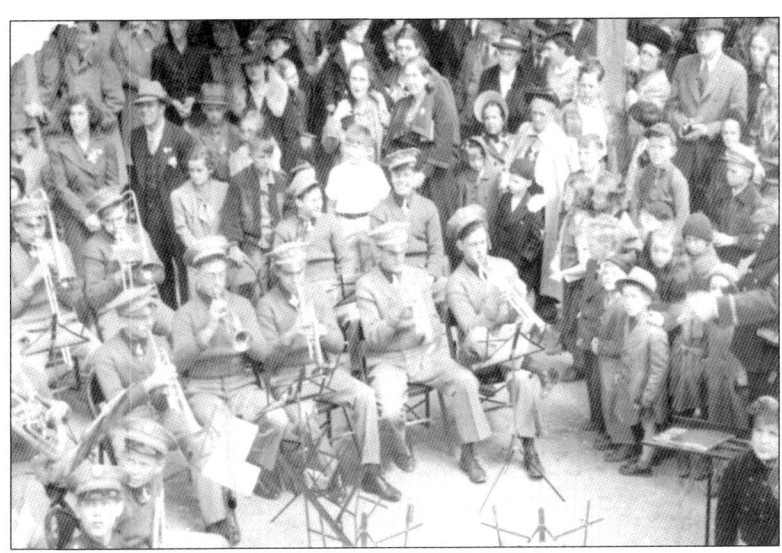

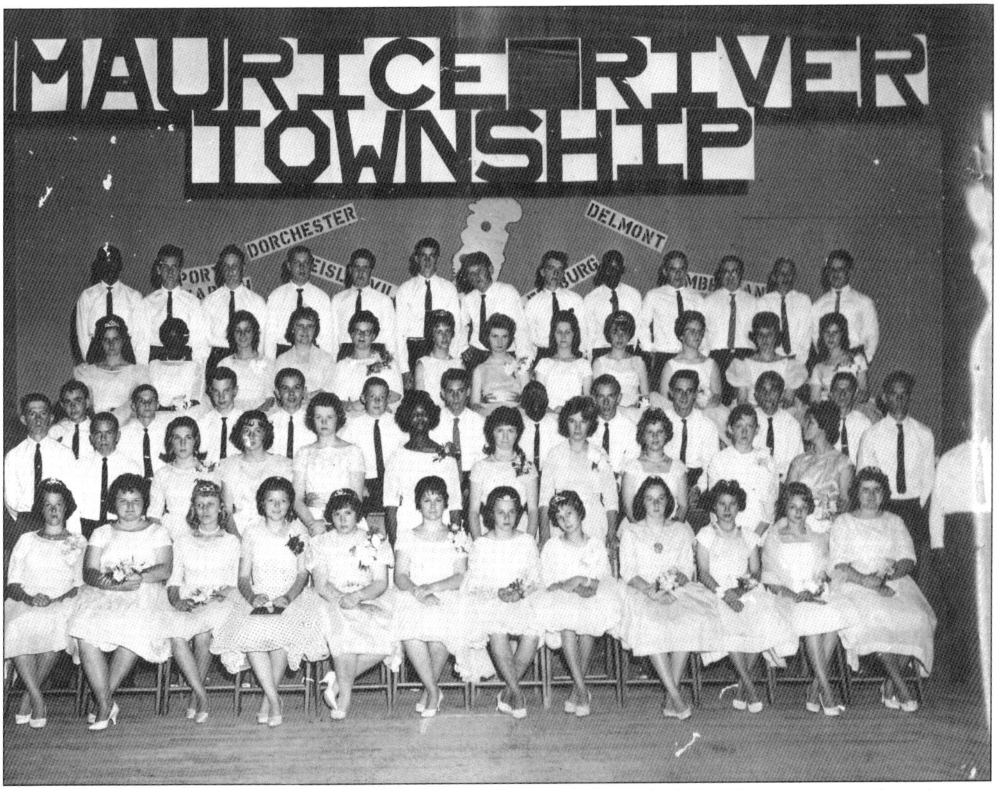

There were 60 students in the eighth-grade graduating class of 1962. This photograph, taken in Leechester Hall, shows handsome young boys in dress shirts and ties and beautiful girls in dresses. Some of the girls are wearing tiaras. The students lived in the surrounding villages of Leesburg, Dorchester, Port Elizabeth, Cumberland, Heislerville, and Delmont, as seen in the signs hanging on the wall in the background. Drew Tomlin is in the fifth row, third from left. (Courtesy of Drew Tomlin.)

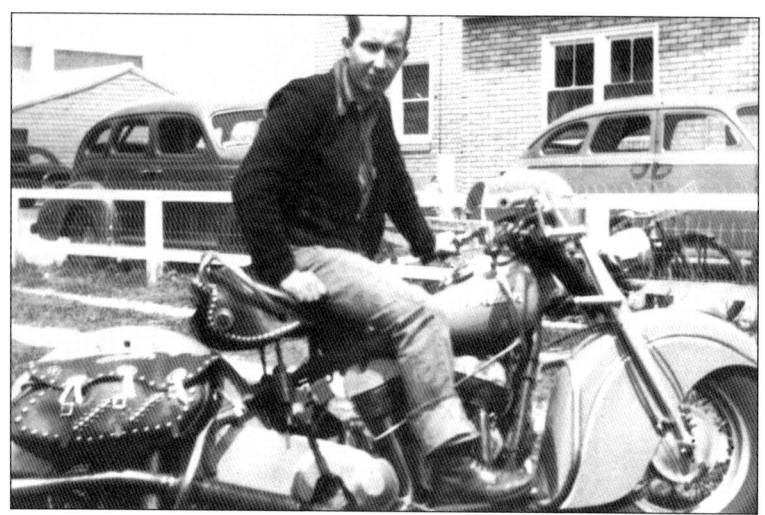

Pictured in 1952 is Charles Foster Sr., a lifelong resident of Leesburg. His wife and children still live in the area. He is seen on his 1948 Indian motorcycle on Olive Street (formerly River Street) in Leesburg. Note the sturdy 1940s cars in the background. (Courtesy Chick Foster Jr. and Mary Hagemann.)

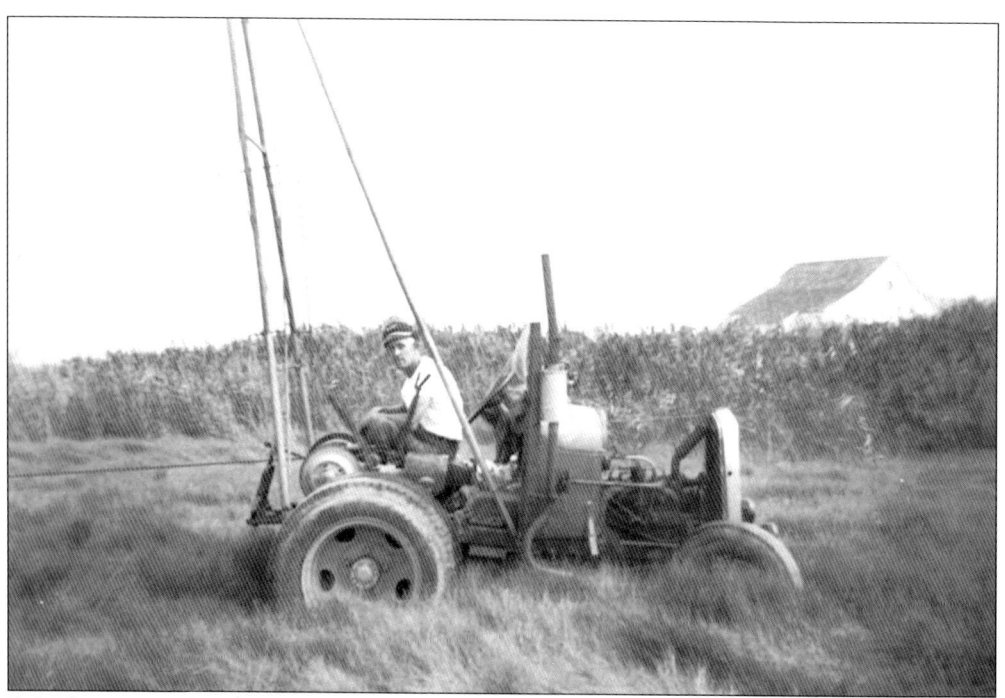

Bob Harris was a Leesburg legend. He was a man who defied the odds. He was a victim of polio and was paralyzed from the waist down, but that did not hold him back. He got around town by moving himself along the ground with his arms and riding on his tractor. He created and drove the most unusual motorized vehicle. Local resident Bill Hawn recalls the rumble of his tractor coming down the road. It reminded him of a contraption in a Rube Goldberg cartoon, and he says it would have fit into the Mad Max movies. It was made from a Ford Model A chassis and was welded together from bits and pieces of pulleys, gears, and chains. Harris put in many wells throughout town and moved many homes through meadows at Thompsons Beach. (Courtesy of Ronald Flynn.)

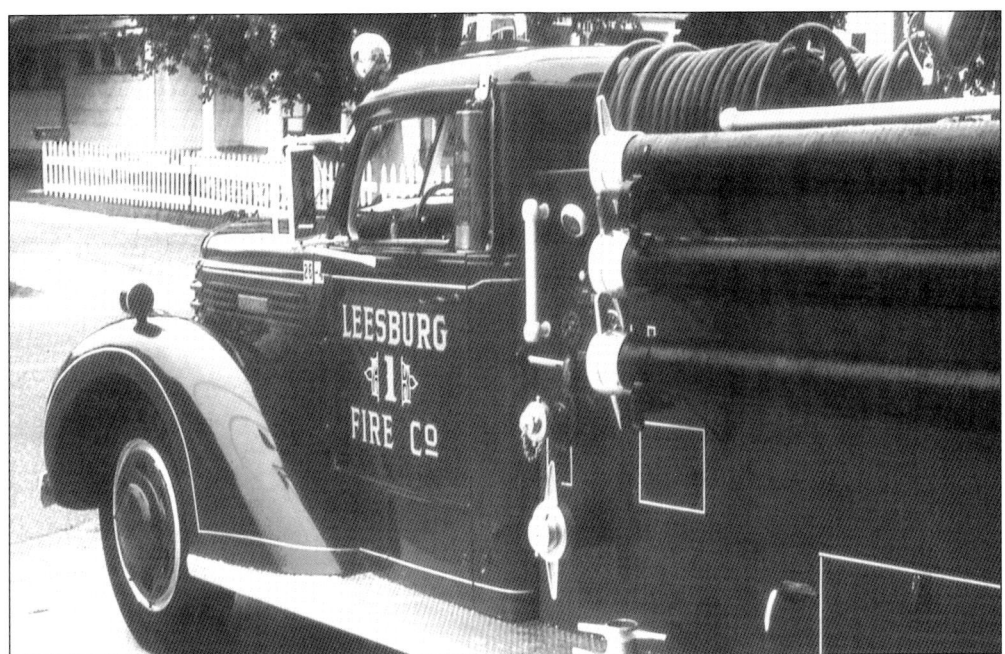

On March 11, 1943, a brand-new Diamond T fire truck with a Hercules engine was delivered to the Leesburg Fire Company to replace the first truck that served the township well since 1926. The Diamond T was a 500-gallon-per-minute pumper, which was a large amount of water for that time. The cost of this new beauty was $5,270. (Courtesy of Drew Tomlin.)

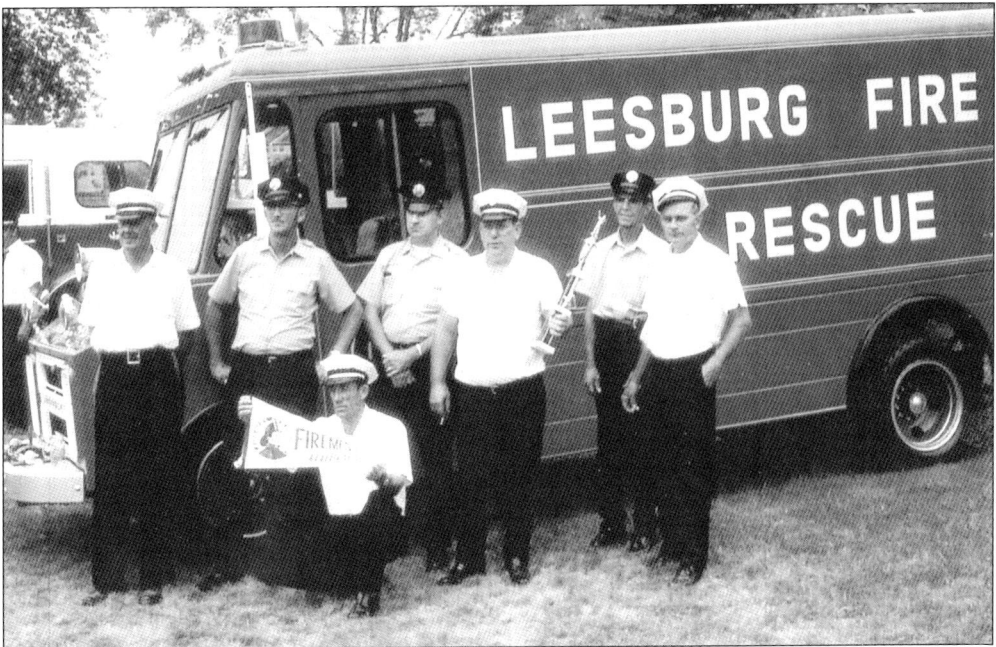

Members of the Leesburg Fire Company are preparing for a parade to celebrate the purchase of a 1972 rescue truck. From left to right are Milinor Wright, Nelson Branin, Harry "Trinkle" Trout (with pennant), Mike Froelich, fire chief Roland Hoffman, Carl Hanby, and Mel Pfirman. (Courtesy of Drew Tomlin.)

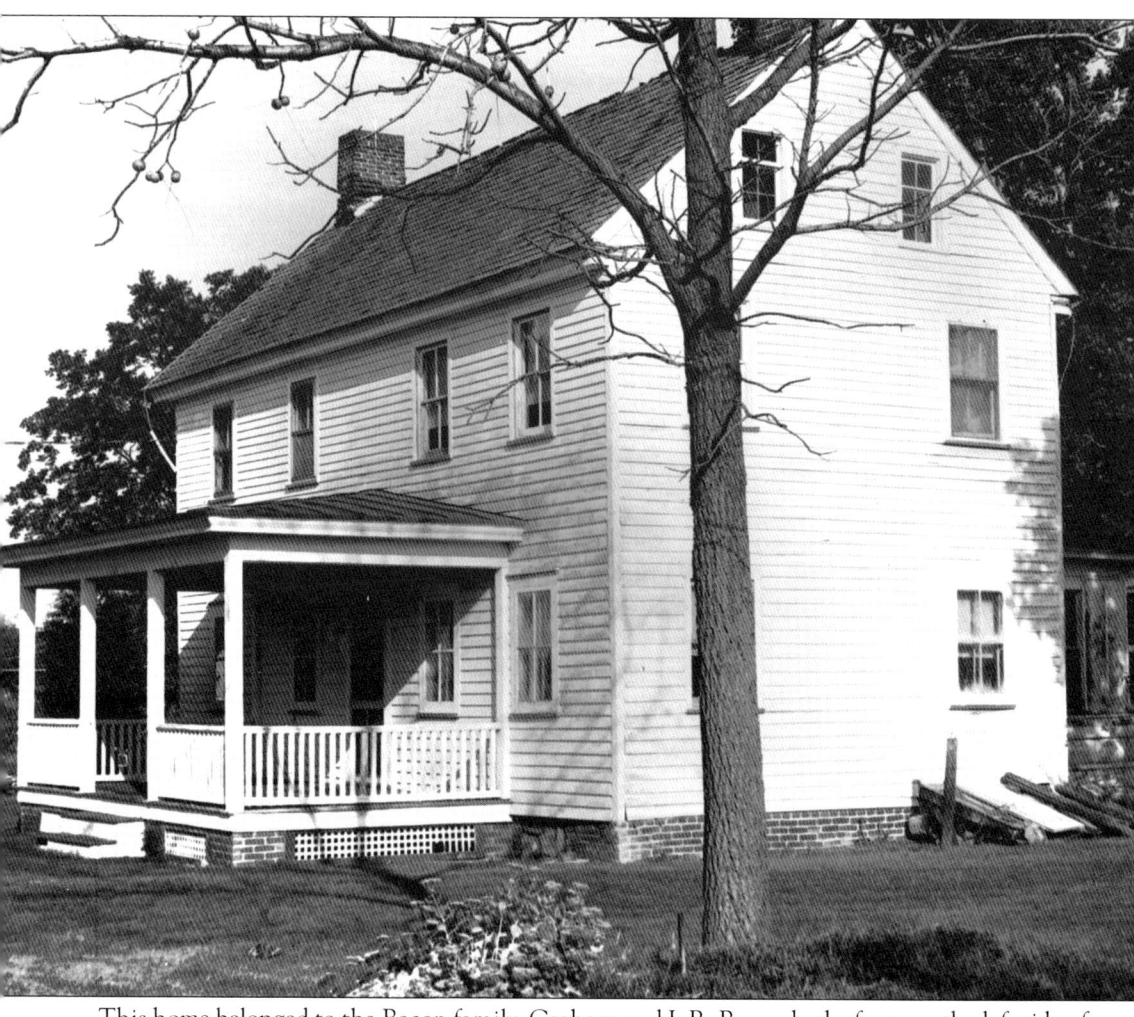

This home belonged to the Bacon family. Graham and L.R. Bacon had a farm on the left side of River Road, just south of the Delaware Bay Shipbuilding Company in Leesburg. The house has since been torn down. (Courtesy of Drew Tomlin.)

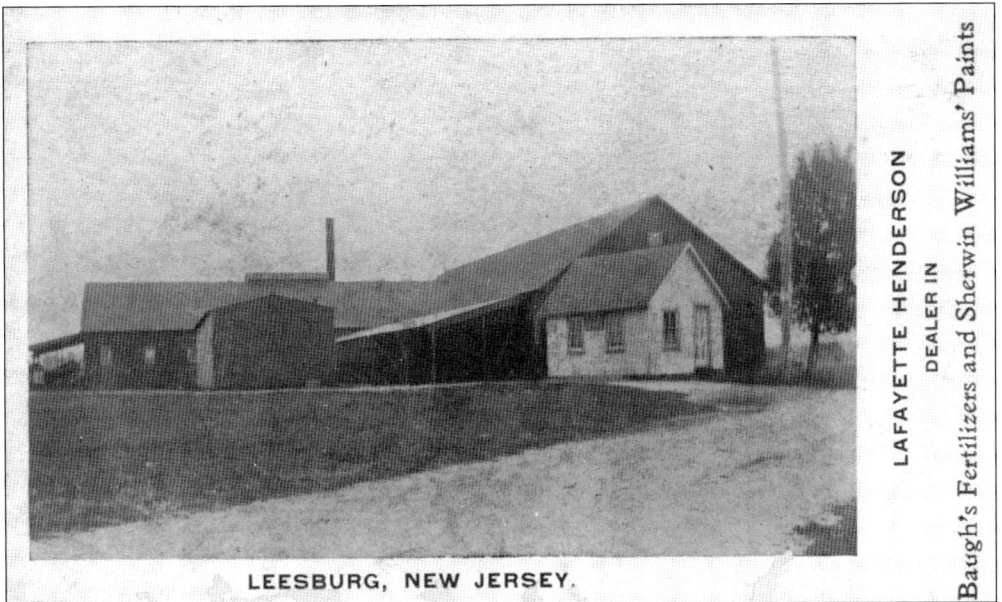

This postcard shows a one-time local business. Lafayette Henderson was a dealer in Baugh's fertilizers and Sherwin Williams paints. Lafayette Henderson's tombstone lists that he lived from 1853 to 1936. (Courtesy of Drew Tomlin.)

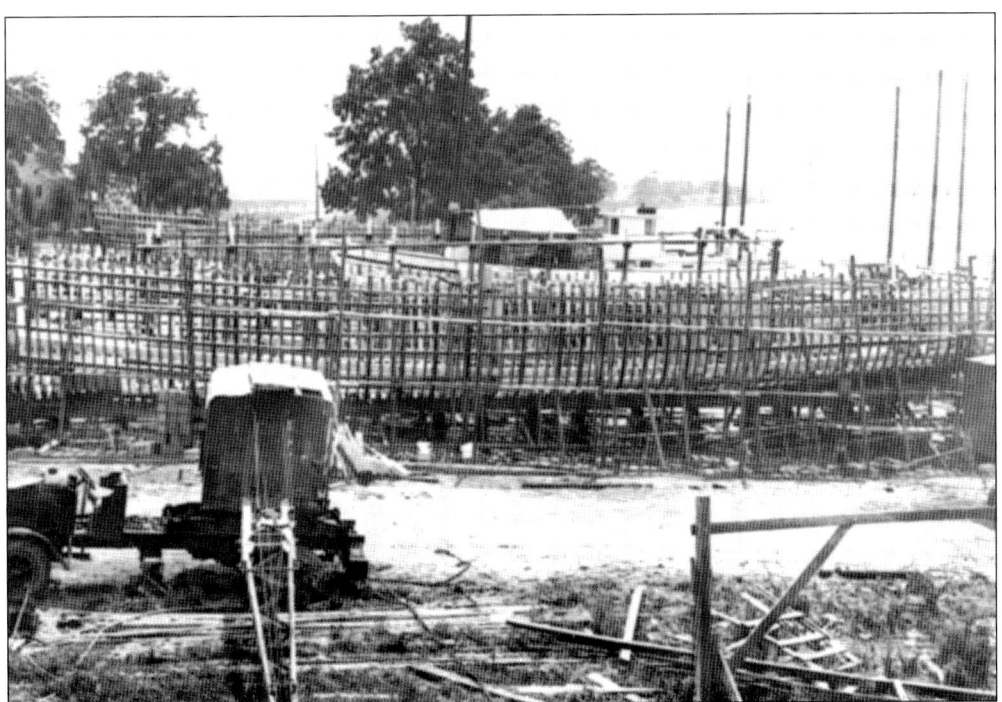

This World War II–era picture shows the wooden, skeletal frames of two boats being constructed at Delaware Bay Shipbuilding Company. (Courtesy of Drew Tomlin.)

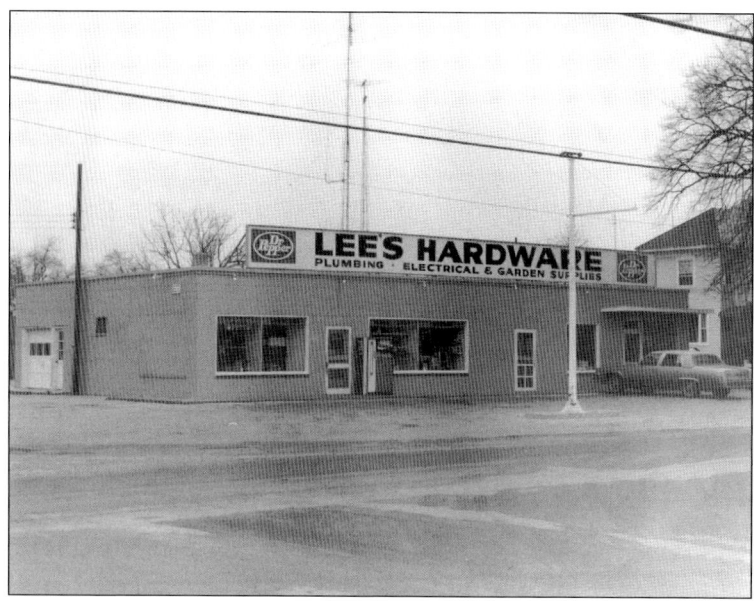

Lee's Hardware was a landmark in Leesburg in the 1960s. Leesburg residents did not have to go uptown (to Millville) more than once a week, since local businesses like this met their needs. This hardware store was a real convenience for Leesburg and surrounding villages. (Courtesy of the Herb Lee collection.)

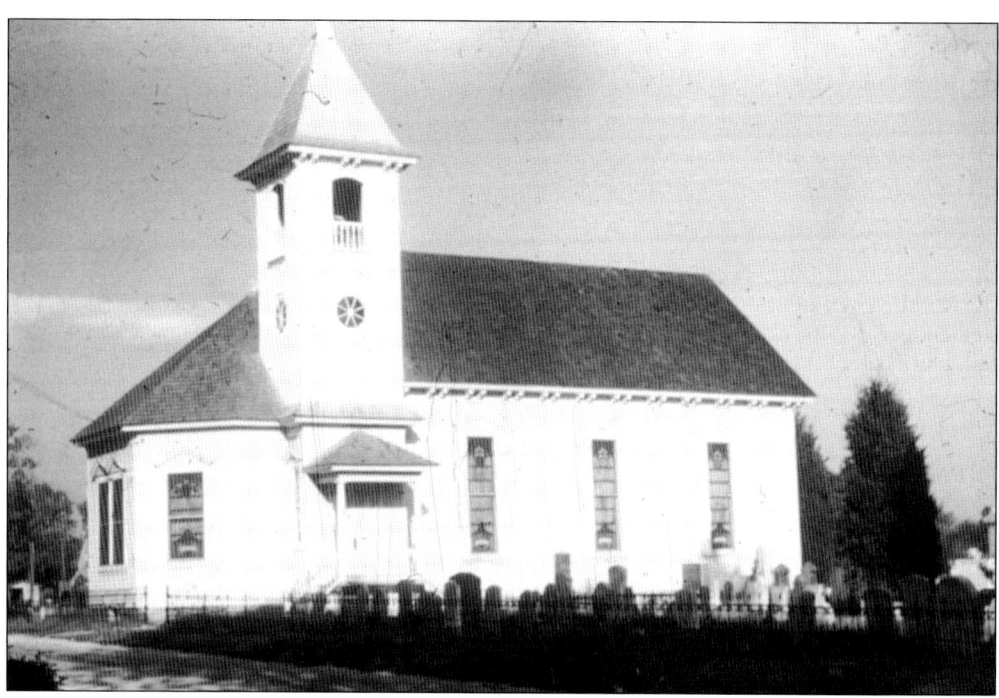

The Leesburg Methodist Church and cemetery are shown in this c. 1950 photograph. A new building was erected to replace the original Methodist church in 1862. In 1882, the spire and a front Sunday school room were added at a cost of $1,500. In 1959, another room was added for additional classroom space. Today, the church is still meeting the spiritual needs of local people. (Courtesy of the Herb Lee collection.)

Four
WORKING THE WATER

The lure of the salt air, the lapping waves, and the endless expanse of the horizon have been a siren call to many watermen. Early explorers came to the region by ship to trade with Native Americans. Gathering oysters was first carried on by the Indians. The oysters were eaten, raw or smoked, and used for trading with inland tribes.

Early explorers settled along the riverbanks, and Port Elizabeth became a designated port in 1789. Large vessels carrying lumber, coal, iron, and brick used this busy port. Many goods were transported by water. In Maurice River Township, shipbuilding took root with the founding of the small villages along the Maurice River. The ships were made entirely of wood and were propelled by the wind. Maurice River, as well as Delaware Bay, was once considered the "oyster capital of the world." The extension of the railroad to Maurice River and Bivalve greatly contributed to the tremendous growth of the oyster industry. At times, hundreds of oyster vessels were seen under sail. During Prohibition, many oystermen made a lot of additional revenue using their vessels to smuggle alcohol.

The area also became known in the early 1900s as "Fisherman's Paradise" due to the abundant local fish in the bay. It was a popular area for recreational and commercial fishermen. There was once a busy fish factory along the river. The bay was also home to eels and horseshoe crabs, which were once used for fertilizer. Commercial crabbing developed as a viable occupation. Blue claw crabs are plentiful in the bay. Watermen tend to be hearty souls who work hard, start their days early, and love being on the open water. They often contend with unpleasant weather, winds, tides, issues with their vessels, and ongoing maintenance concerns. They also enjoy their independence, solitude, and the sense of freedom on the bay. One could say that they have the bay in their blood.

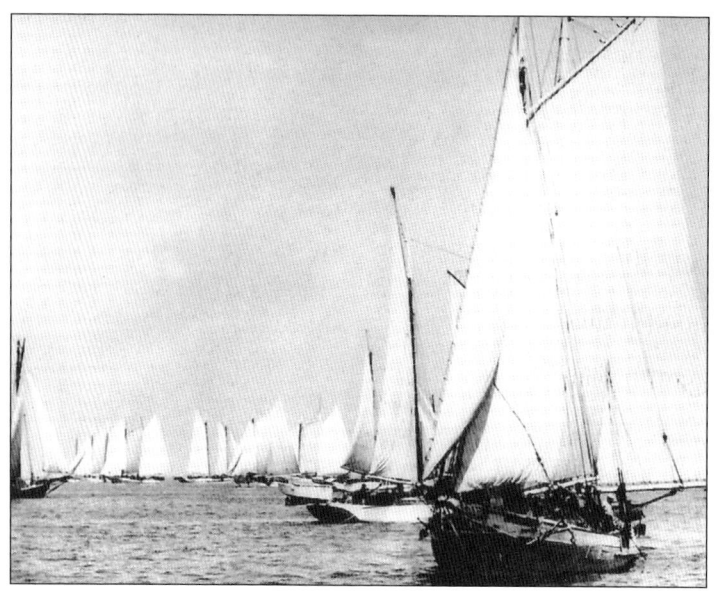

In the early 1900s, the Maurice River at the mouth of Delaware Bay was described as a forest of masts. In this photograph, it is easy to see why. The water is thick with sailing oyster vessels. It is indeed a magnificent sight. At one time, there were around 500 working oyster vessels in this area. (Courtesy of Drew Tomlin.)

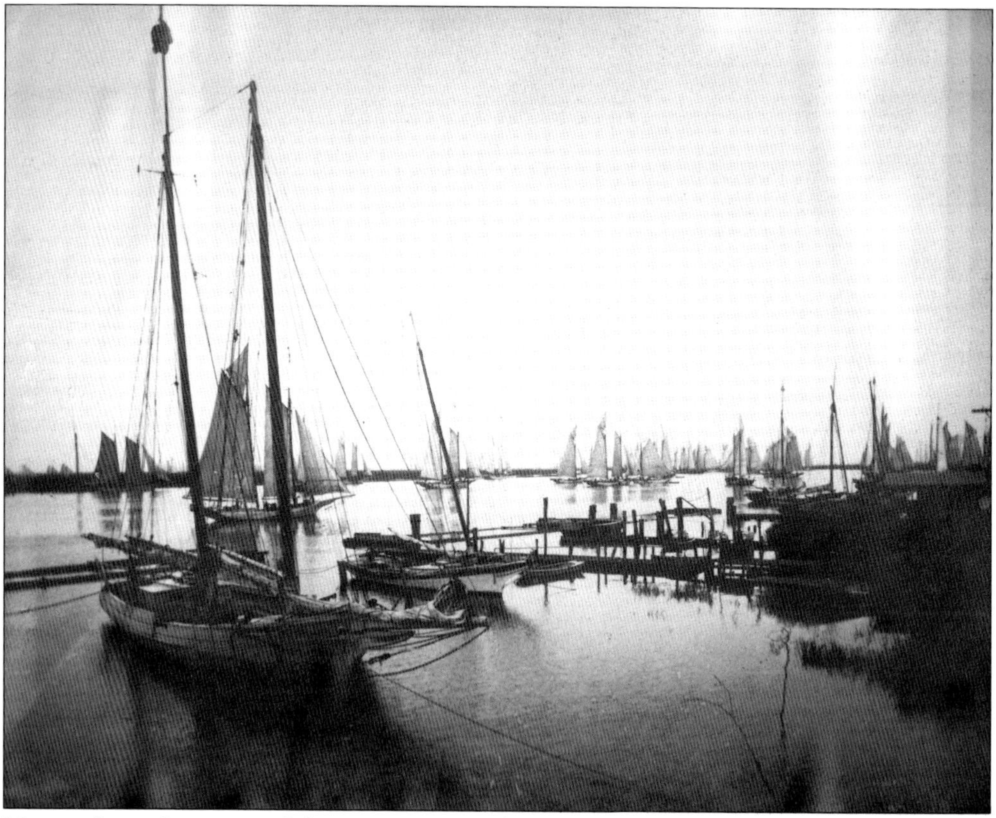

Many sailing schooners and sloops are seen on the Maurice River in this postcard, postmarked 1910. The water is as smooth as glass. It is easy to imagine the warmth of the day and the sounds of the seagulls soaring overhead. It is a peaceful scene during the spring oyster planting season known as "bay season." (Courtesy of Bayshore Center at Bivalve, gift of Bill Biggs.)

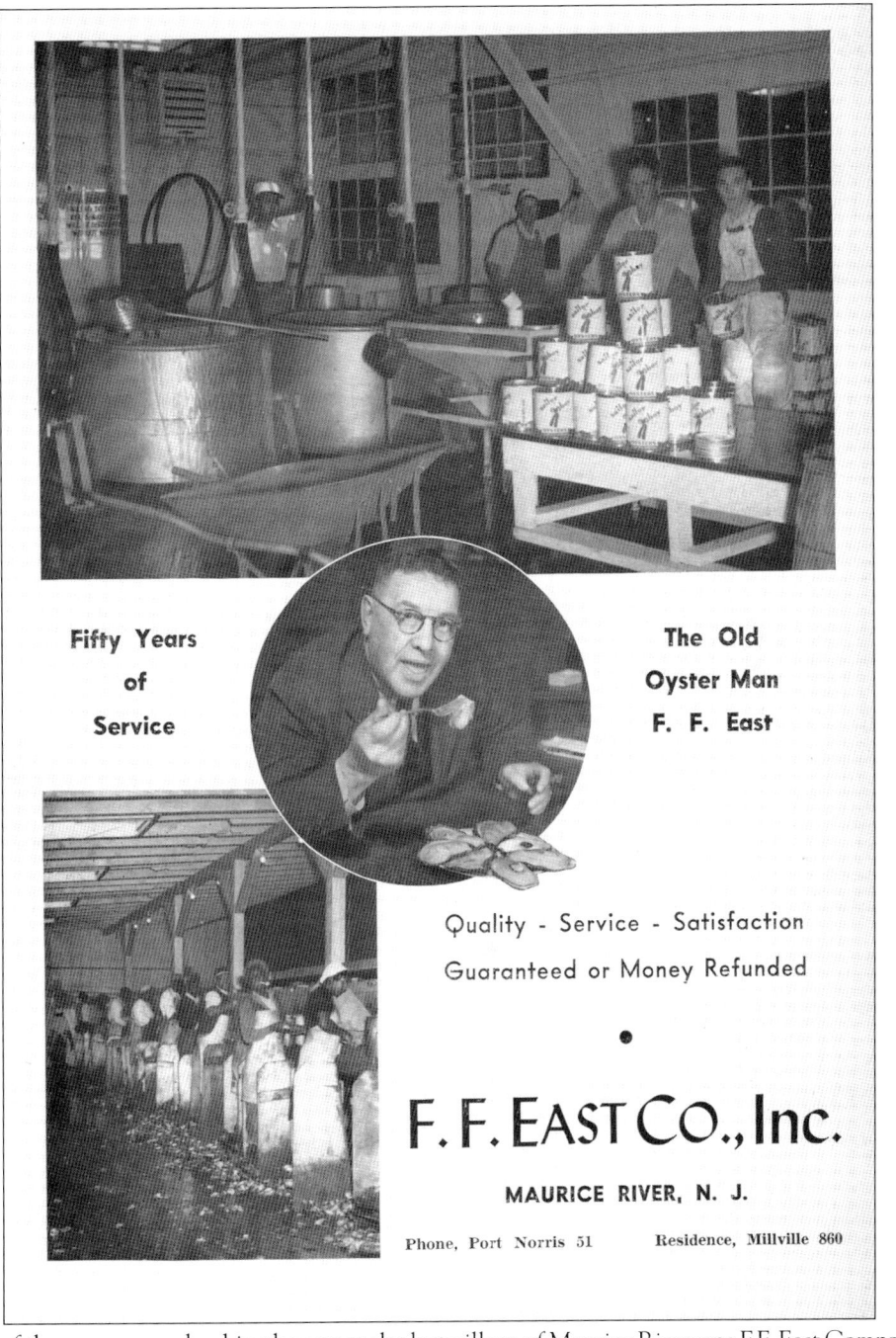

One of the prosperous shucking houses at the lost village of Maurice River was F.F. East Company. At the time of this advertisement, "old oysterman" F.F. East (center) had been in the business for 50 years. Stacks of canned oysters, along with workers, are pictured at the shucking house, located across the river from Bivalve. According to an article in *Reading Railroad* magazine in 1926, Maurice River, as well as Delaware Bay, was once the "oyster capital of the world," which seems hard to believe today. There were more oysters grown in this area than the combined production of New York, Connecticut, and Rhode Island. (Courtesy of Bayshore Center at Bivalve.)

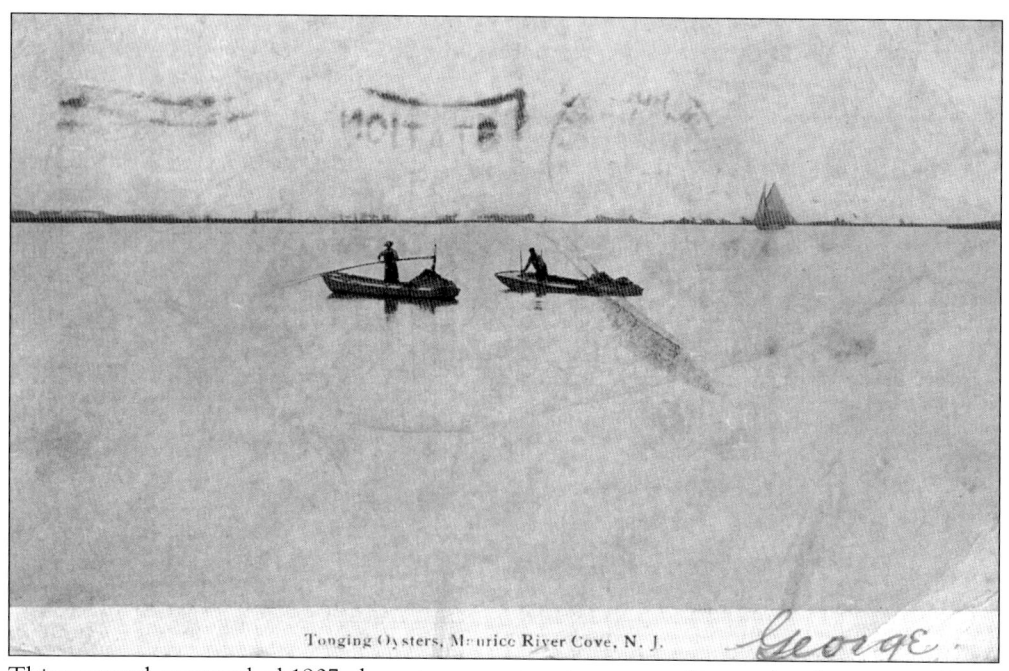

This postcard, postmarked 1907, shows two men tonging oysters. Former local oysterman Louis Peterson defines tongs as long wooden staves with a metal basket at the end with metal teeth; the tongs are used to gather oysters from the bottom of the bay. There are different types of baskets and different lengths of tongs, typically 12 to 14 feet. Tonging requires a lot of upper body strength, and especially wrist strength. (Courtesy of Bayshore Center at Bivalve, gift of Bill Biggs.)

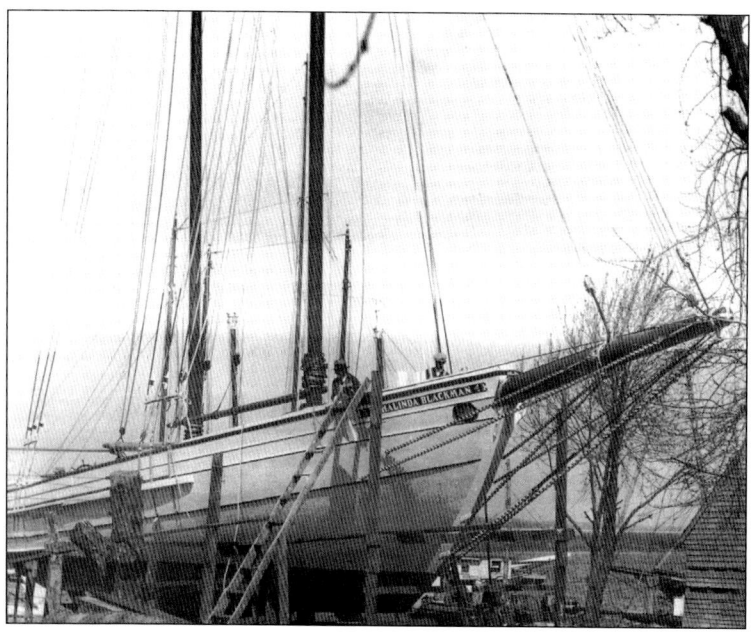

The *Ethalinda Blackman* was the largest oyster dredge boat built on the Maurice River. She was built in Dorchester in 1929. According to Rachel Dolhanczyk, curator at Bayshore Center at Bivalve, boats are often thought of as family and as having personalities, usually stereotypical female characteristics. (Courtesy of Bayshore Center at Bivalve, gift of Vincent J. Piecyck.)

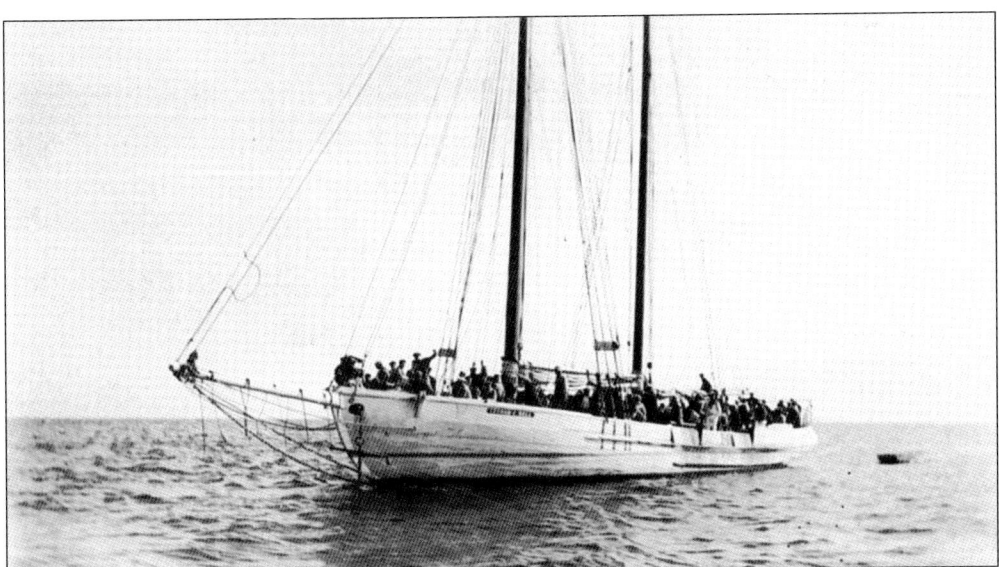

The *George C. Bell* is seen here on an excursion on the bay. She was built in Dorchester in 1929 and would have been one of the last schooners built. She had two sets of dredgers. During the great schooner race in the same year, she was skippered by George Armstrong and won both A Class and third place overall. (Courtesy of Drew Tomlin.)

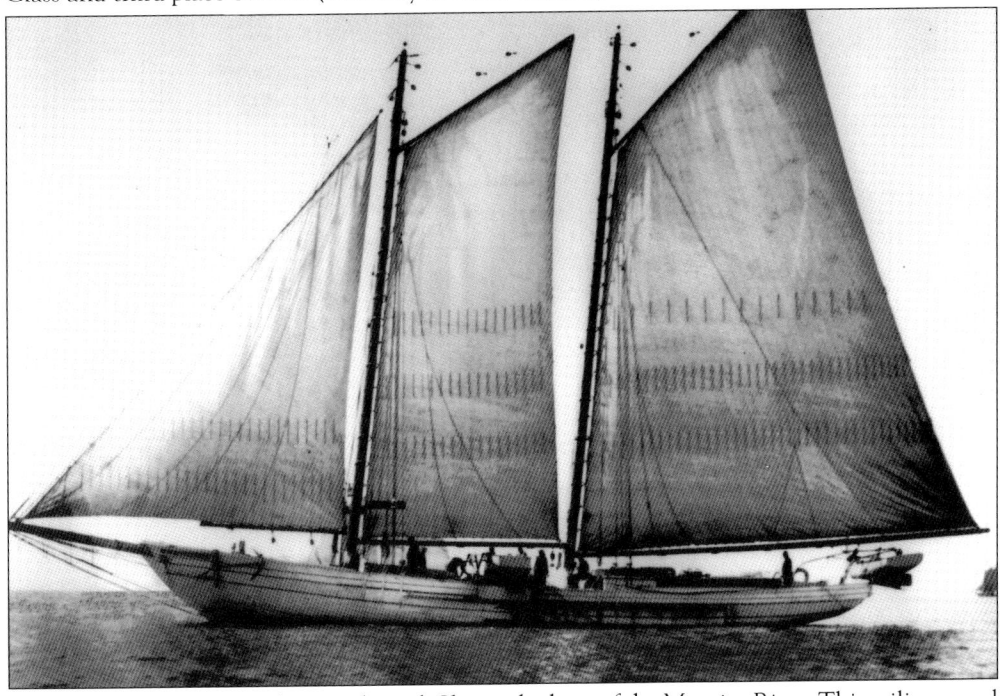

The *A.J. Meerwald* is seen here under sail. She worked out of the Maurice River. This sailing vessel was a new style of schooner built with an engine in 1928. She was one of the last schooners built between 1925 and 1930 and was converted to power in 1945. She was saved by Meghan Wren, now director of Bayshore Center at Bivalve. With dedicated volunteers and shipwrights, Wren restored her to her original beauty in the late 1990s. She now sails around the region as the official tall ship of the state of New Jersey. (Courtesy of Bayshore Center at Bivalve.)

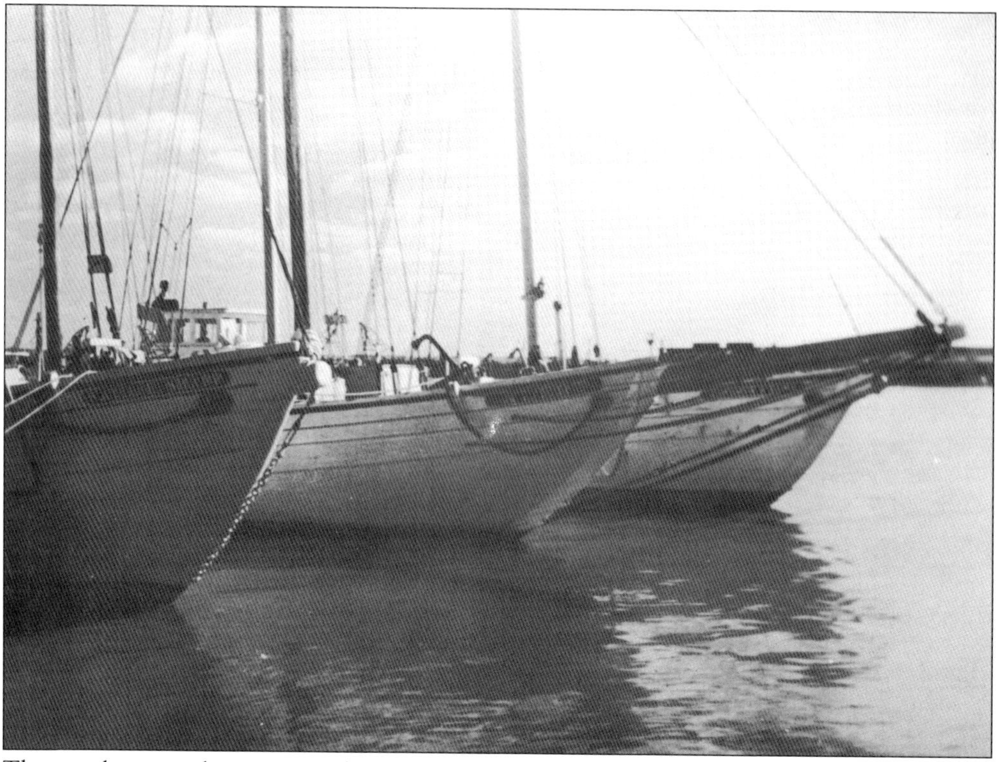

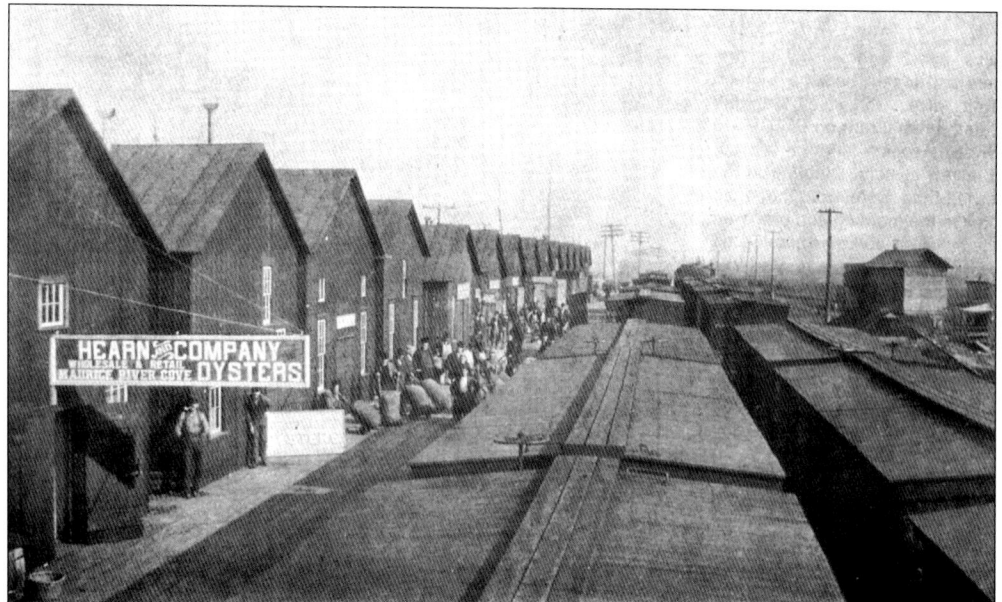

Three sailing vessels are pictured in the Maurice River. A captain can be seen at the helm of the center ship. It looks like it might have been a day without much wind due to the water being smooth and calm. (Courtesy of Drew Tomlin.)

Hearn Company Oysters in the lost village of Maurice River is seen here. Workers with loaded bags of oysters are next to the train cars in the late 1800s. (Courtesy of Bayshore Center at Bivalve, gift of Richard Smith.)

This is an oyster fleet in Maurice River Cove seen from East Point on May 18, 1941. This gorgeous view would not have been an unusual sight at that time. (Courtesy of Nelson Klein.)

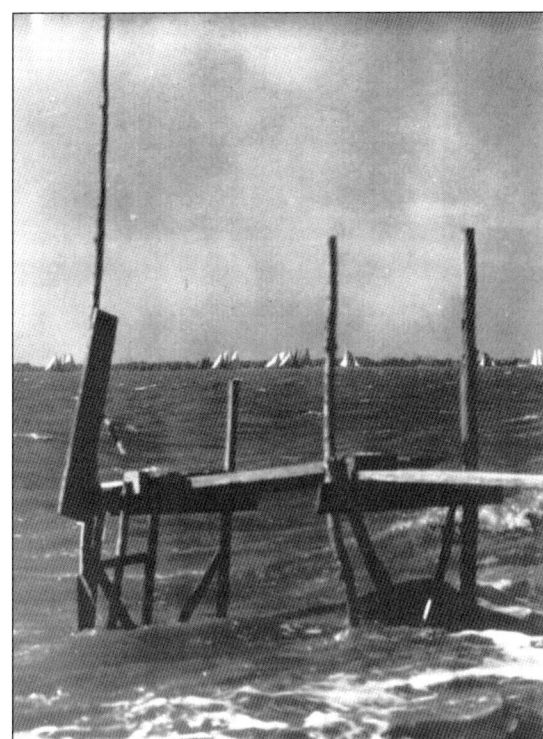

Here is an oyster schooner under sail. She is fully loaded with oysters and crew members. It must have been a great day on the water. (Courtesy of Drew Tomlin.)

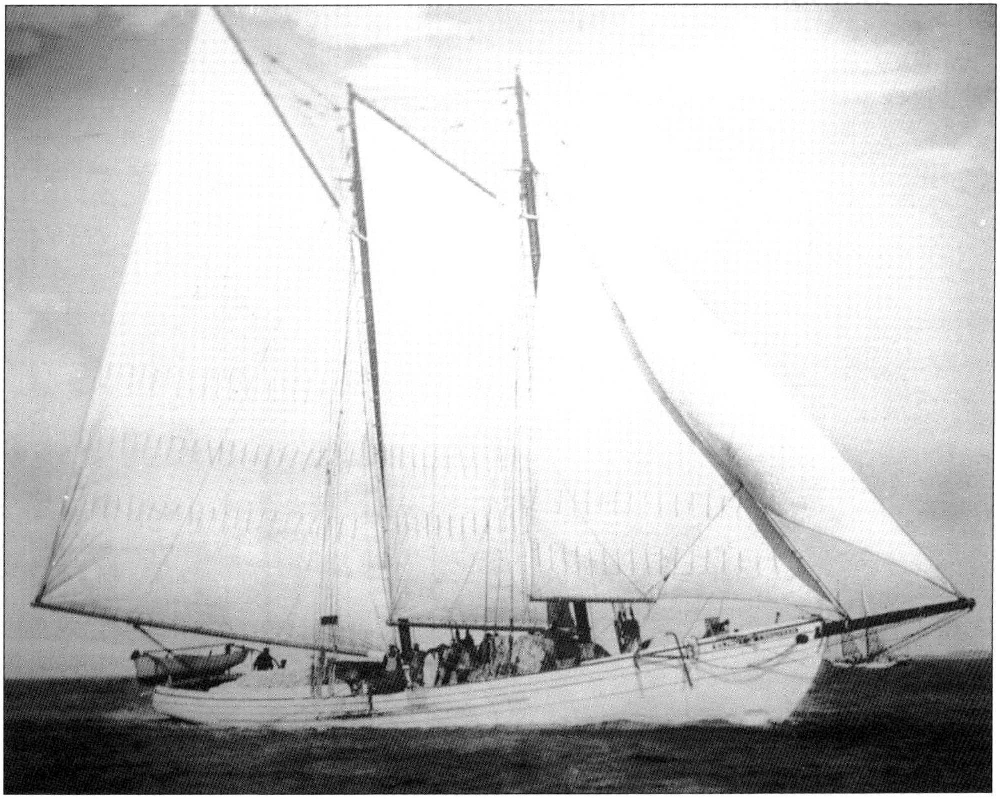

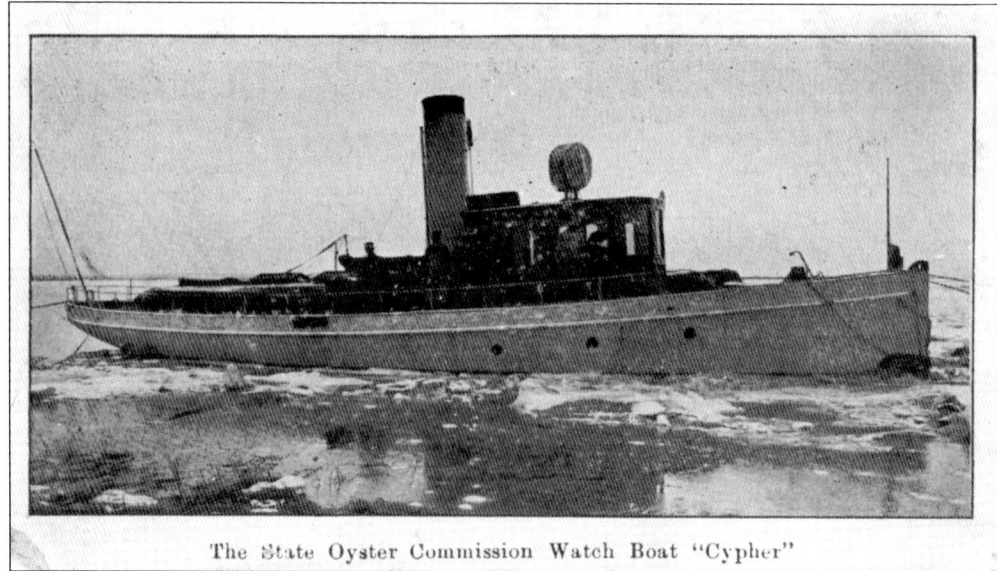

The State Oyster Commission Watch Boat "Cypher"

The New Jersey State Oyster Commission's watch boat *Cypher* was responsible for making sure that the oystermen were in the correct locations and only harvesting oysters from their leased grounds. According to a 1926 article in the *Reading Railroad* magazine, in the 1920s, 40,000 acres of oyster grounds were laid out into plots from 10 to 100 acres each and leased to growers by the state. This postcard is postmarked 1908. (Courtesy of Bayshore Center at Bivalve, gift of Bill Biggs.)

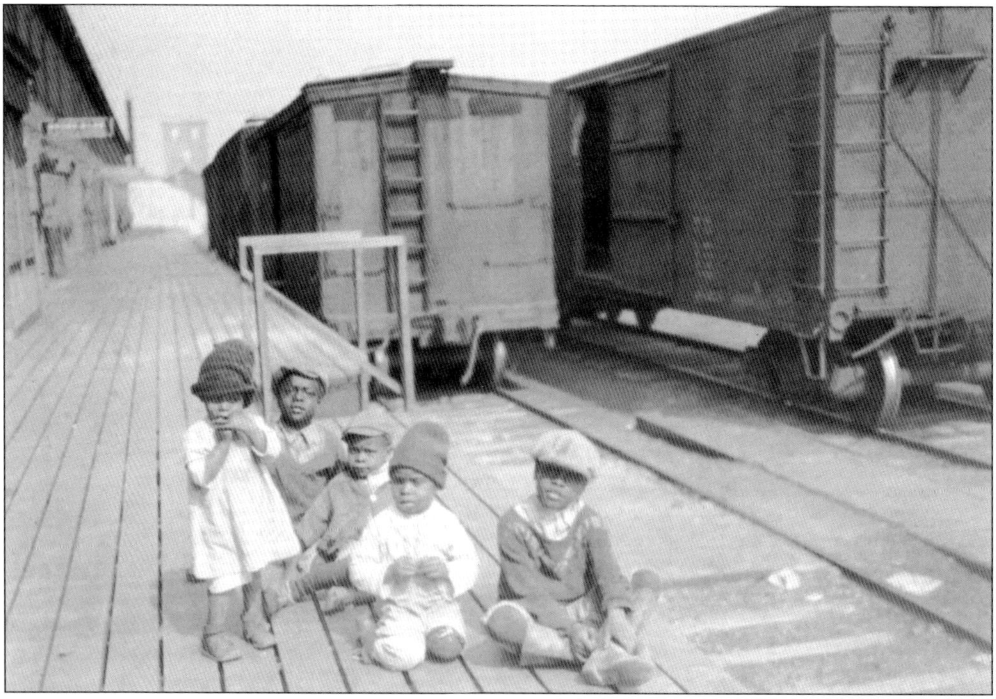

Pictured around 1920 is a group of oyster shuckers' children. The oyster workers and their families all lived in small houses called shanties near the wharves and railroad station. The children were accustomed to playing near the railroad and around the property. (Courtesy of Bayshore Center at Bivalve, gift of Olin McConnell.)

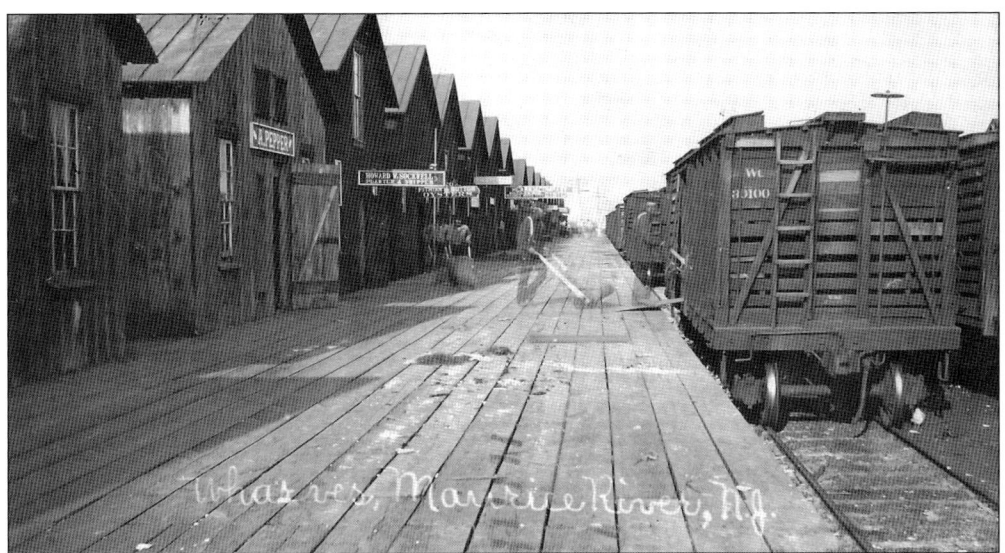

In this postcard, oyster workers are seen in ghostly form pushing loads of oysters to waiting train cars. Several oyster business signs can be seen over doors along the wharf. It was a thriving time for the oyster business. In the early 1920s, an average of 7,000 train carloads of oysters went out each year. Each carload contained 100 bags each, with 800 oysters per bag. The annual output of 56 million oysters was valued at $8 per bag, as stated in *Reading Railroad* magazine. (Courtesy of Bayshore Center at Bivalve, gift of Bill Biggs.)

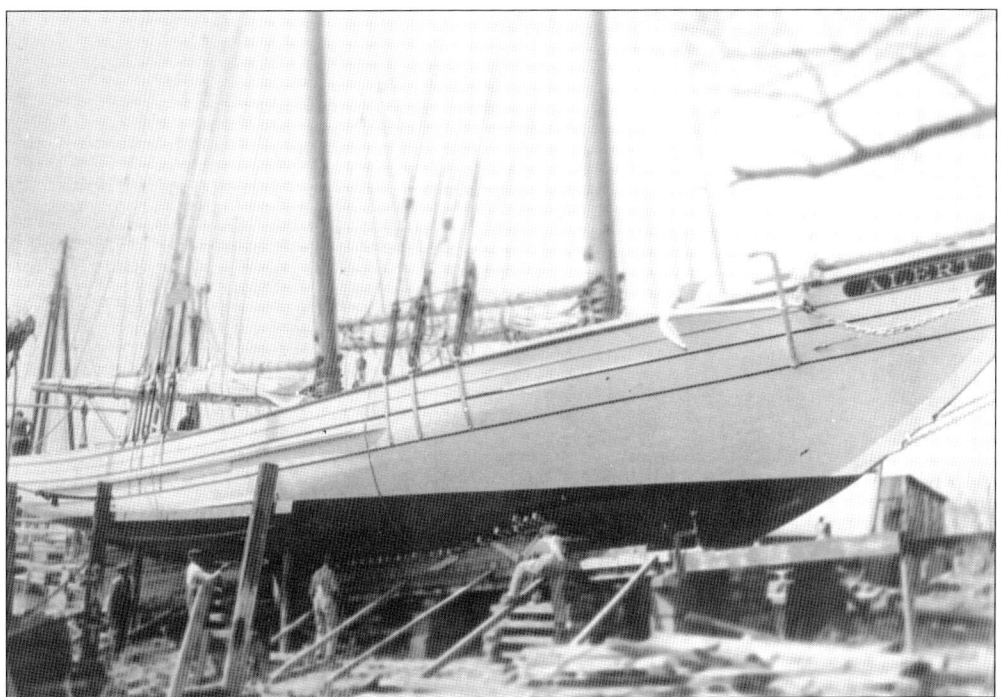

According to *Under Sail: The Dredge Boats of the Delaware Bay*, by Donald H. Rolfs, *Alert* was a spoon-bow schooner, built and launched at Dorchester for Capt. Frank Hinson. (Courtesy of Drew Tomlin.)

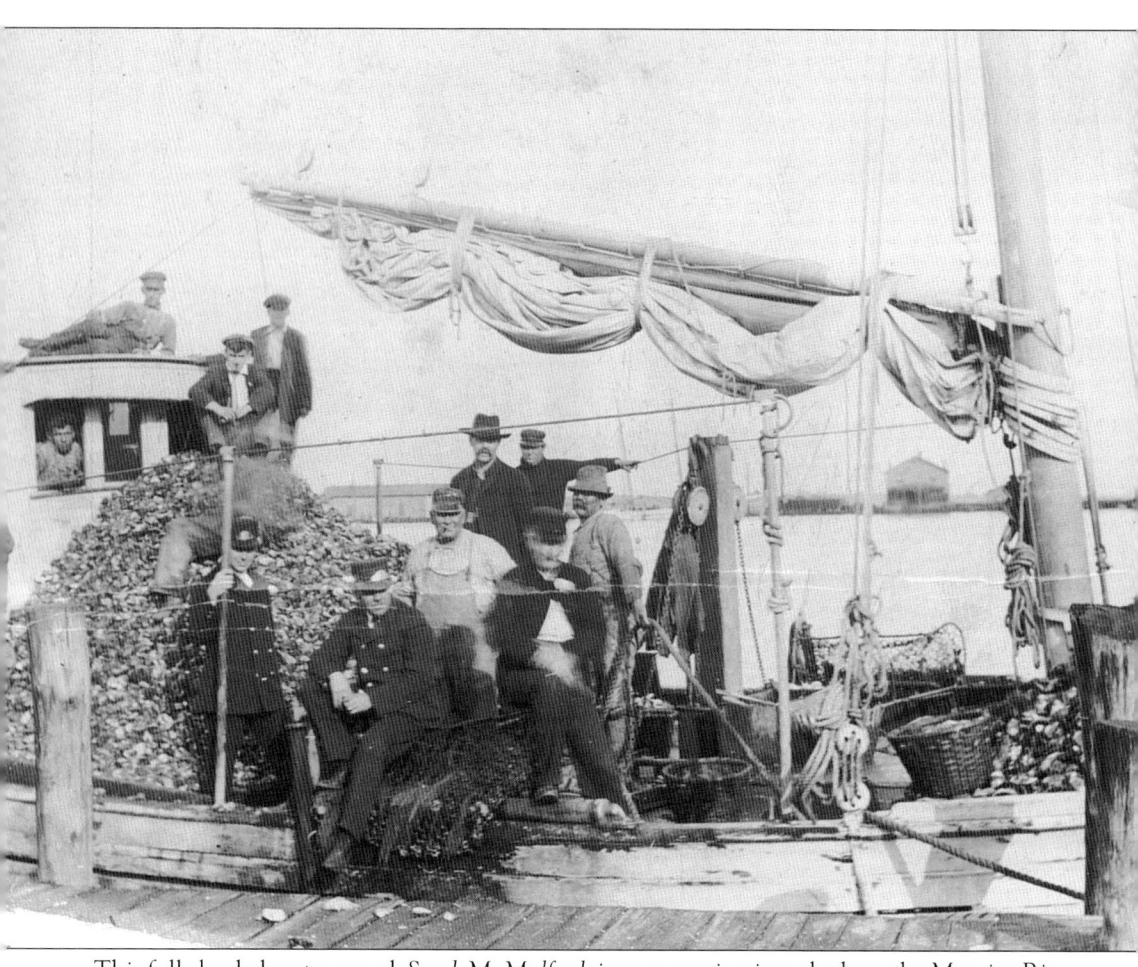

This fully loaded oyster vessel, *Sarah M. Mulford*, is seen coming into dock on the Maurice River. It was a good catch. This would have been a typical sight during the heyday of the oyster industry. Note the two inspectors. (Courtesy of Drew Tomlin.)

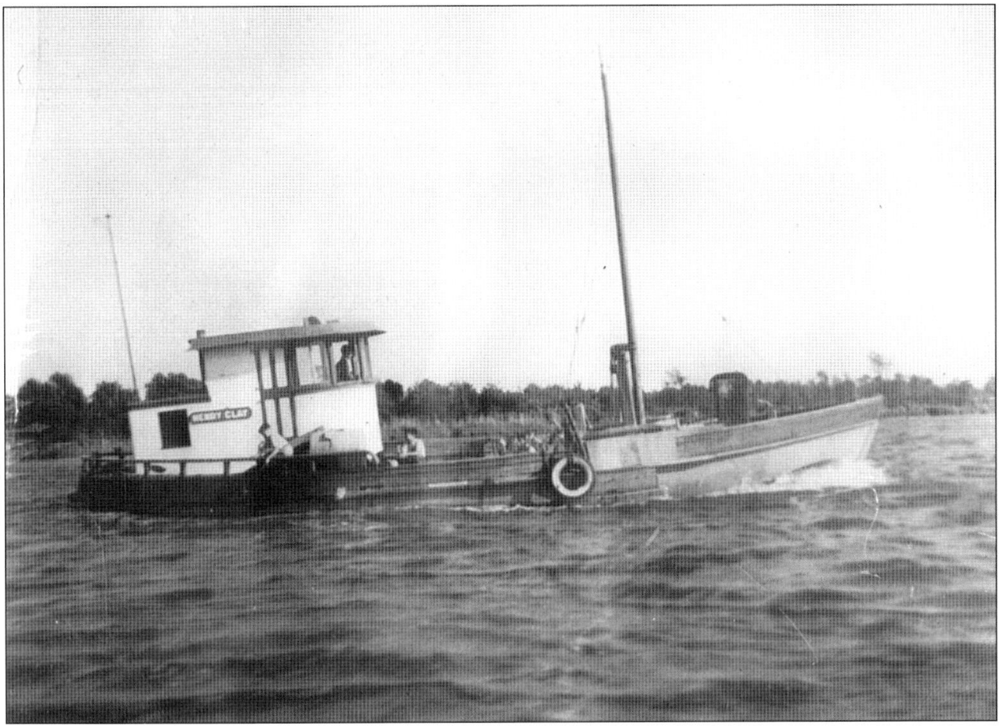

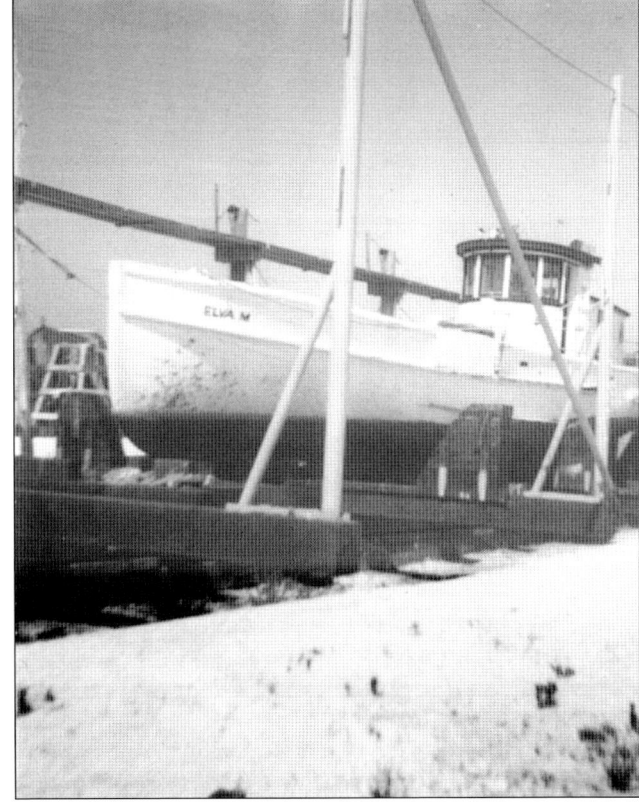

The *Henry Clay* was a dredge boat owned by Fred Peterson. In this photograph, Fred is at the helm. On the left is his son Fred, who was 10 years old, and on the right is his brother Louis, who was 12 at the time. The picture was taken in 1947. The boat is headed downriver. Louis is watching the bilge for water. (Courtesy of Louis Peterson.)

The *Elva* M was Louis Peterson's first oyster boat. Louis was in the oyster business from 1975 to 1998. In this photograph, the *Elva* M is on a railcar to be transported out to be refurbished. Peterson said he had paid off his farm and went to the bank to get a production credit loan. He bought the *Elva* M from Dan Hines. (Courtesy of Louis Peterson.)

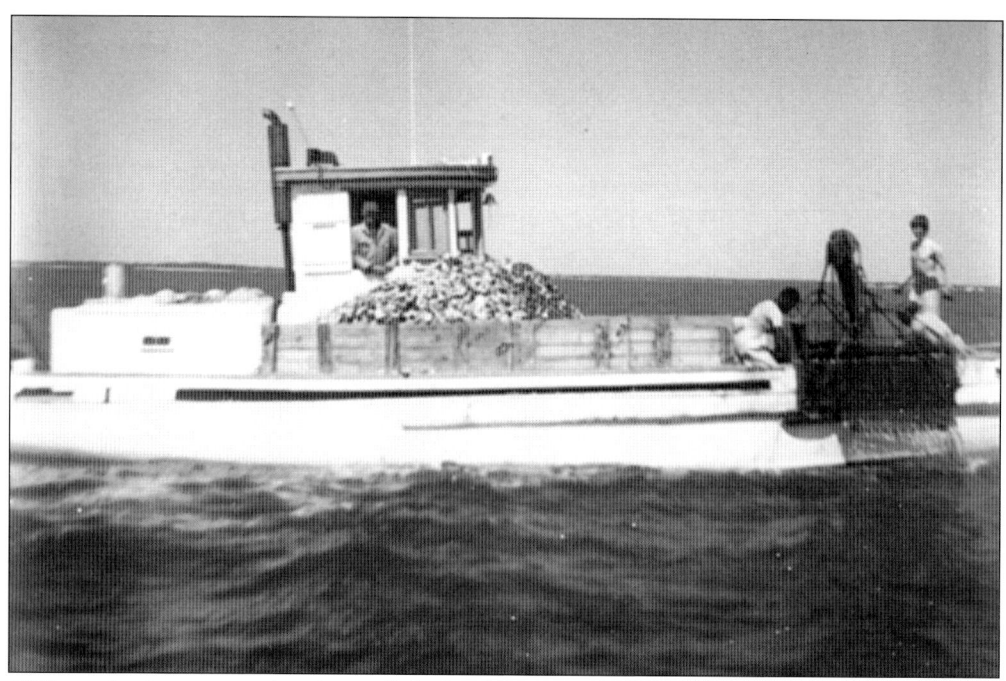

1975 was the first spring of working off the bay for Louis Peterson. In this picture, the men at right are crew members picking and separating oysters. (Courtesy of Louis Peterson.)

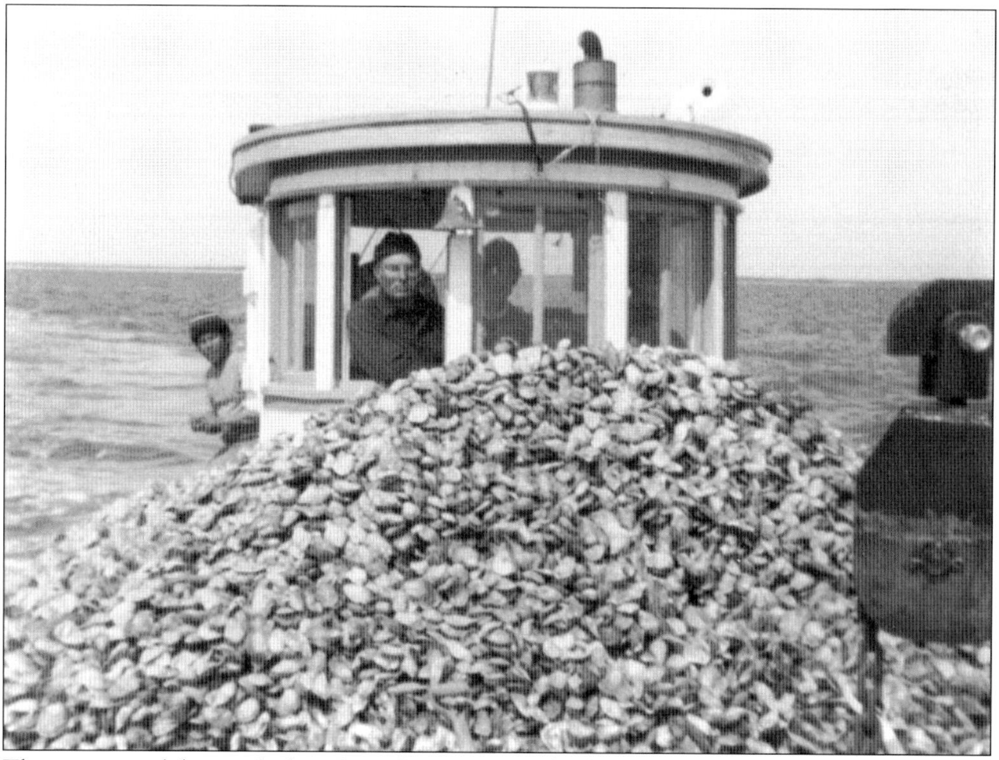

This was a good day on the bay. Louis Peterson is at the helm with a catch of about 300 bushels of oysters. (Courtesy of Louis Peterson.)

Oysterman Louis Peterson is standing outside the workshop on his farm holding tongs. The wooden stave on the left was about 14 feet in length, and the one on the right is about 18 feet long. At the time, Peterson also made machinery for boats. Oystermen needed to have other employment during the off-season since the oyster business was not year-round. This photograph was taken in the late 1970s. (Courtesy of Louis Peterson.)

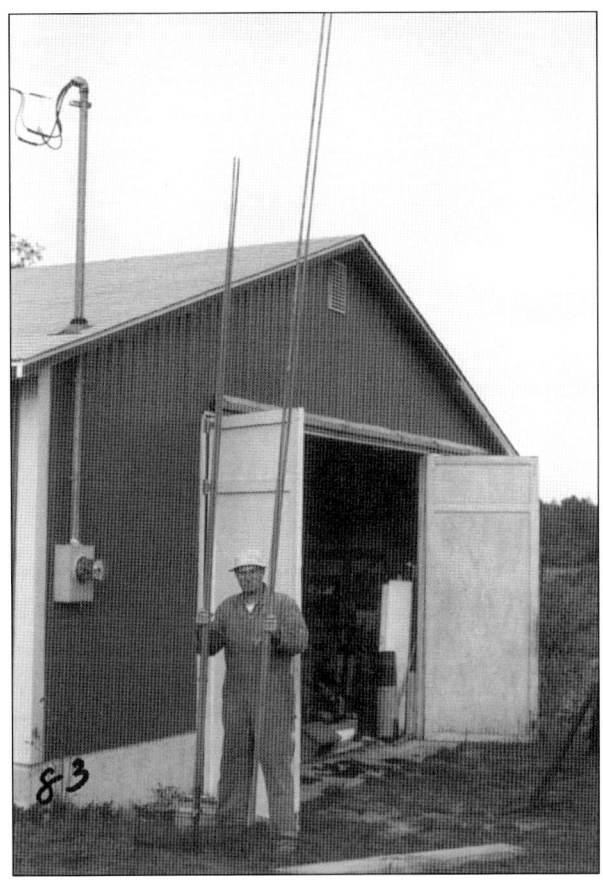

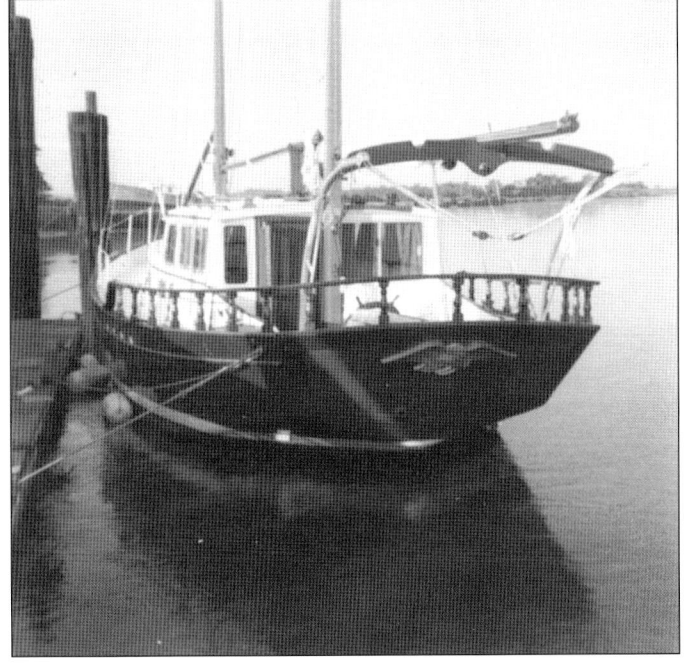

This boat with the eagle insignia was built at the Leesburg shipyard, which was not the Delaware Bay Shipyard at the time. Louis Peterson put the planks together and added the hardware for the masthead and masts. (Courtesy of Louis Peterson.)

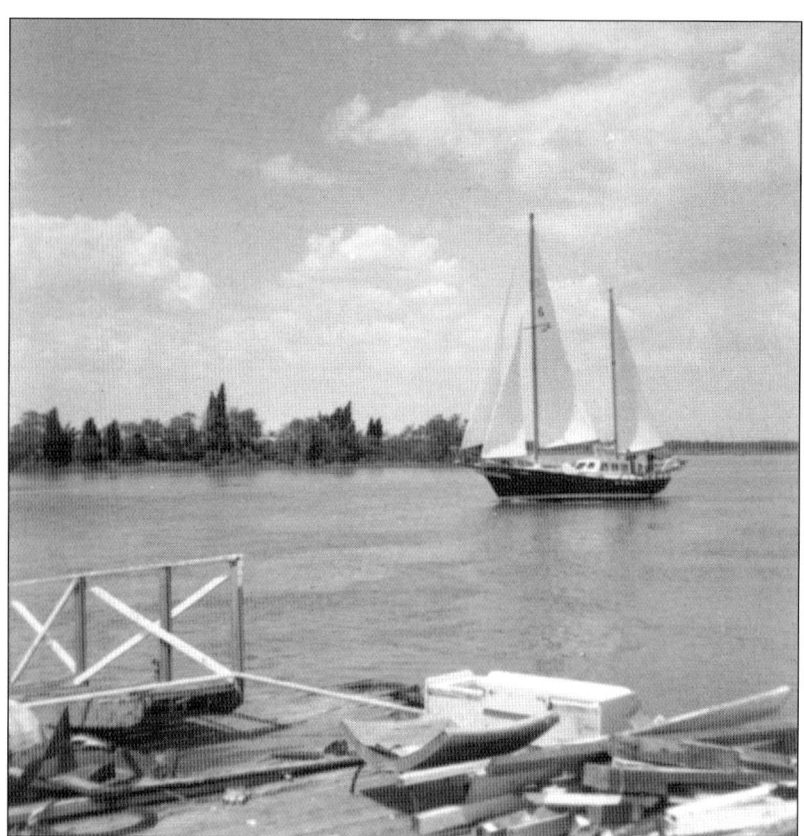

This is another view of the boat with the eagle. It is under sail on the Maurice River. She was a beauty. (Courtesy of Louis Peterson.)

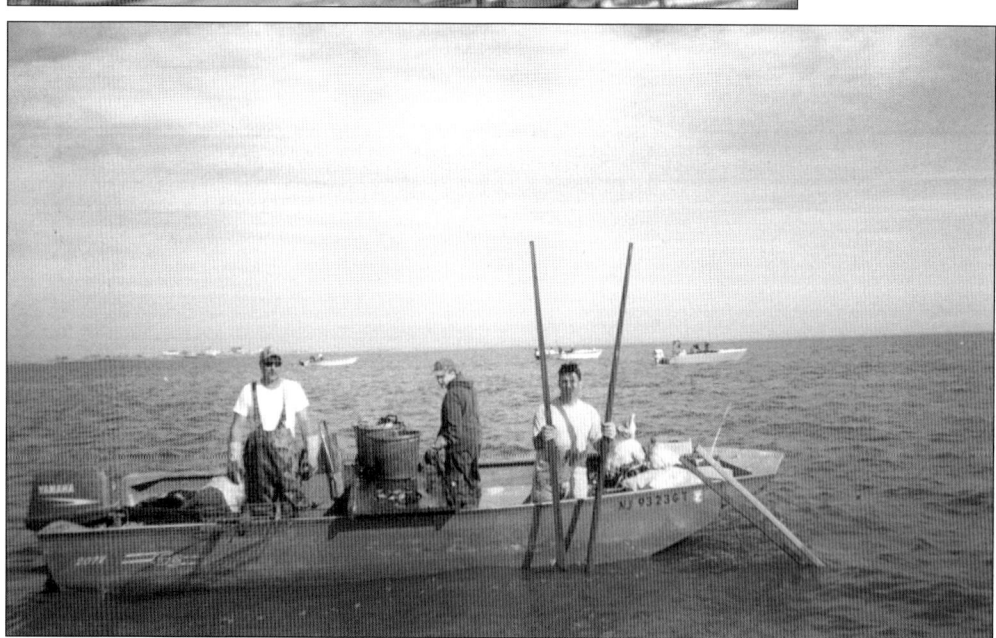

In the background of this photograph of a tonging crew is East Point. There were different types of tong baskets for different types of bottoms, like sandy or muddy. At the time, the tongs cost $2 per foot and were made locally by a man named Robert "Bobby" Lee. (Courtesy of Louis Peterson.)

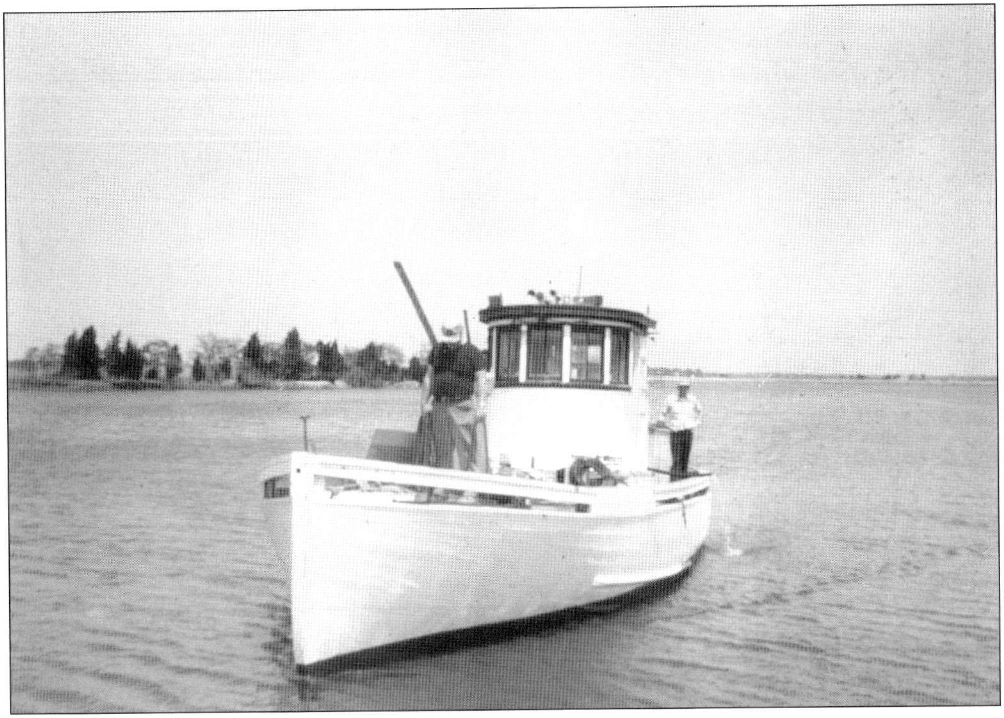

Oyster boat *Elva M* was working in the Maurice River near the Leesburg shipyard when this photograph was taken in 1976. Two crew members are seen. (Courtesy of Louis Peterson.)

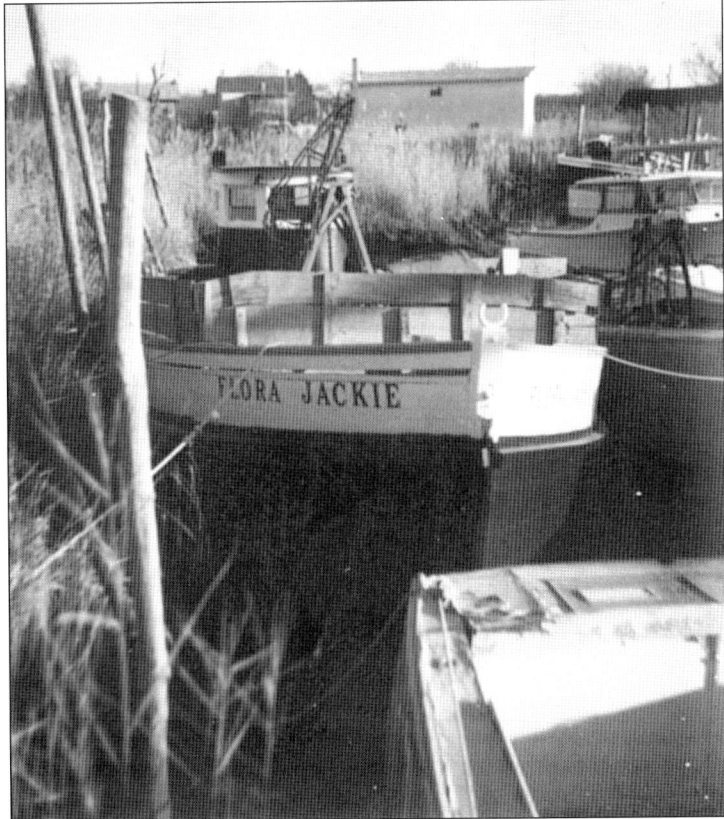

Louis Peterson's second oyster boat was the *Flora Jackie*. This picture was taken in Cedar Creek. He bought her in 1978 because she could carry more oysters. He could stay out working the bay for a longer day with a boat that had greater capacity. (Courtesy of Louis Peterson.)

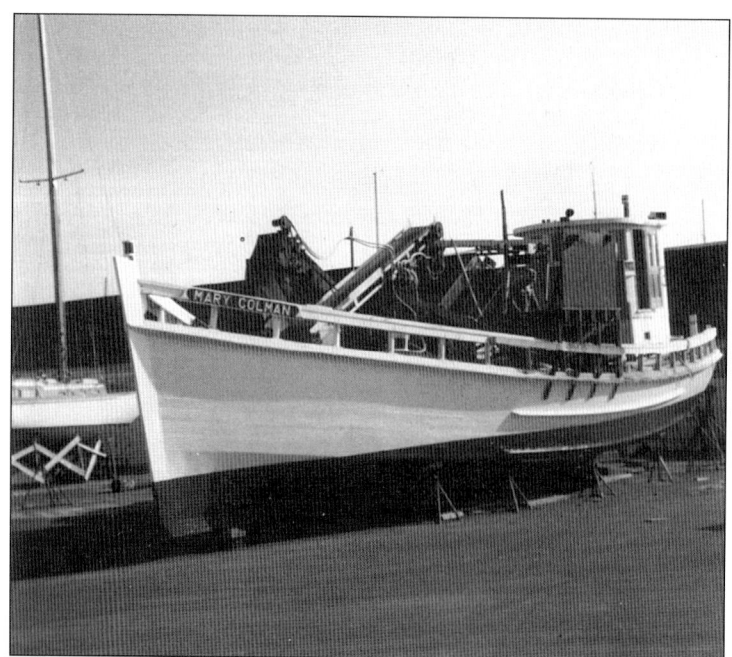

The *Mary Coleman* was Louis Peterson's third oyster boat. She was a type of boat known as a dead rise bateau. Louis bought her from Charles Hanby, but she needed to be restored. A man named George Jenkins at Bivalve Packing Company oversaw the restoration, which amounted to $250,000. Louis paid in oysters, which was a common practice in the business. (Courtesy of Louis Peterson.)

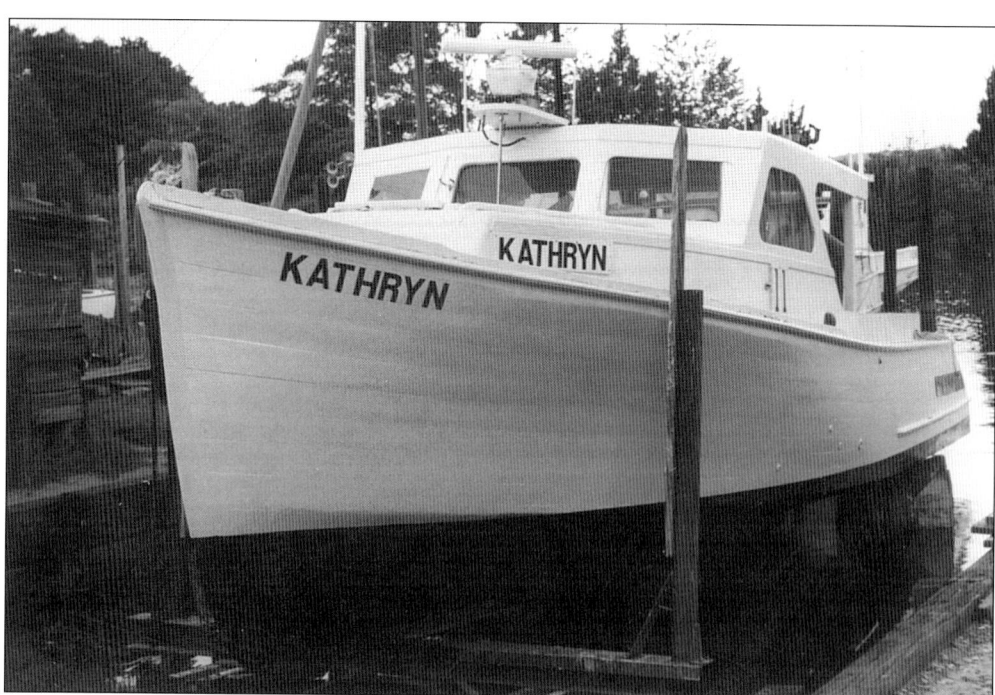

The last oyster boat that Louis Peterson purchased was in 1997. She was a burned-out party boat that was on sale for $4,000. Peterson overhauled and restored her himself. He named her *Kathryn*, after his wife. The *Kathryn* was only worked one season, since Peterson retired in 1998. (Courtesy of Louis Peterson.)

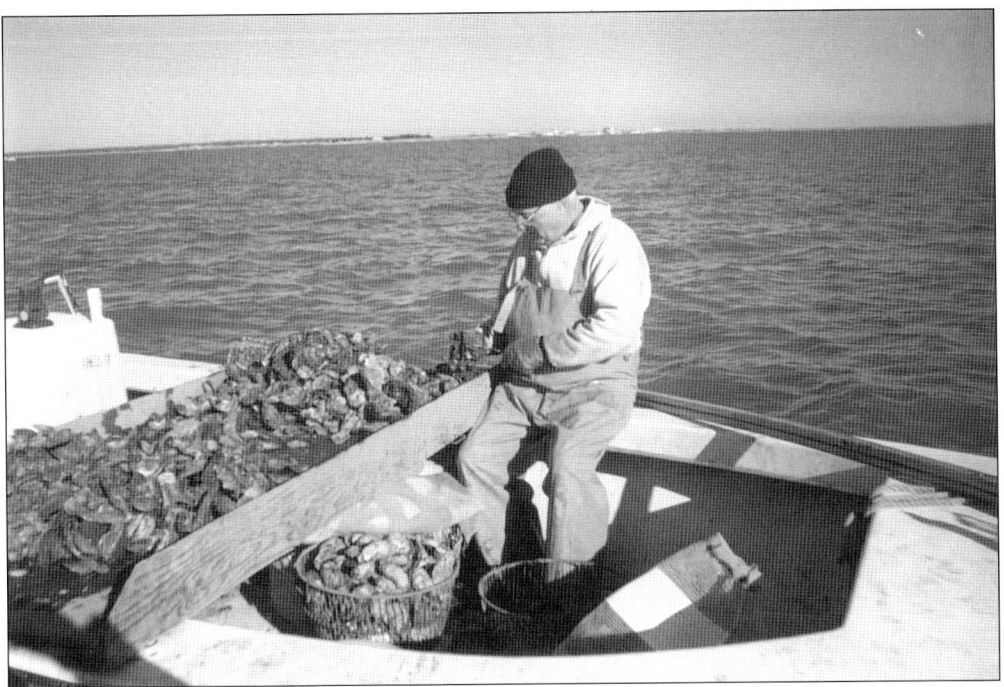

After retiring in 1998, Louis Peterson is seen here in a 20-foot seahawk, tonging for oysters. While no longer officially in business, he would occasionally go out. He could get $45 a bushel. (Courtesy of Louis Peterson.)

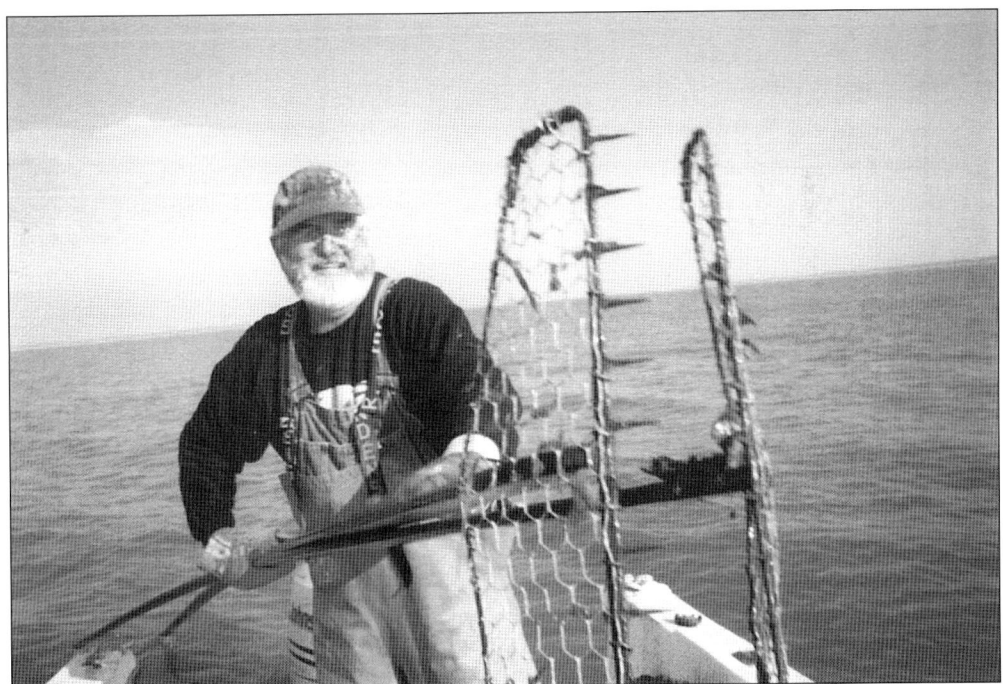

Robert Peterson is tonging oysters on the Delaware Bay. It looks like a calm day on the water. Imagine the strength needed to handle tongs of this size and length. (Courtesy of Louis Peterson.)

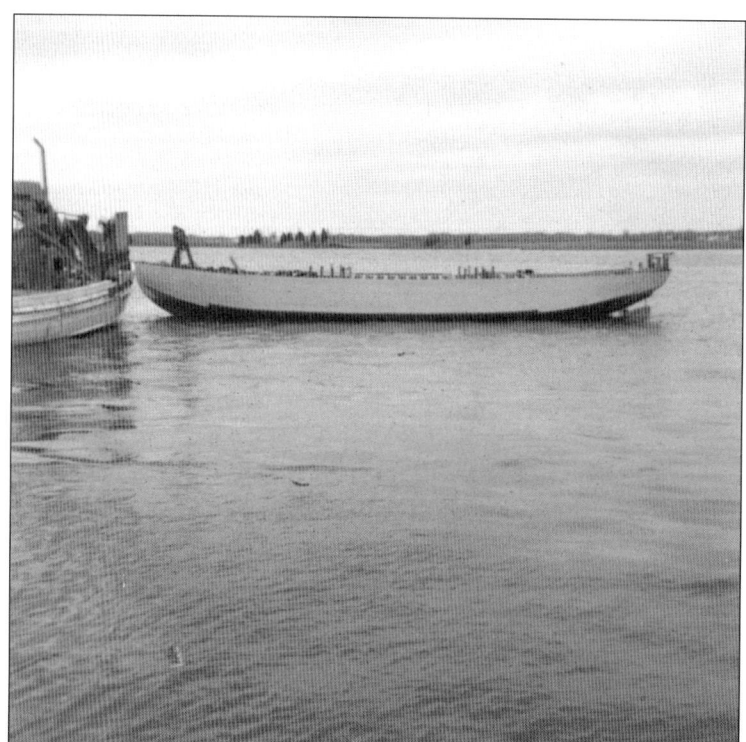

This clam boat at the Penny Hill Boatyard in Dorchester was made from standard lumber. In 1983, when Louis Peterson was working at Bivalve Packing in the off-season of the oyster business, he was asked to make the boat larger by adding 20 feet of lumber to the middle section of the boat. He accomplished that task, which made a 40-foot clam boat into a 60-foot vessel. (Courtesy of Louis Peterson.)

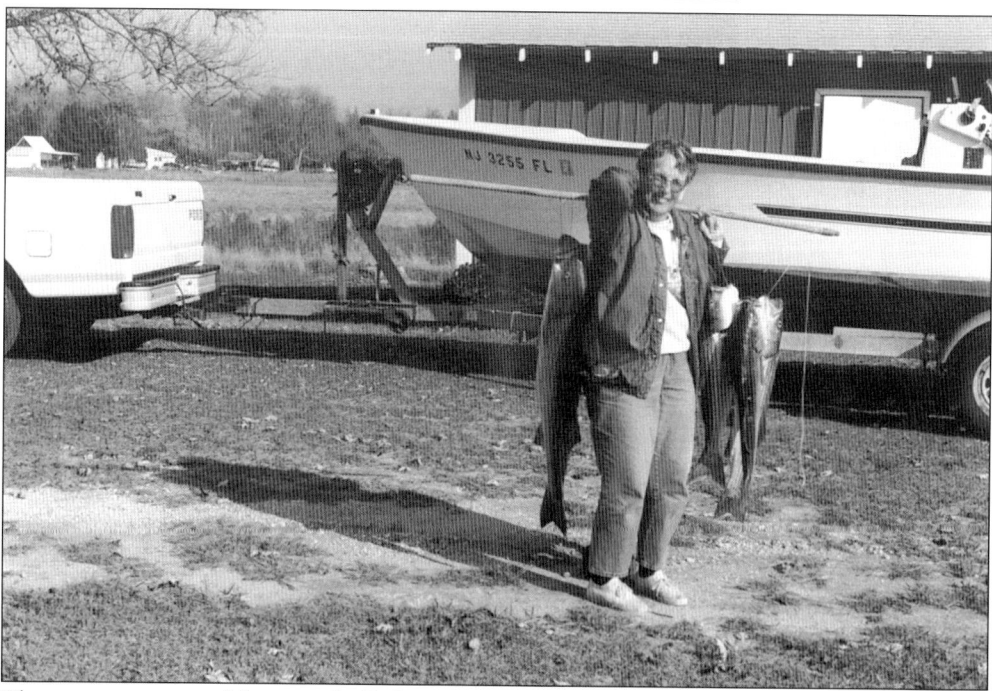

There was some great fishing on the Delaware Bay in the 1980s and 1990s. Kathryn "Kit" Peterson is showing the stripers that she caught on her fishing excursion with her husband, Louis. Stripers are Atlantic striped bass, also known as rockfish, and are predominately found along the Atlantic coast. They have a rich flavor and a large, firm flake. (Courtesy of Louis Peterson.)

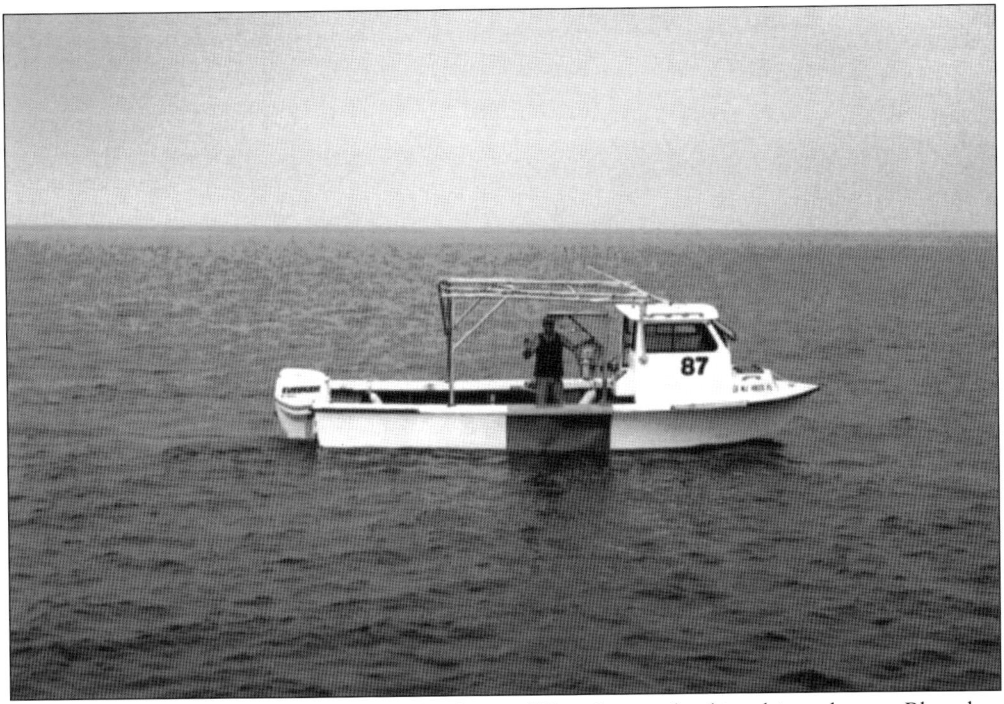

Commercial crabber Nelson Klein is in his boat off East Point, checking his crab pots. Blue claw crabs are abundant in Maurice River Township. They grow large and are delicious. Crab season typically runs from April through November. (Courtesy of Nelson Klein.)

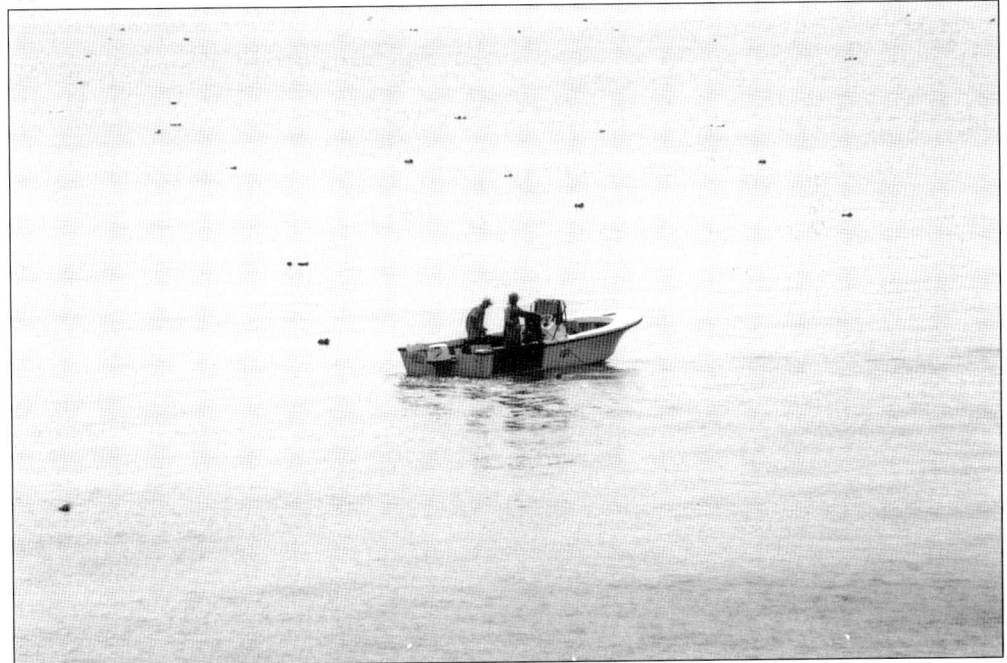

Commercial crabbers are checking their catch for the day in front of East Point Beach. The dots in the water are commercial crab traps. In the summer, the floating crab buoys are like an obstacle course for recreational boaters. (Courtesy of Richard St. Aubyn.)

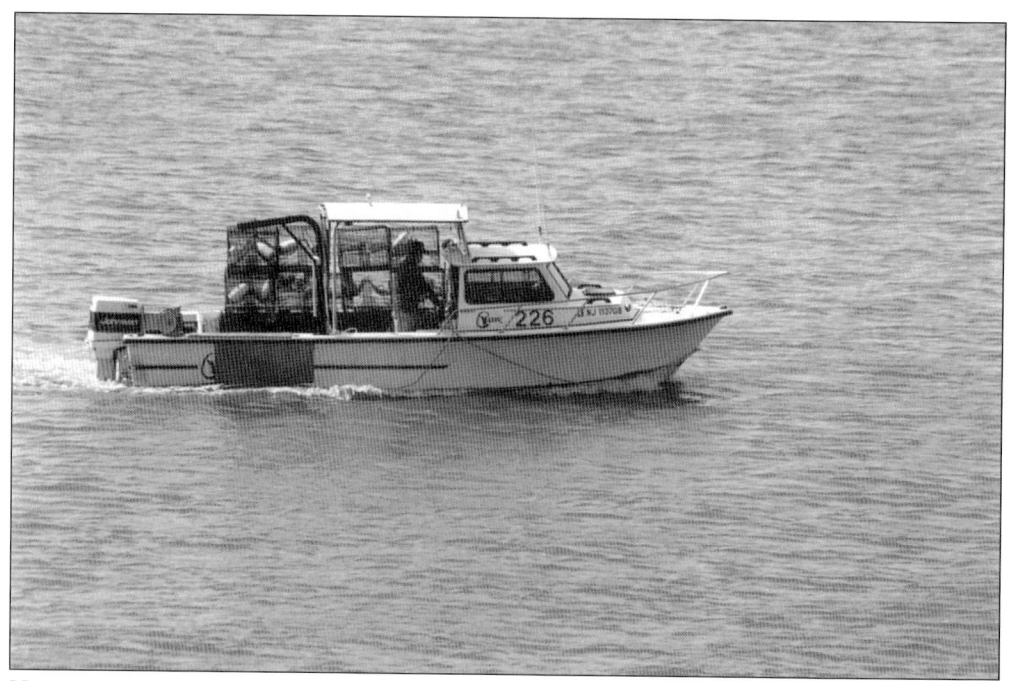

Here is a commercial crabber on the bay in front of East Point Beach, heading in with his crab pots. Blue claw crabs are plentiful in the area. Commercial crabbers generally take their catch to Flag Fish Company at Anchor Marina/Matts Landing, where they are sold and distributed to restaurants and the public. (Courtesy of Richard St. Aubyn.)

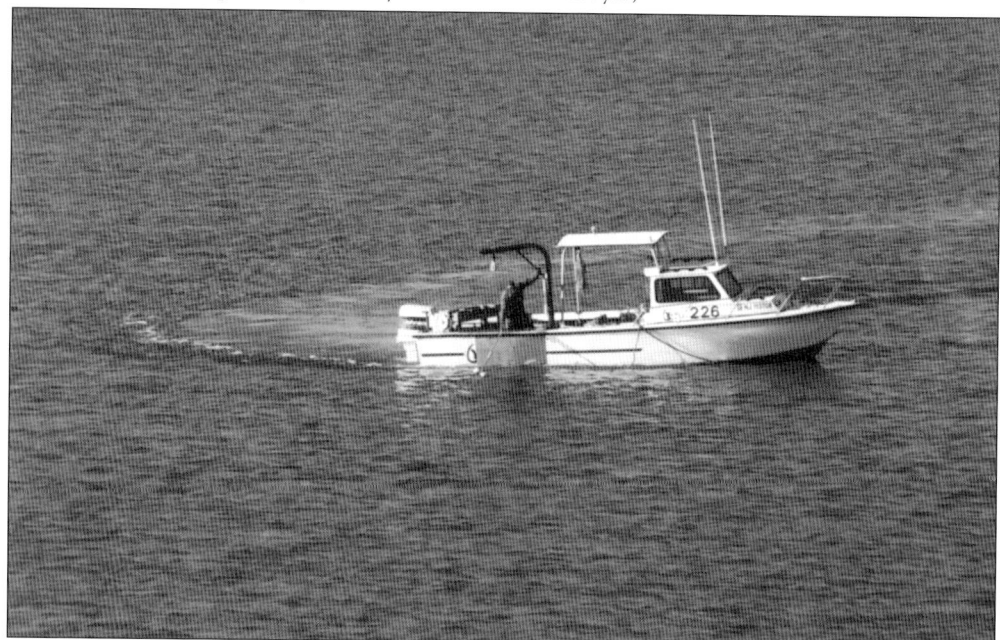

This commercial crab vessel is seen on the bay. Even though crab season is eight months, there is year-round work for commercial crabbers. Boats and crab pots require maintenance throughout the year. During crab season, these hardworking individuals typically start their day around 4:00 a.m. (Courtesy of Richard St. Aubyn.)

Five

THE LOST VILLAGES

Maurice River Township has several lost villages, which include Halberton, Maurice River, Moores Beach, and Thompsons Beach. The oldest of these was Halberton, which was in the pine barrens between Woodbine and Manumuskin. It was one of several Russian refugee colonies in New Jersey in 1894. Jewish immigrants working in sweatshops in New York were taken to various parts of the United States and given land to settle small communities; this was done in the hope that they could develop industries and make better lives for themselves. At one point after 1883, there were 60 cottages, a cloak factory, and a school in Halberton. Unfortunately, the population did not have the means to survive, the factory closed, and the village was sold in a sheriff's sale. While this community did not prosper, there were others in southern New Jersey that did, such as Alliance, Rosenhayn, and Carmel. Today, nothing remains of Halberton.

The village of Maurice River once stood along the river's edge across from and competing with Bivalve as a place where the oyster industry thrived. Trainloads of oysters were shipped from both sides of the river in the late 1800s and early 1900s. Much of the area was lost to erosion, and nothing remains of Maurice River today. Another community that once thrived prior to the flood of 1950, but shows no signs of existence currently other than cinder blocks, drain pipes, and miscellaneous rubble, was a beach community along Route 47 known as Moores Beach. Today, there is a rough, unpaved road, passable only at low tide with a four-wheel drive vehicle. The area is now owned by the New Jersey Division of Fish and Wildlife and is a part of the Heislerville Wildlife Management Area.

Another nearby community that no longer exists is Thompsons Beach. Prior to the 1950 flood, there were over 100 homes, a boardwalk, boat rental facilities, restaurants, and rental cottages. Due to several unfortunate situations including storms, erosion, an unprotected coastline, the sale of hay meadows behind the beach, a utility company's involvement, and financial constraints, the remaining residents were bought out and forced to leave in 1997. An elevated wooden platform remains.

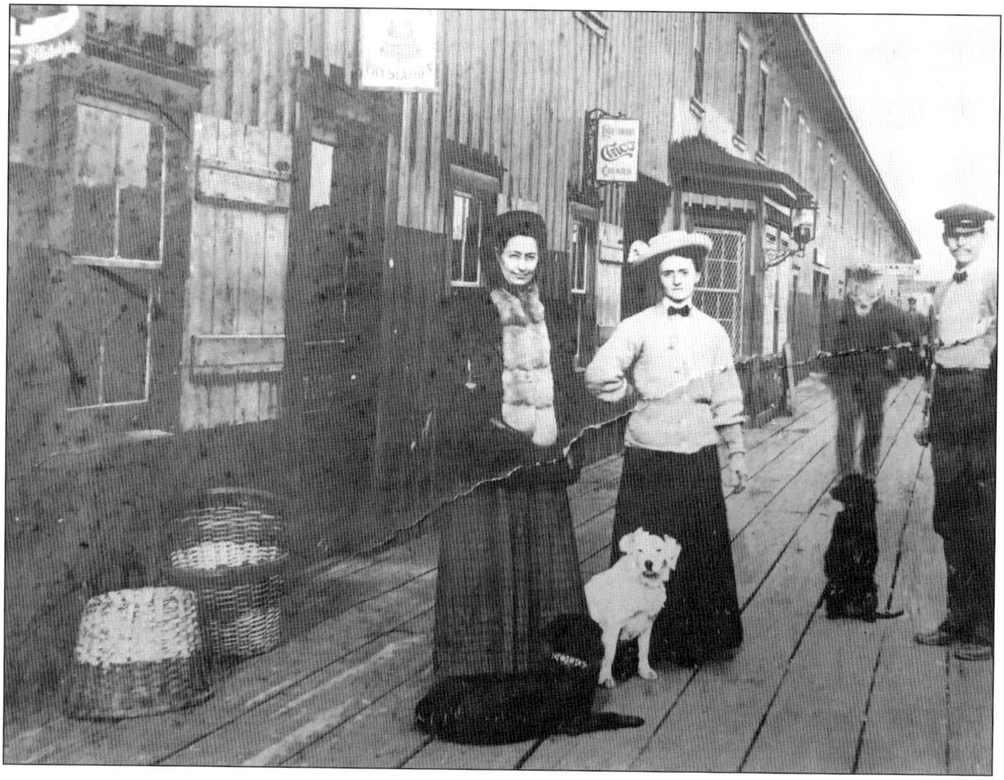

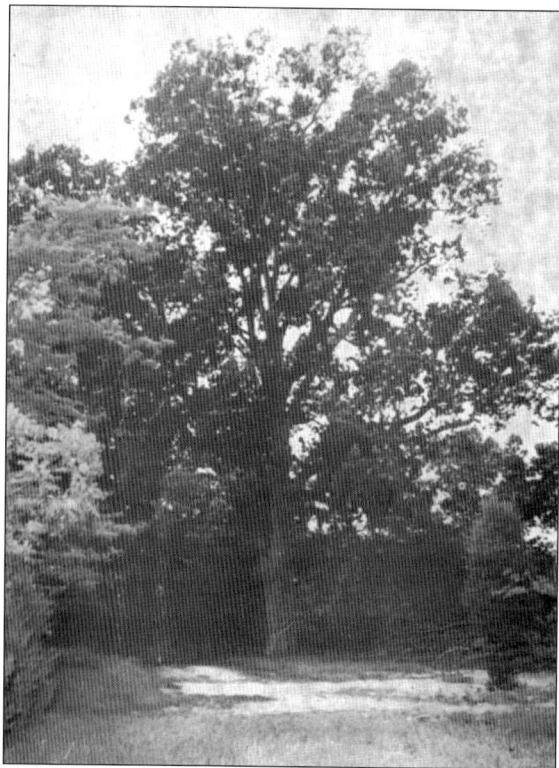

The village of Maurice River was a happening place at the turn of the 20th century. Several people are seen on the wharf on this cool day. Two women, a gentleman, and their three dogs had their picture taken. Other people can be seen in the background at the busy oyster businesses. Maurice River competed with Bivalve in the successful oyster industry. (Courtesy of the Maurice River Township Heritage Society and Bayshore Center at Bivalve.)

The Old Hickory tree was over 300 years old and was in Dorchester on Stagecoach Road. The tree was 88 feet high, with a spread of 74 feet, a diameter of 6 feet, and a circumference of 12.5 feet. It was so old that it is said this tree was 100 years old at the time of the American Revolution. It was recognized for its age, size, and role in history at a dedication ceremony on June 18, 1966. Unfortunately, the tree no longer stands. (Courtesy of Nelson Klein.)

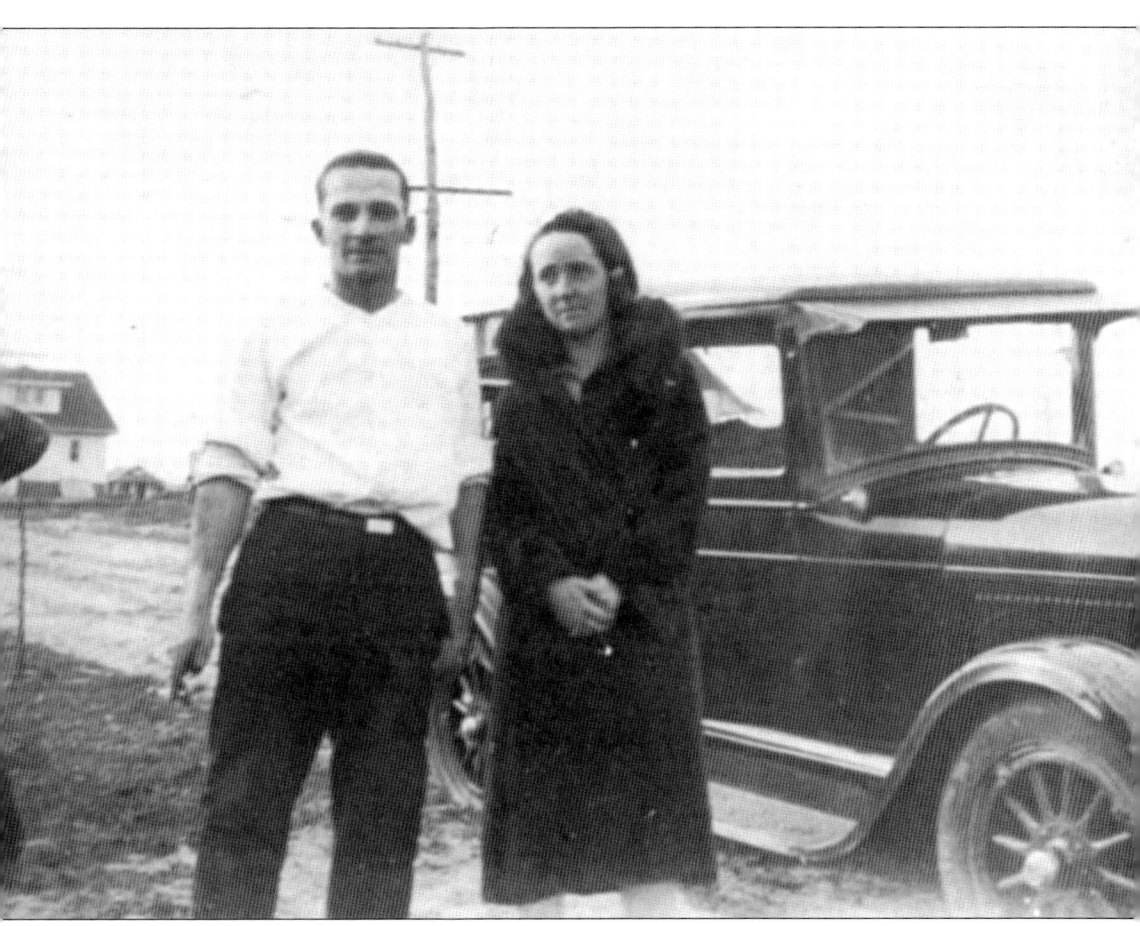

Adolfe (Allie) and Violet Klein are seen standing next to their car at Thompsons Beach in the 1930s. Adolfe owned a thriving boat rental, grocery, restaurant, and cottage rental business at the beach in the 1930s and 1940s. (Courtesy of Nelson Klein.)

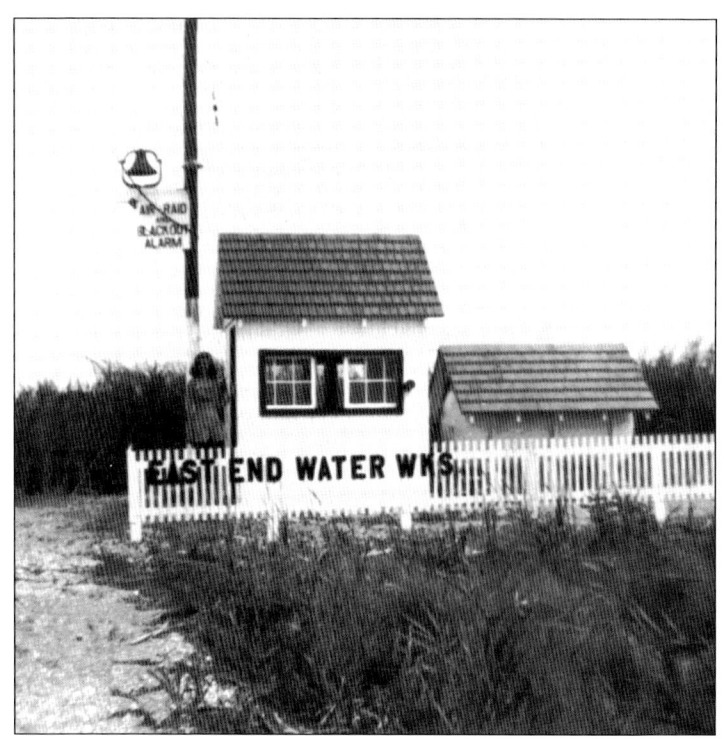

During World War II, Thompsons Beach was popular. The beautiful woman pictured here is Gladys Westcott. She is standing by the East End Waterworks beneath an air raid and blackout alarm sign. (Courtesy of Nelson Klein.)

Adolfe and Violet Klein are seen here in their 1940s car, with large whitewall tires that were popular at the time. Adolfe was called by the nickname Allie due to the widespread disdain for the only other person most people at the time knew of by that name, Adolf Hitler. (Courtesy of Nelson Klein.)

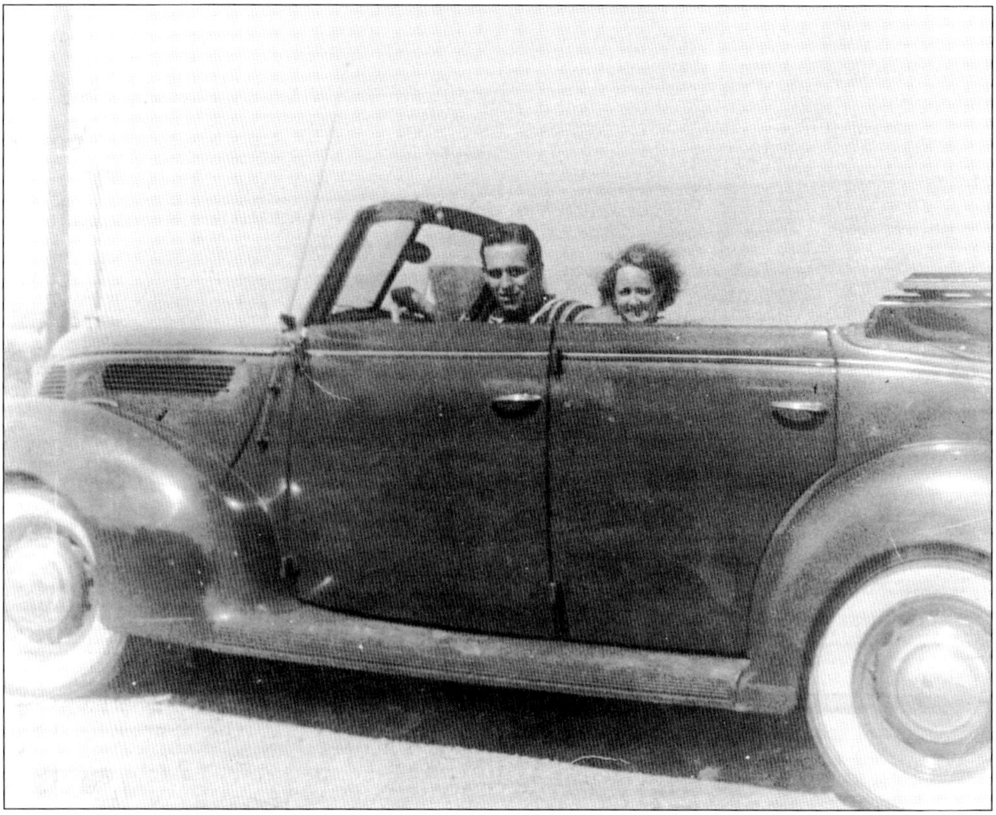

In the 1930s, the Thompson family, after whom the beach was named, had a small hotel and store at the beach. These people are believed to be members of the Thompson family in front of their business. (Courtesy of Nelson Klein.)

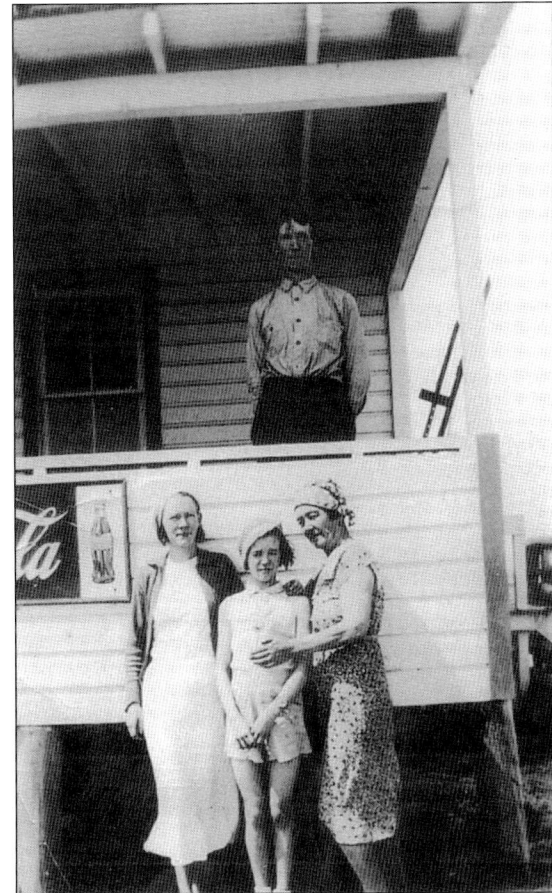

This is a 1930s postcard view of Thompsons Beach from the water showing Butchers Pier and boat rental. Note the large number of homes that can be seen. The place was known as Fisherman's Paradise at the time. (Courtesy of Vic Ballato.)

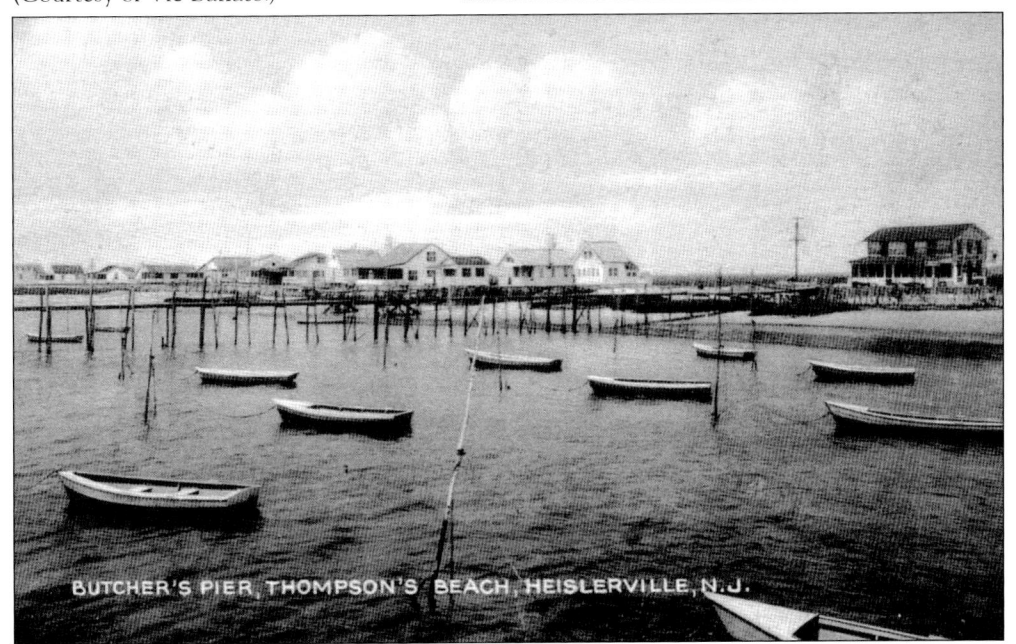

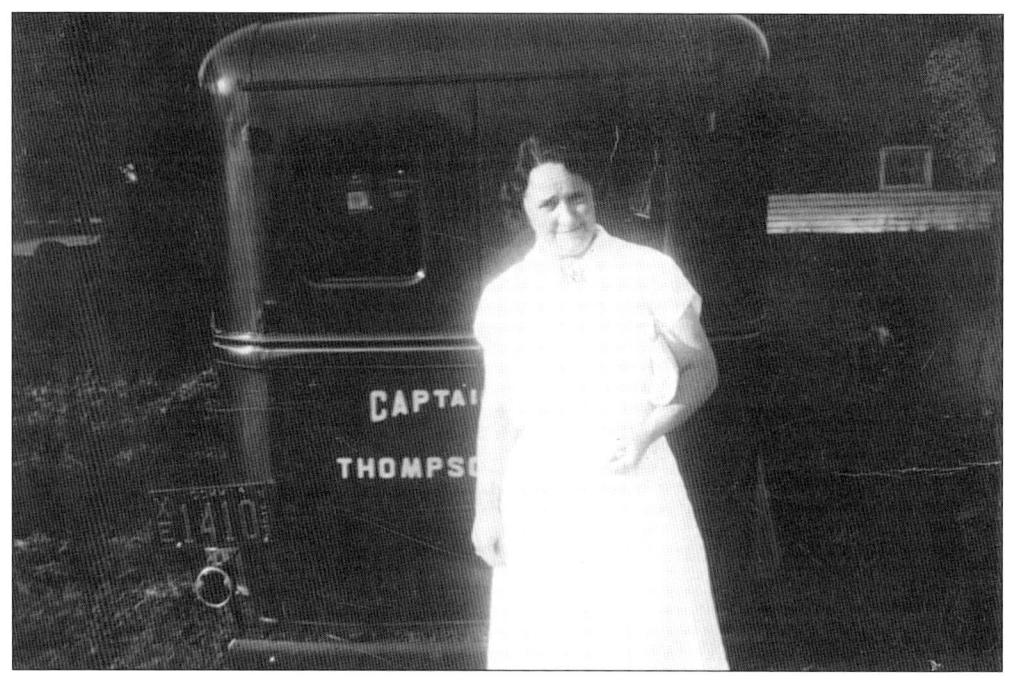

Violet Klein looks like an angel in this photograph. She is standing in front of her husband's company truck, which advertised Captain Klein's Boat Rentals at Thompsons Beach. (Courtesy of Nelson Klein.)

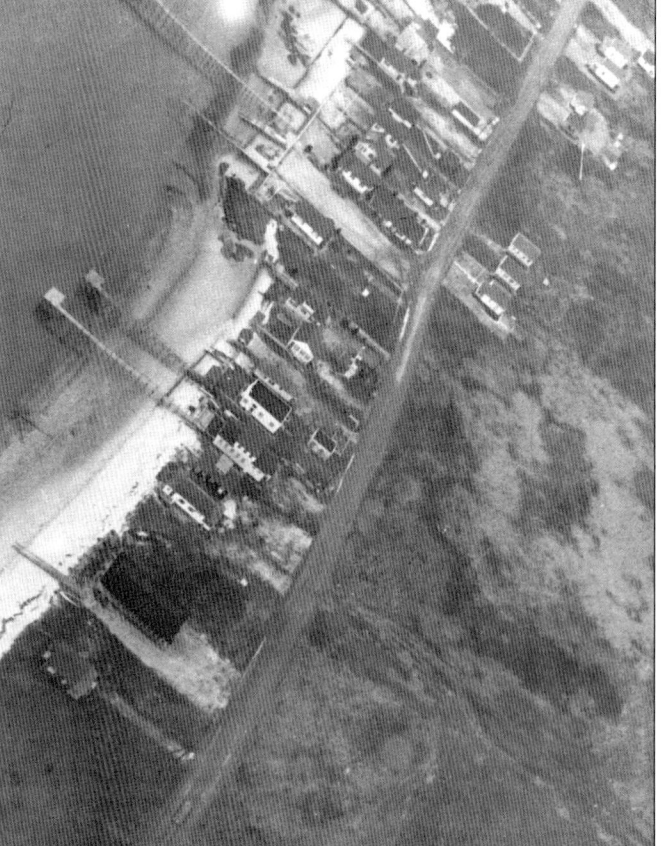

This is an aerial photograph of Thompsons Beach prior to the 1950 flood. It was well developed with many homes with grass in the yards and mature trees on the properties. It was a beautiful community. (Courtesy of Nelson Klein.)

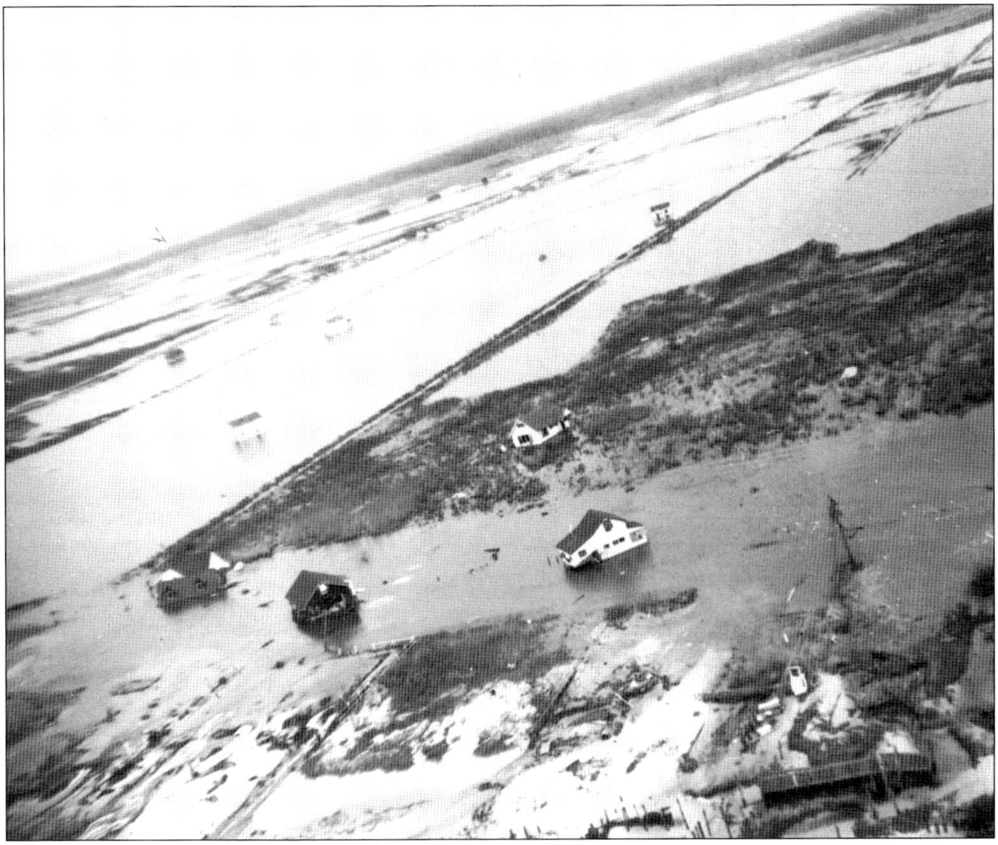

This is an aerial view of Thompsons Beach after the flood in November 1950. Only seven homes remained on their foundations. Interestingly, Nelson Klein's parents, who were at the beach and survived with their baby daughter, counted the homes while they walked the beach the day before the storm. There were 107. (Courtesy of Nelson Klein.)

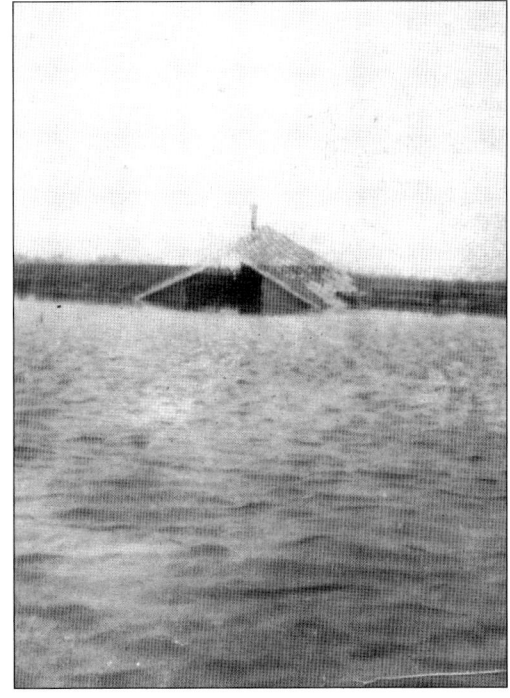

This is the roof of a house in the water after the 1950 flood at Thompsons Beach. Edward H. Thompson, age 100 at the time, was quoted in the *Millville Daily Republic* after the storm as having said, "I told em so. I have said there was no telling when the tide would come in and do a lot of damage." He had owned 350 acres of meadowland including all of Thompsons beach and sold it to a cousin who divided up the land into beachfront lots for development. (Courtesy of Nelson Klein.)

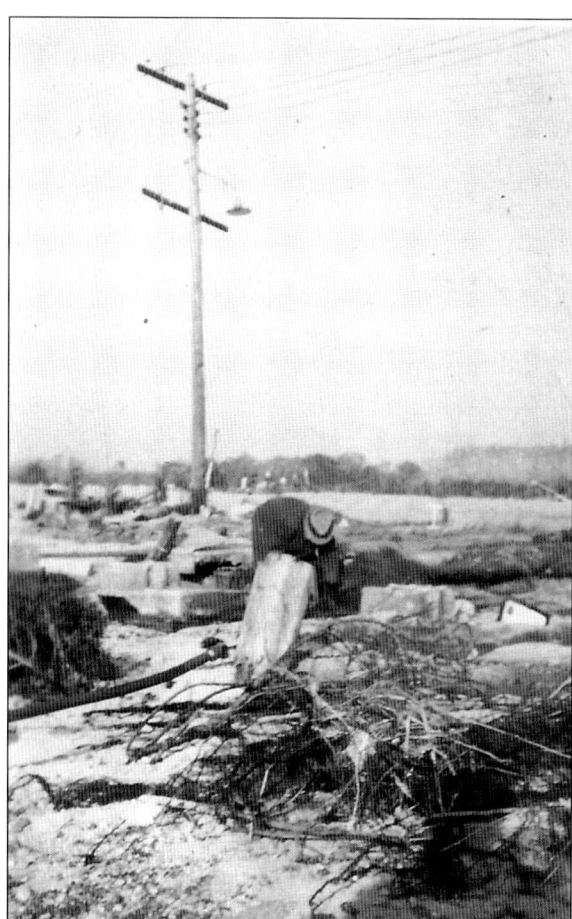

A man is seen picking through the rubble after the flood. He is surrounded by bits and pieces of homes, concrete, and pipes. It was total devastation. (Courtesy of Nelson Klein.)

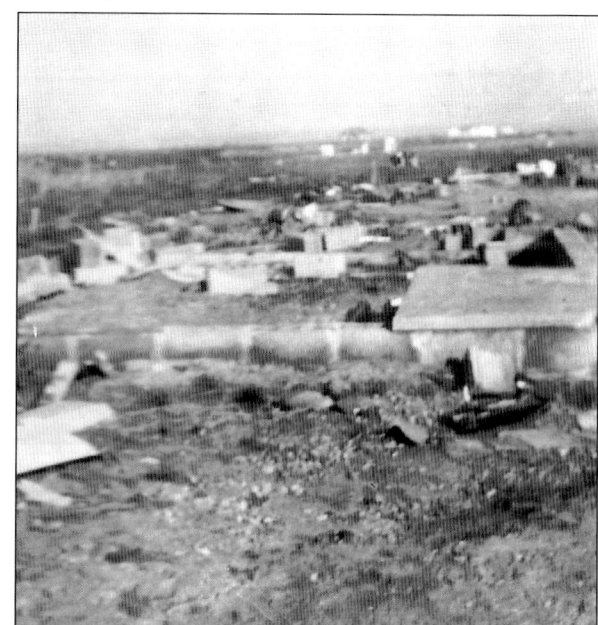

This post-flood photograph shows destruction as far as the eye can see. Tide upon tide came in with heavy winds on that fateful Saturday morning, November 25, 1950. (Courtesy of Nelson Klein.)

A house is being moved out of the meadow after the flood. Several cottages floated near East Point Road and were relocated in Heislerville after this fateful event. Some of the cottages remain there to this day. (Courtesy of Nelson Klein.)

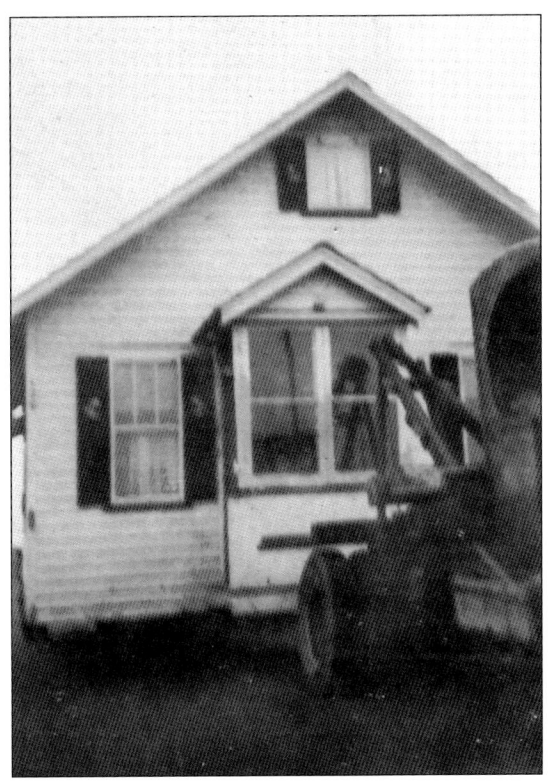

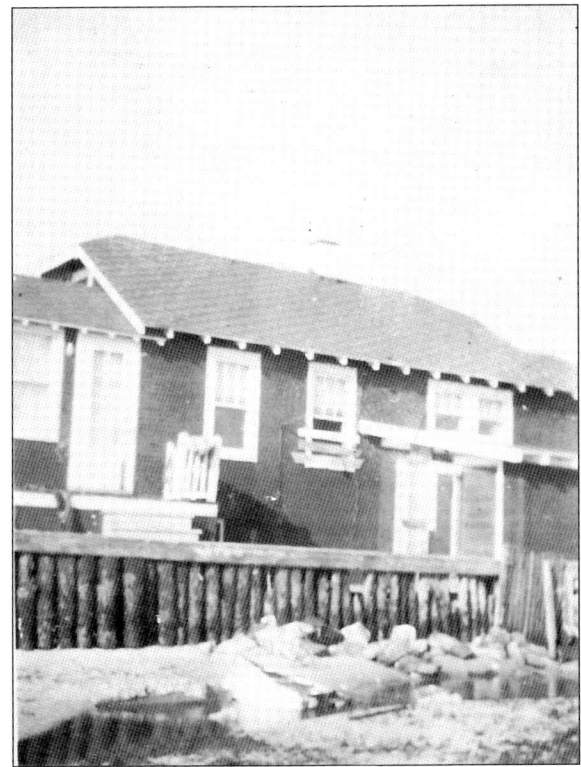

This cottage looks like it stayed in place at Thompsons Beach. Only seven homes remained on their foundations. (Courtesy of Nelson Klein.)

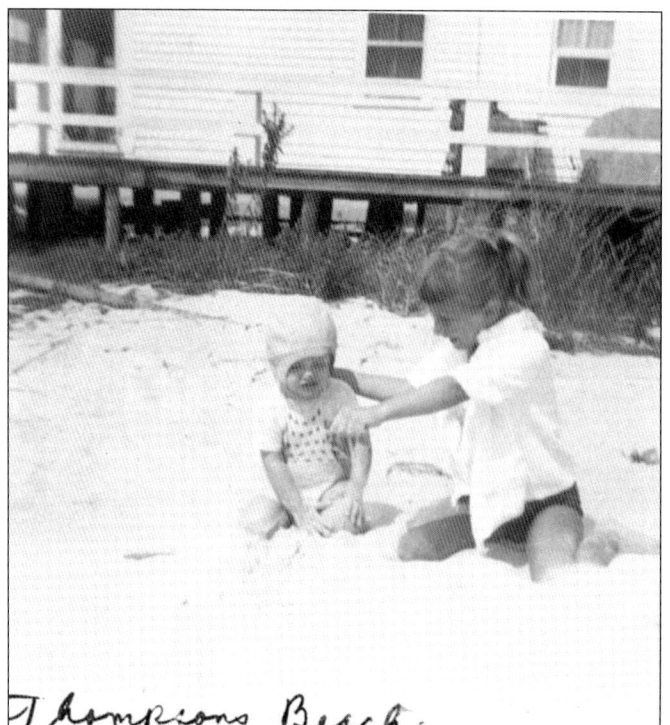

Residents at Thompsons Beach demonstrated the pioneer spirit. After the 1950 flood, a few people pulled houses from the meadows and put them back on pilings at the beach. This photograph was taken in 1957. It shows Christina (right) and Julie Rumbold sitting on the beach by their great-aunt Pearl and uncle Orville Rumbold's home. (Author's collection.)

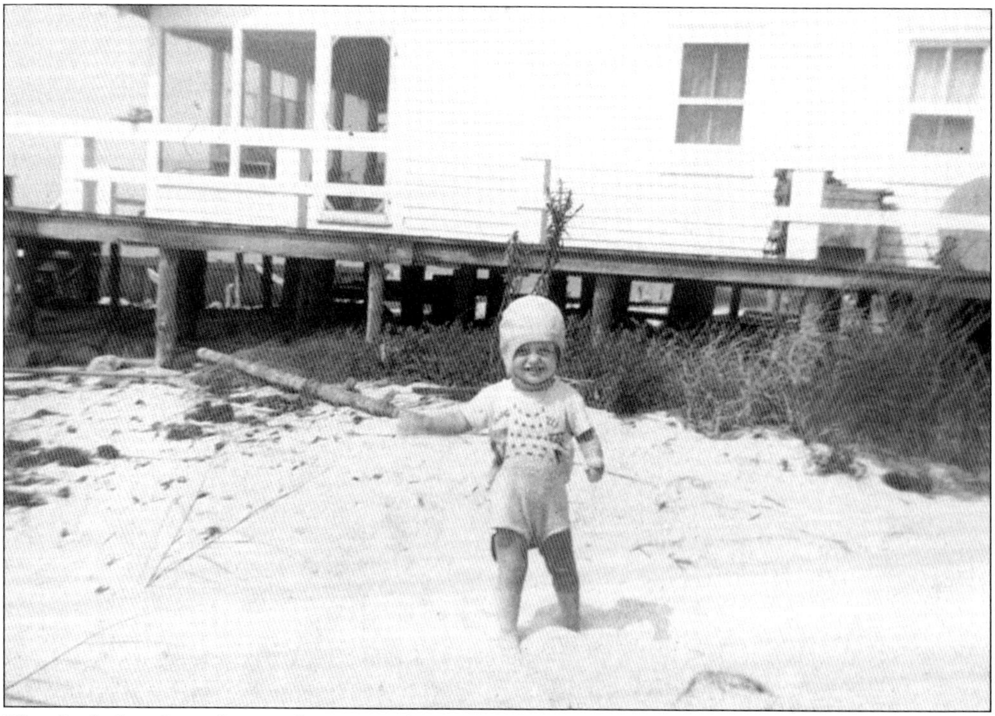

This little beachcomber is playing in the sand in 1957. At the time, the author's grandparents also had a cottage across the gravel road from this location at Thompsons Beach. They got their cottage by buying it out of the meadow after the 1950 flood. (Courtesy of Ronald Flynn.)

This Easter picture was taken around 1960 and shows Ronald Rumbold with daughters Julie and Christina. The Shaw family cottage is seen in the background. Many people took a chance on placing cottages at Thompsons Beach even after the devastating storm of 1950 and another significant storm in 1960. (Courtesy of Ronald Flynn.)

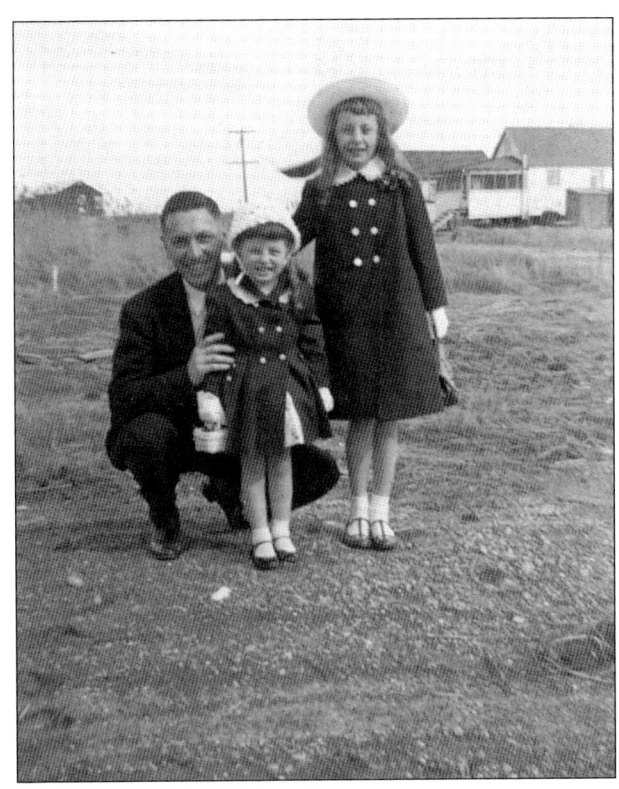

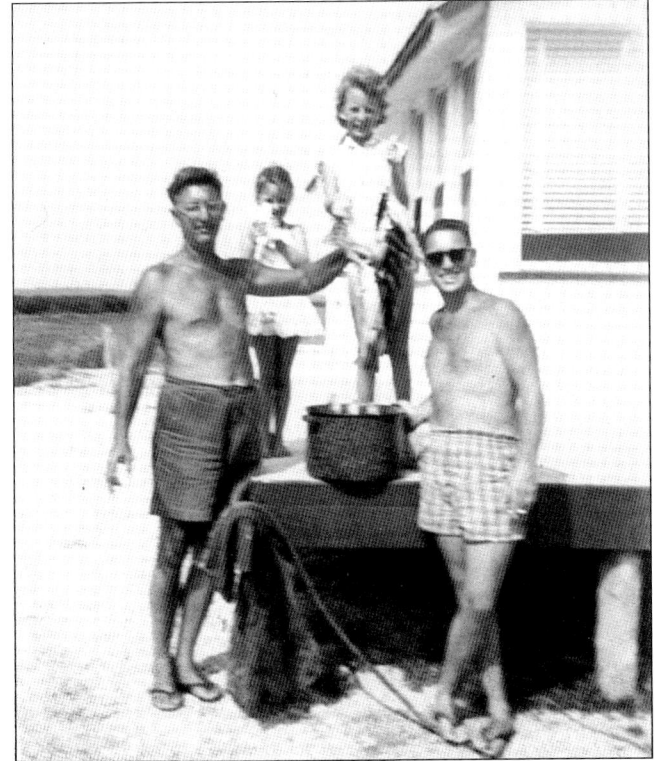

A good catch was had on this summer day. From left to right, Wade, Julie, Christina, and Ronald Rumbold are by Wade and Lilian's cottage at Thompsons Beach around 1961. Fish were abundant, and fishing was a regular activity in this era. (Author's collection.)

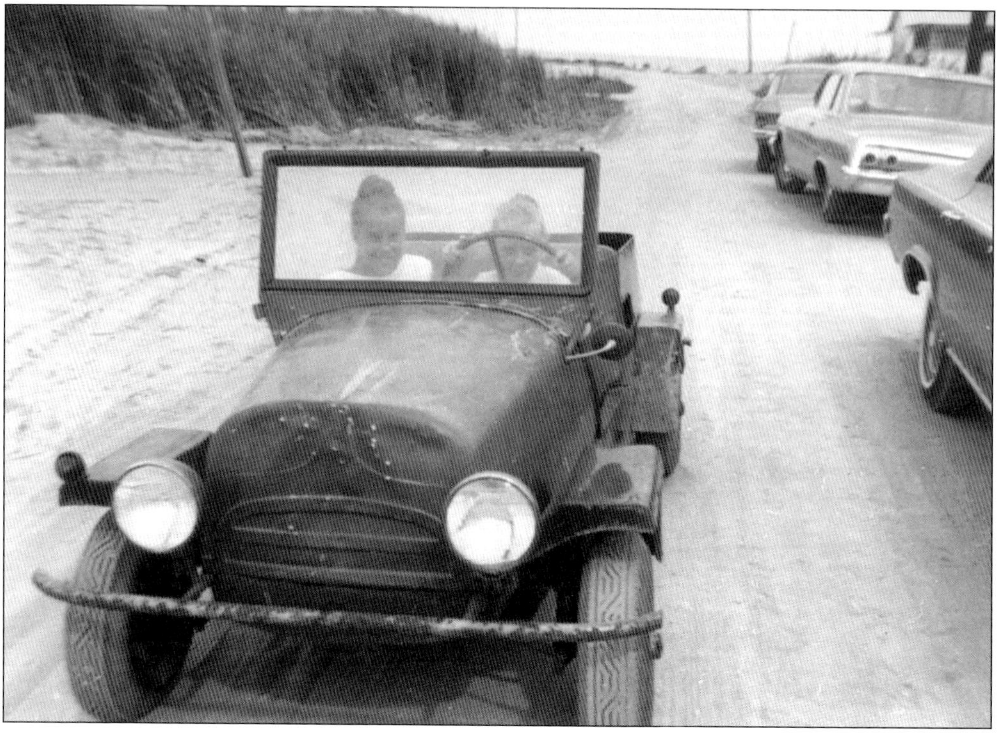

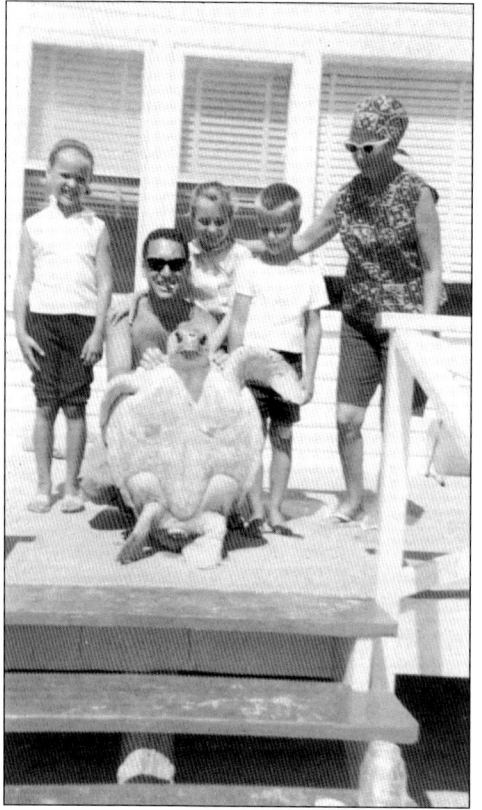

The Laxton family had a cottage on the waterfront in what was once Pearl and Orville Rumbold's place. Linda Laxton's father, Frank, owned an automobile repair shop in Chester, Pennsylvania. He got his daughter this cool, miniature-size antique car, which was frequently driven on the gravel road at the beach. Julie Rumbold is driving and Linda Laxton is the passenger on this trip. There are many cars parked along the road because it was the day of a communal beach party at Thompsons Beach. This was a tradition that was carried on for a few years. The party always had music, dancing, drinking, and lots of carrying on. (Courtesy of Ronald Flynn.)

From left to right, Ellen, Ronald, Julie, Mark, and Lilian Rumbold pose with a giant turtle on the porch of Wade and Lilian's cottage. After the picture was taken, the turtle was released back into the bay. (Author's collection.)

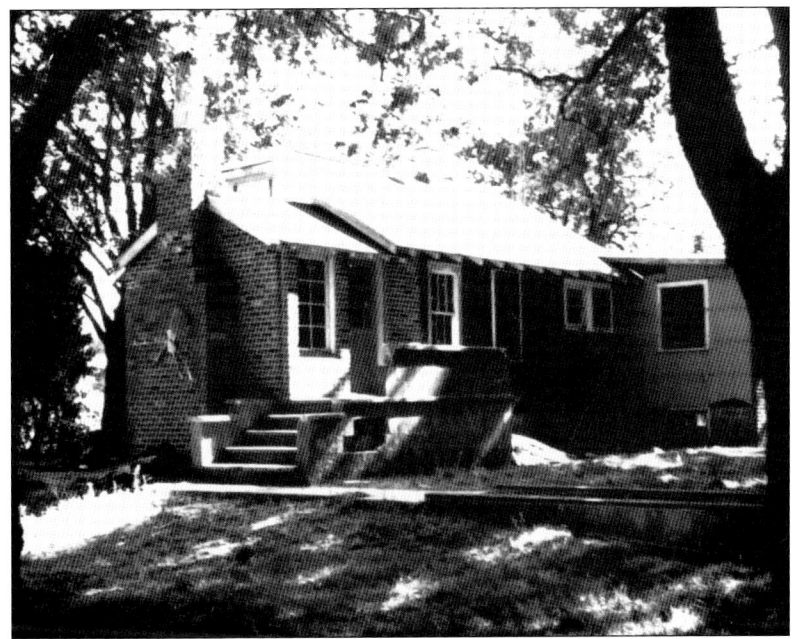

Ed Krupa briefly owned this home on Thompsons Beach Road. It was purchased by eminent domain when all the residents were made to leave the beach in 1997. (Courtesy of Ed Krupa.)

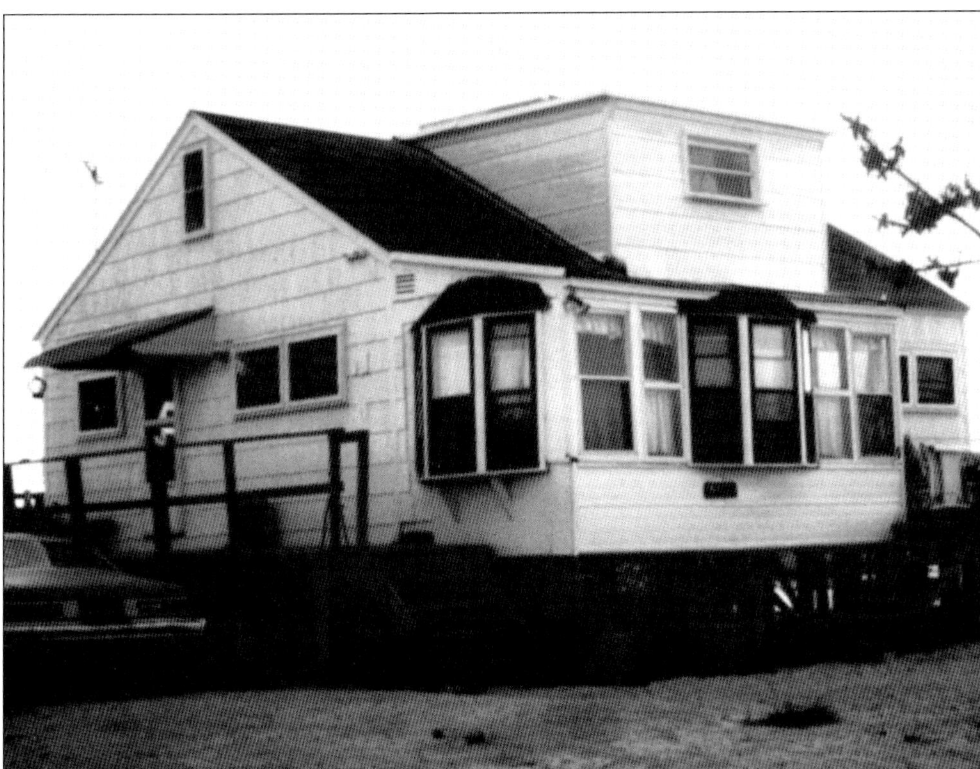

This was the Krupa family cottage at Thompsons Beach. The family lost their home in the 1980 storm. They took shelter in the home of a neighbor, whose house was high off the ground on pilings. (Courtesy of Ed Krupa.)

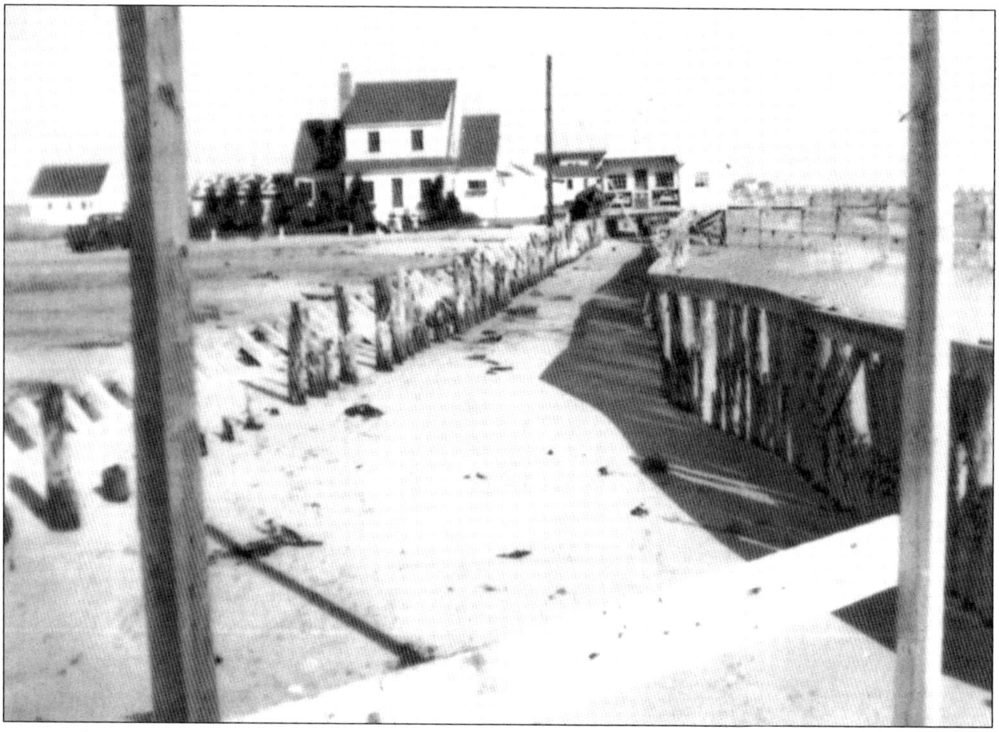

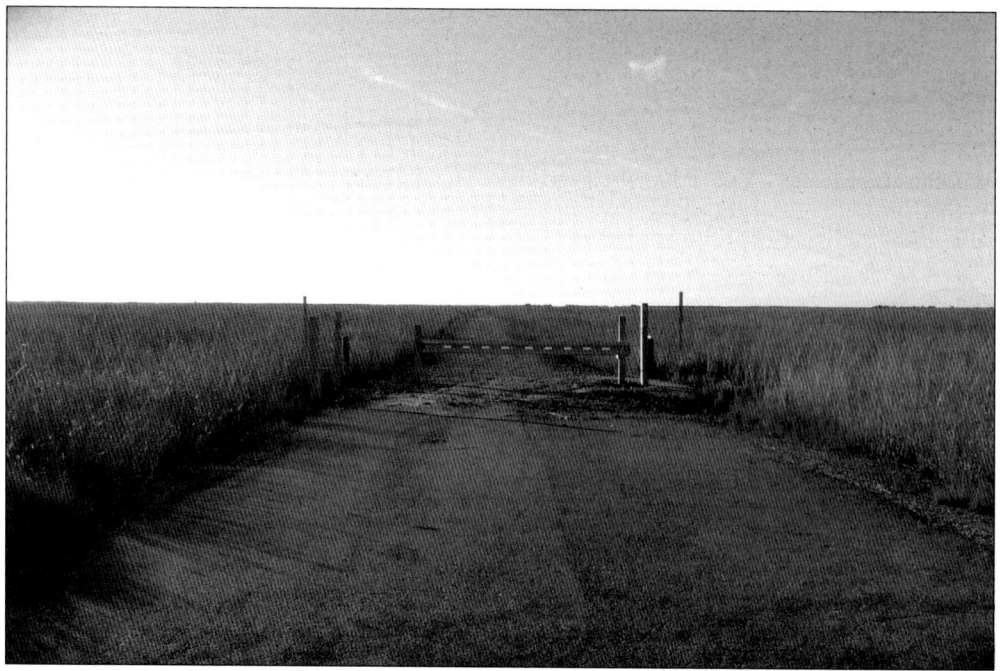

Pictured is a cottage at Thompsons Beach near one of the boat rental places. Some washed-out bulkheads can be seen. Storms often battered the area. (Courtesy of Drew Tomlin.)

This is the road that leads to Thompsons Beach. Nothing remains of the homes and community that once existed there, except for one old fireplace and some pilings. (Author's collection.)

Six
HEISLERVILLE AND MATTS LANDING

The quaint village of Heislerville was known as Maurice River Neck until 1860. This location was and is surrounded by lowlands and marshland known as the "glade." This glade separates Heislerville from the neighboring community of Delmont. Glade Road runs through a desolate area with vast expanses of meadows and marshes. Heislerville is a small town in a rural location with a population of less than 500 people. The community borders the Maurice River and Delaware Bay. It is a lovely, peaceful setting.

In its heyday, it was known for a thriving salt hay industry. The salt hay was harvested from parts of a huge area formerly known as the Cadwalader Estate. That area is now the Heislerville Wildlife Management Area. It has also been known for agriculture. When the railroad was active, in the late 1800s and early 1900s, loads of Heislerville strawberries were shipped out to larger cities from "Link City," a railroad station on Matts Landing Road. The railroad also serviced the thriving oyster industry along the river. For many decades, fishing was a thriving industry in the area as well.

Around 1793, George Heisler Jr. homesteaded in Heislerville and was known to hold Methodist meetings there. Heisler Memorial Methodist Church was built in 1855. The whole Maurice River Township area is known for its numerous Methodist churches. In more recent history, the area is also known for its marinas and for an area known as Matts Landing.

Matts Landing Road leads out from Heislerville to Heislerville Wildlife Management Area and several marinas. These marinas currently include Anchor, Haase's, and Popeyes. These businesses service boaters, fishermen, commercial crabbers, and individuals who wish to launch jet skis and kayaks. This area is referred to as an impoundment because the body of water is confined within an enclosure.

Visitors and those wanting to sightsee can observe birds and waterfowl including bald eagles, cormorants, egrets, and herons, just to name a few varieties. There are areas to walk and ride bicycles.

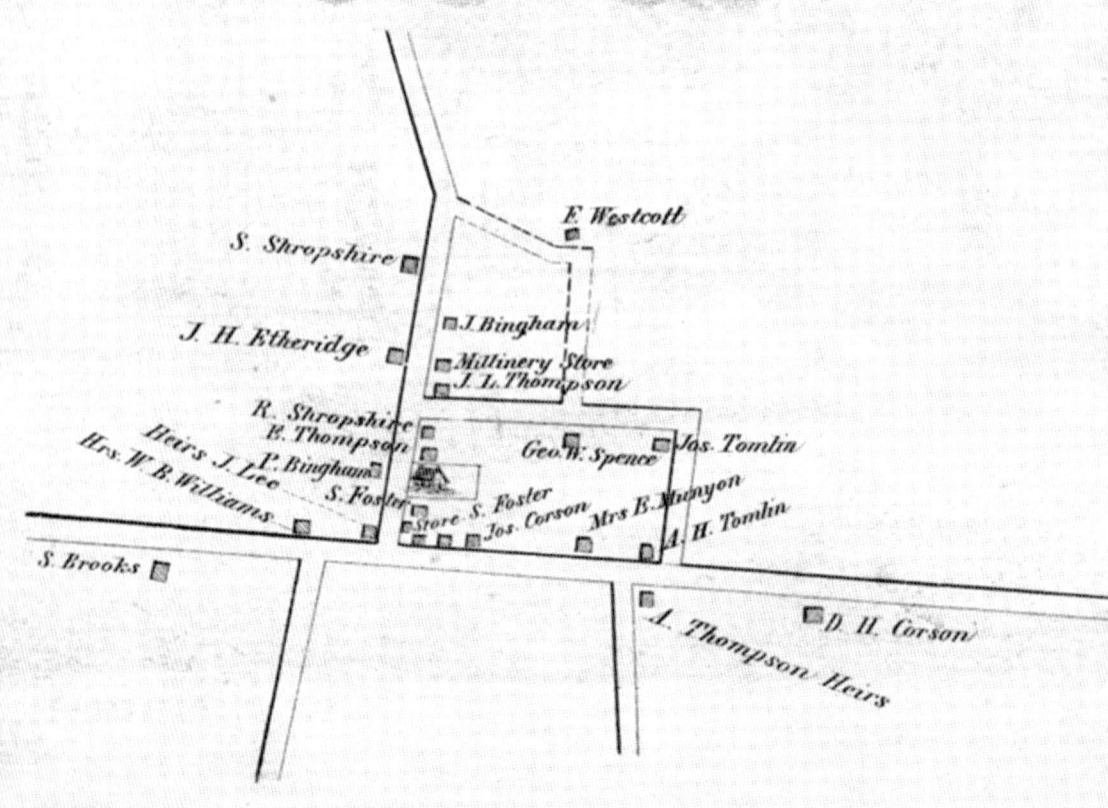

This is a map of Heislerville from 1876. The town was just slightly developed based on the number of homes. There were a couple of businesses listed included a millinery store and a store owned by S. Foster. The church is not identified, but was there at the time. The first church was constructed in 1839 when the town was known as Maurice River Neck. The second church building was begun in 1853 and completed in 1855. The second building stood 75 feet behind the present location. In 1864, the trustees voted to change the name of the church to the Union Methodist Episcopal Church of Heislerville. The current church is named Heisler Memorial United Methodist Church. (Courtesy of Library of Congress.)

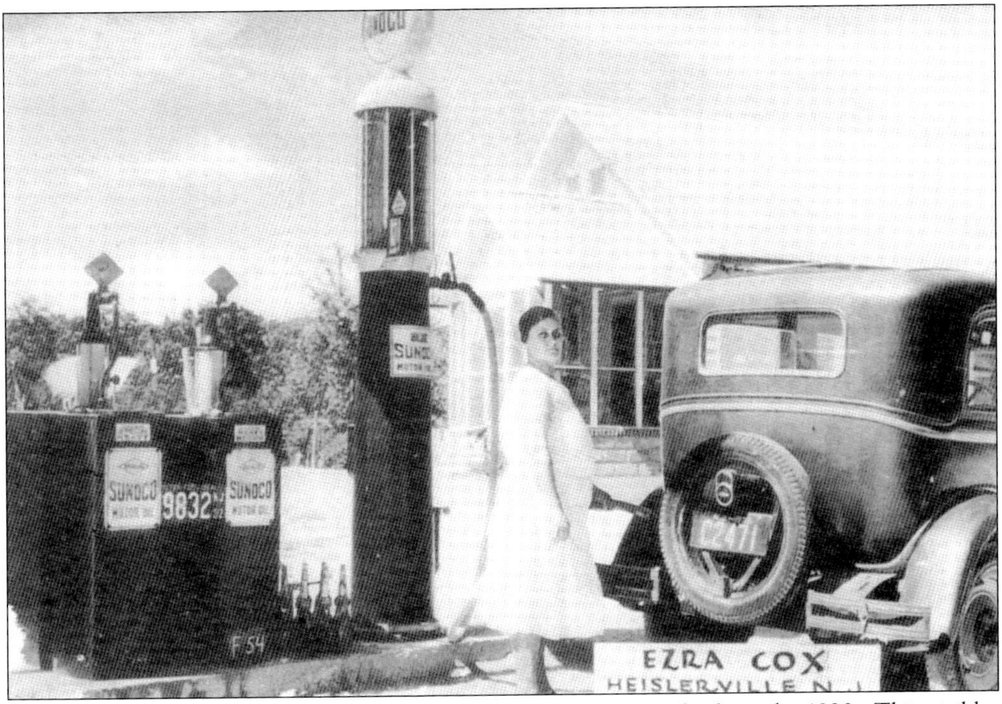

This photograph labeled "Ezra Cox, Heislerville, N. J.," appears to be from the 1920s. This visible-type gas pump was prevalent at that time. Visible gas pumps are now selling online for anywhere from $1,250 to $9,000. Sun Company also became Sun Oil Company in 1920. Currently, people do not typically pump their own gasoline in New Jersey due to state laws. (Courtesy of the Maurice River Township Heritage Society.)

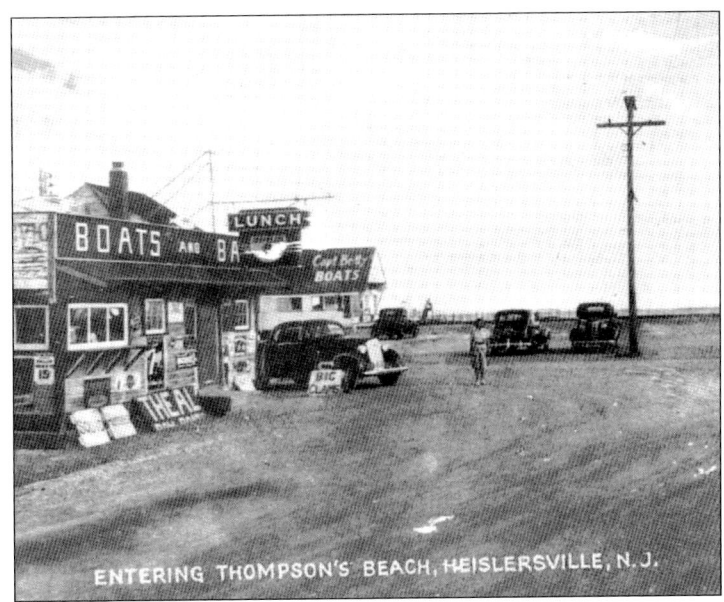

This is a photograph of Thompsons Beach in Heislerville. There is a boat and bait rental facility that belonged to Captain Betty. The picture shows an unidentified woman wearing capri-style pants, which came into vogue in the late 1940s. Women liked them for the freedom of movement they had during activities such as bicycle riding or gardening. (Courtesy of Nelson Klein.)

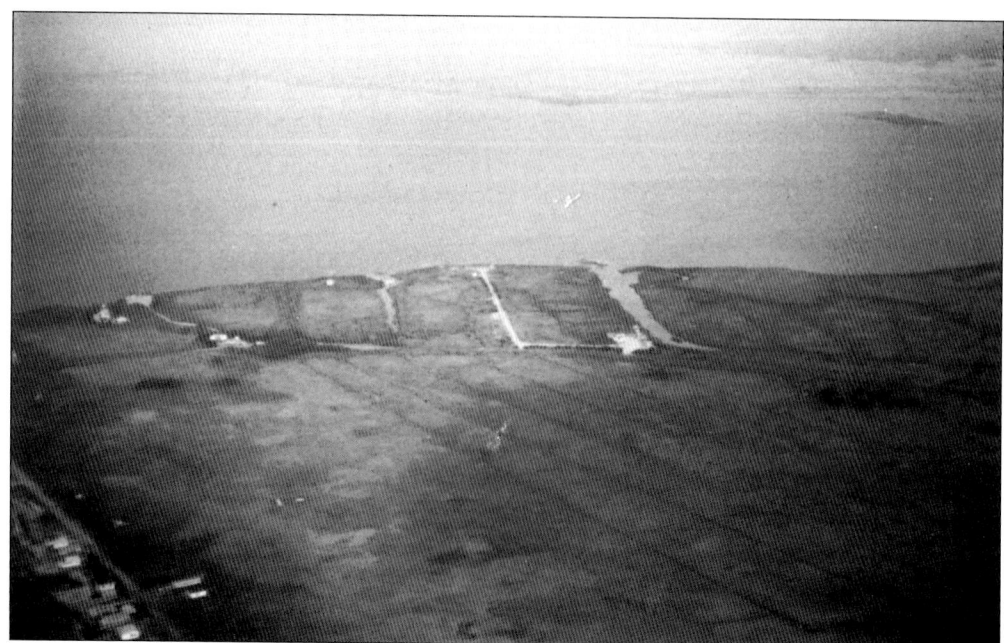

In this aerial view taken in the mid- to late 1960s, a large expense of salt hay meadow can be seen. Captain Klein's property and much of the Maurice River Cove are visible. (Courtesy of Nelson Klein.)

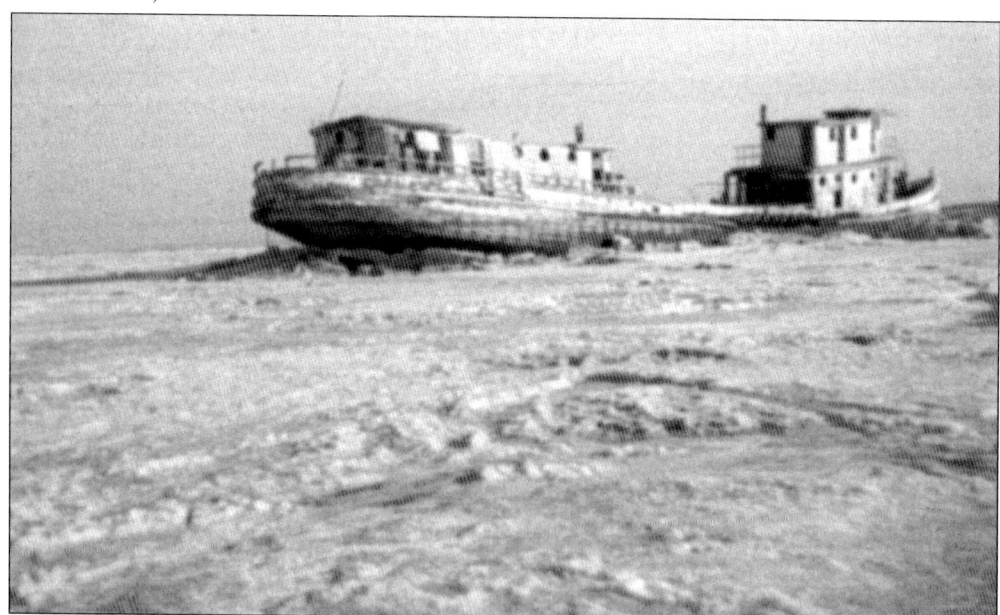

The *Fairmont* is seen here iced in. This bunker boat was purchased by Capt. Nelson Klein Sr. in the late 1960s from the Dorchester shipyard. He intended to float her upriver and establish her as a coffee shop and luncheonette. Unfortunately, the tugboat that towed the *Fairmont* missed the tide, and she became grounded at the mouth of the creek. Several attempts were made by the family to get her to float again. There is not much left of the boat, also known as the "sunken ship" today, but she has been captured in paintings and photographs throughout the years. (Courtesy of Nelson Klein.)

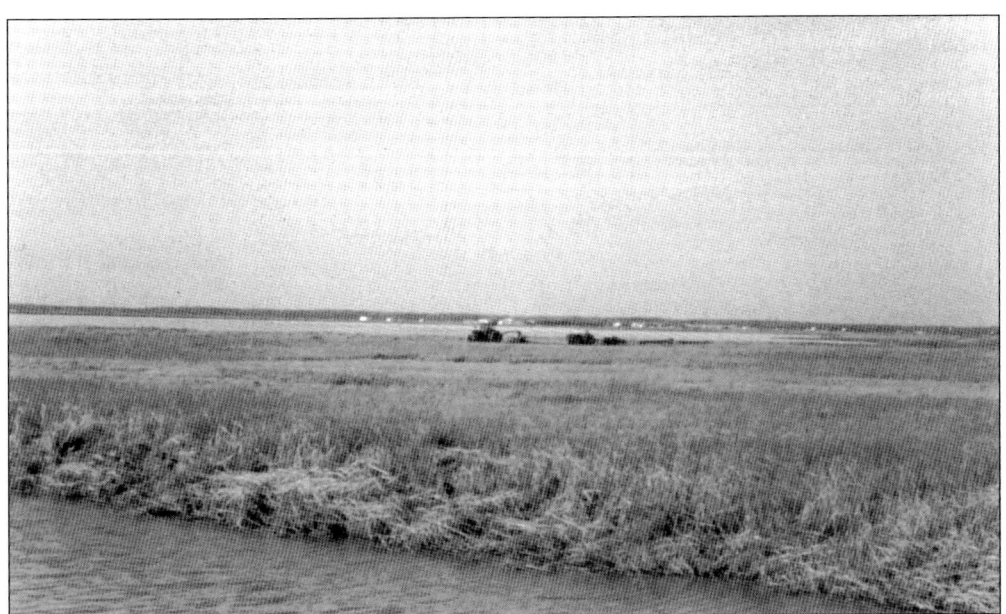

Farming hay was a big industry for several decades in Maurice River Township. Its use dated back to colonial days. Some of the uses for salt hay included insulation for crops and icehouses, packing materials for the glass industry, and bedding for stables. Salt hay also helped prevent erosion in construction sites. This photograph, taken from Captain Klein's property in Heislerville, shows farmer Ezra Cox on a tractor. (Courtesy of Nelson Klein.)

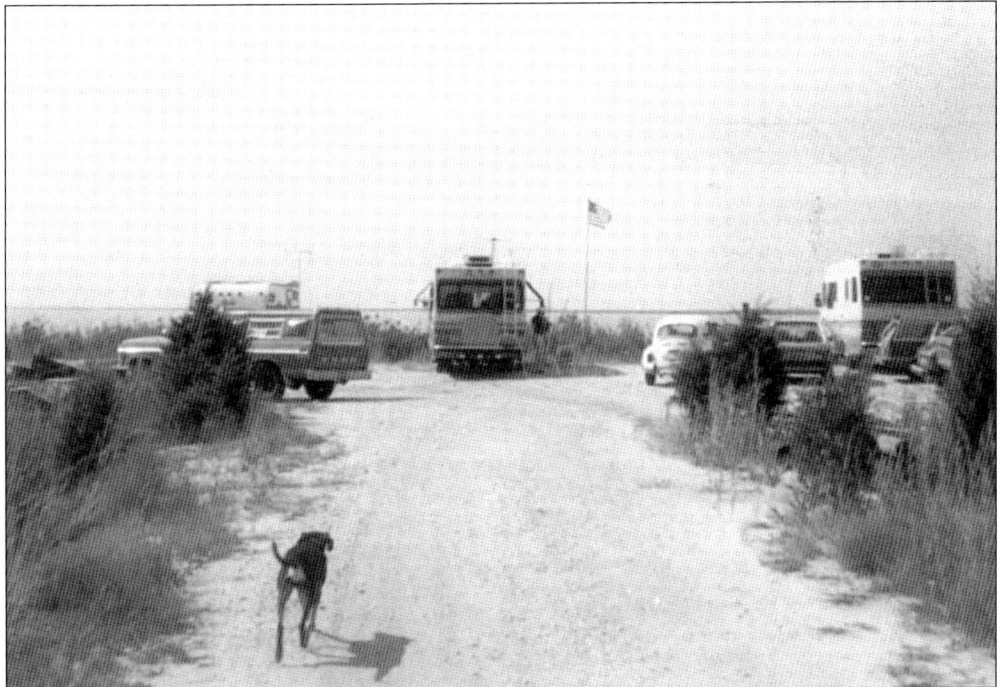

In the beginning of Captain Klein's Campground, in the late 1960s, transients would pitch their tents or park their RVs near the water. It was a pleasant place to vacation along the bay at the Maurice River Cove. (Courtesy of Nelson Klein.)

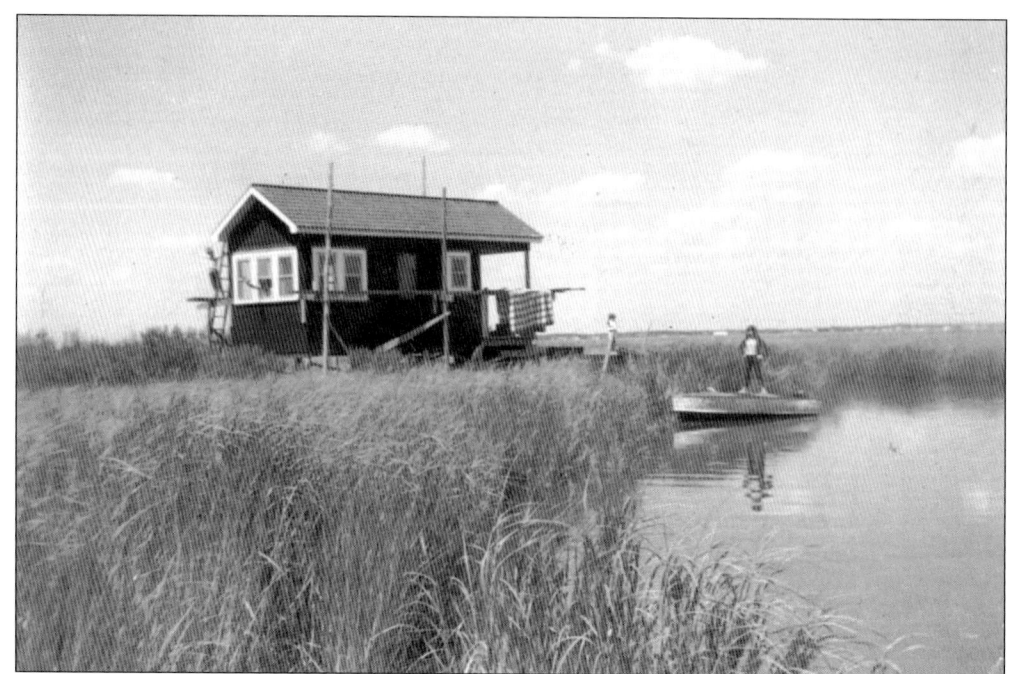

The Klein family had a small summer cottage at the campground around 1966. In this photograph, Maryanne Klein is seen standing in a small boat in the inlet. The days were filled with fun and relaxing activities. The family would come down for weekend getaways. (Courtesy of Nelson Klein.)

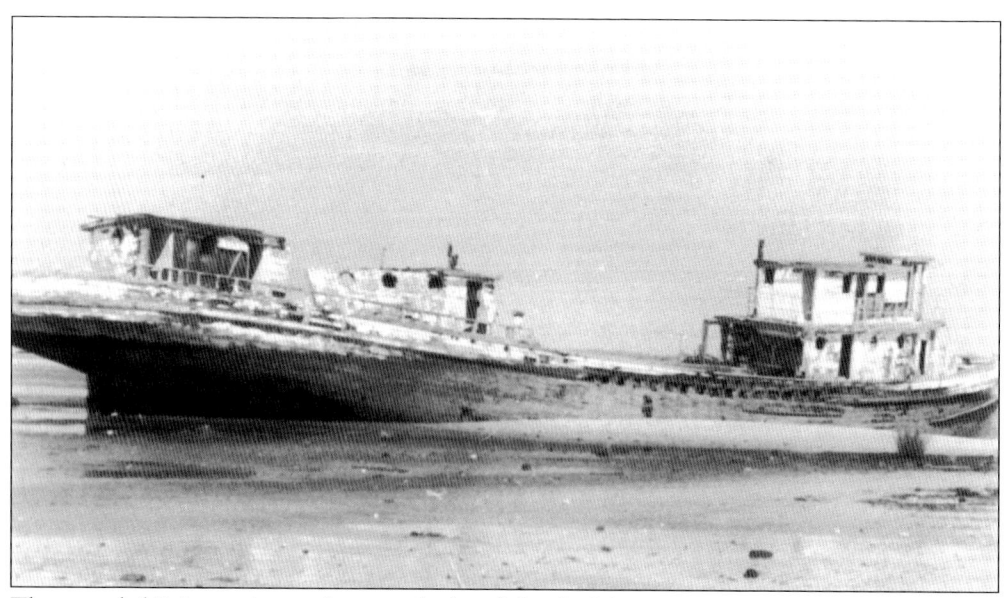

The stranded *Fairmont* is seen here on the beach by the Maurice River Cove in the early 1970s. As a young boy, Nelson Klein used to camp on it with his friends and dive off it at high tide. It was a place for great adventures and imagination. (Courtesy of Nelson Klein.)

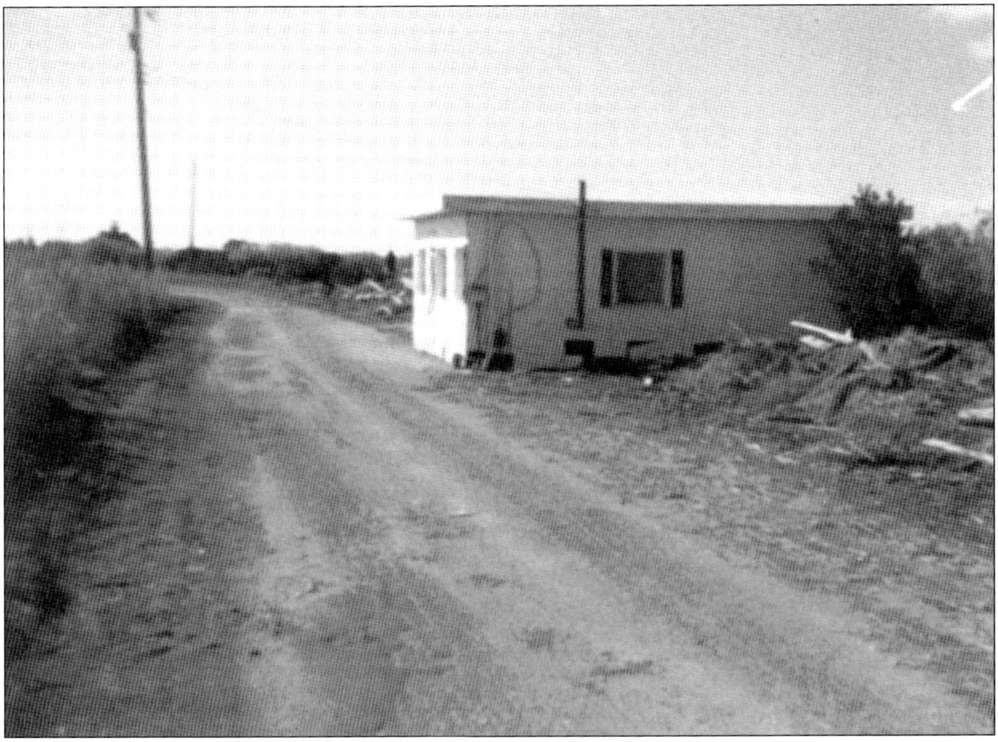

A storm in 1980 did much damage at East Point and Thompsons Beach. This house is literally on East Point Road in Heislerville. It washed from East Point Beach. (Courtesy of Nelson Klein.)

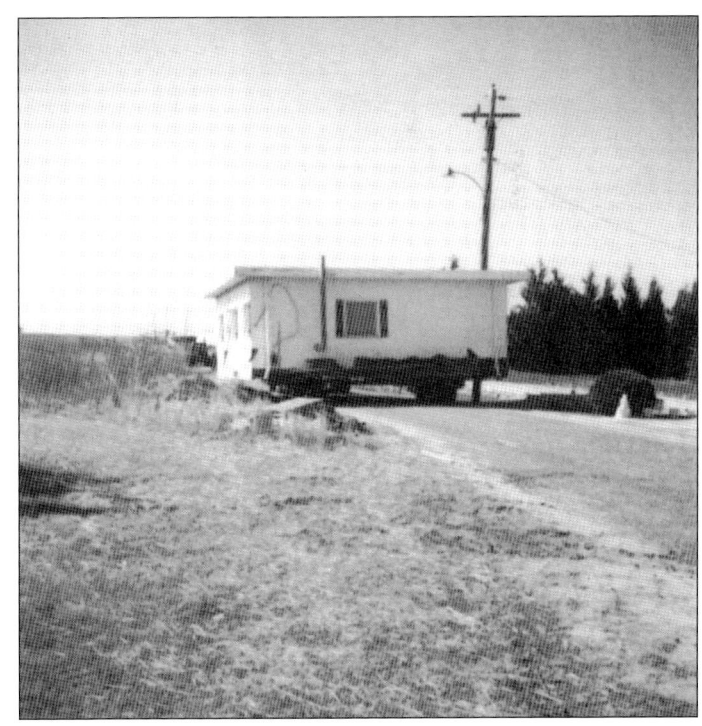

Here, the house is being moved back from East Point Road in Heislerville near Captain Klein's Campground to East Point Beach. One thing that can be said about the residents of the bayside beach communities is that they had persistent, pioneer spirits. (Courtesy of Nelson Klein.)

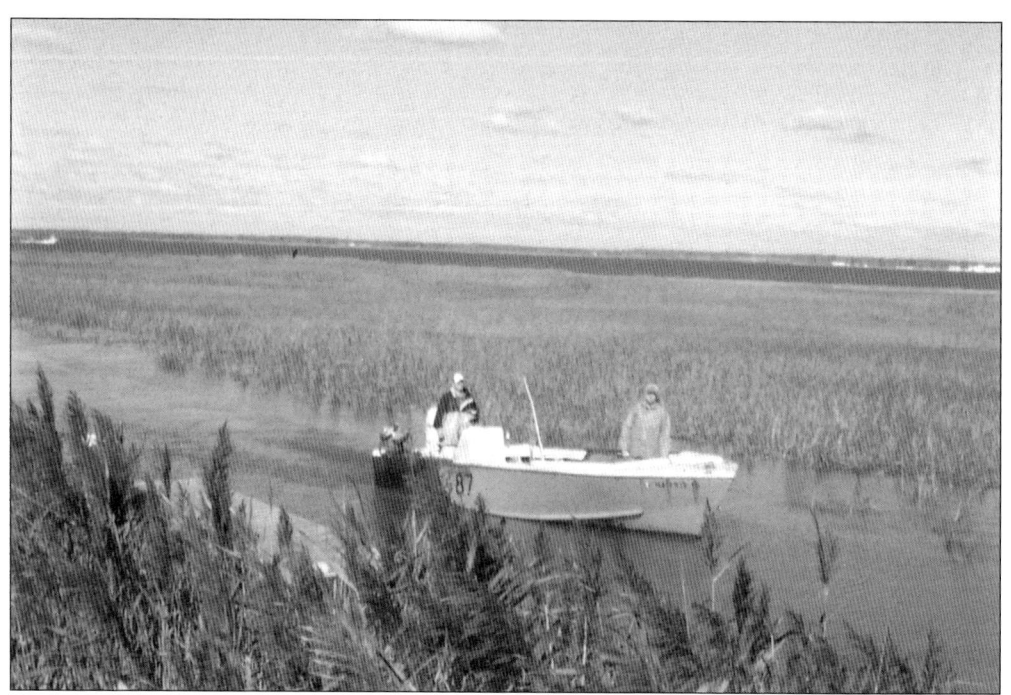

There is an inlet that runs behind Captain Klein's Campground in Heislerville. In this photograph, Nick (left) and Jimmy Gruff are returning from the tonging grounds after a day of oystering. (Courtesy of Nelson Klein.)

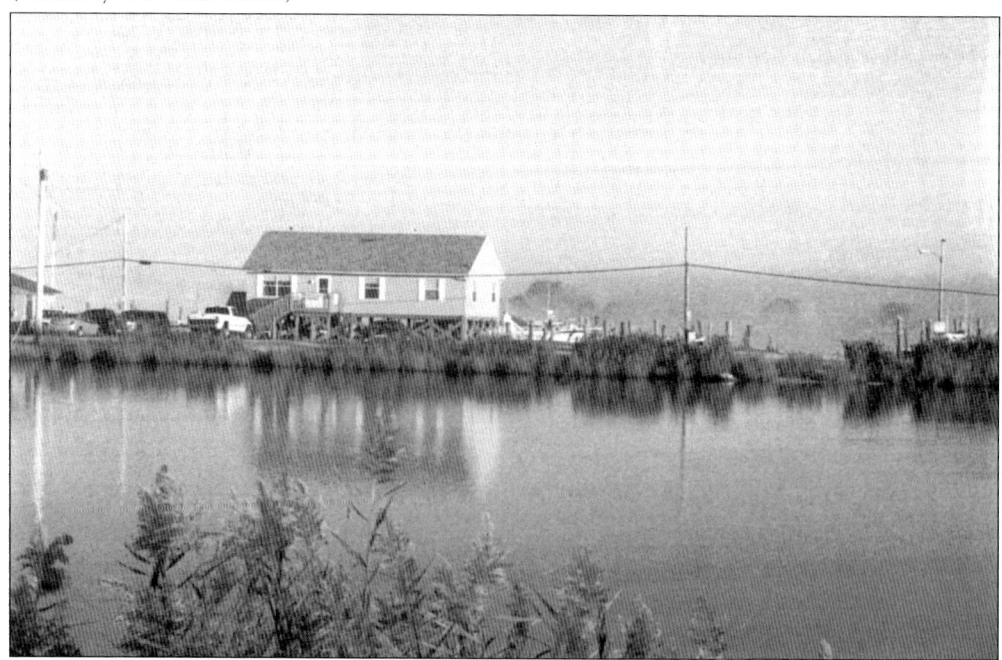

There is a rough, gravel, dike road around the saltwater impoundments at Matts Landing. It can be driven with four-wheel drive vehicles and is often the chosen spot for crabbers in the summer. In this view is Fish Tales Marina, which is no longer in operation. (Courtesy of Richard St. Aubyn.)

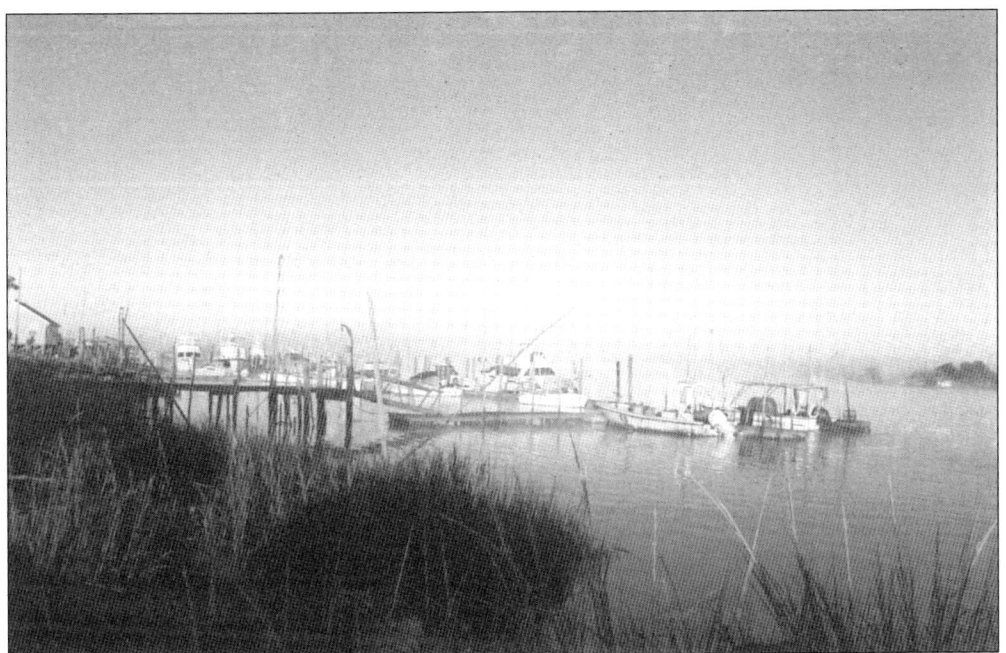

This picture was taken near the water at Matts Landing, which is home to Anchor Marina, Haase's, and Popeyes. There is a haze on the water in this dreamy photograph of anchored boats. (Courtesy of Richard St. Aubyn.)

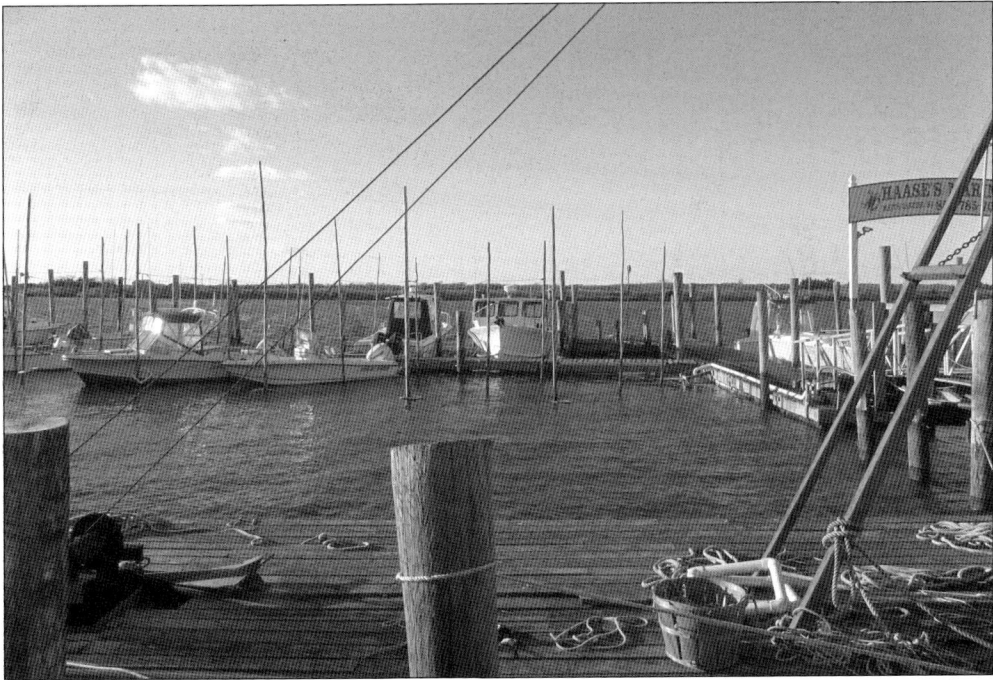

Boats are anchored at Haase's Marina at Matts Landing. The marinas here offer bait, tackle, boat slips, crabs for purchase, and a boat ramp for public use. A boat trip along the scenic Maurice River is a great way to spend a day. The river leads out to the mouth of the bay for fishing and recreational excursions. (Author's collection.)

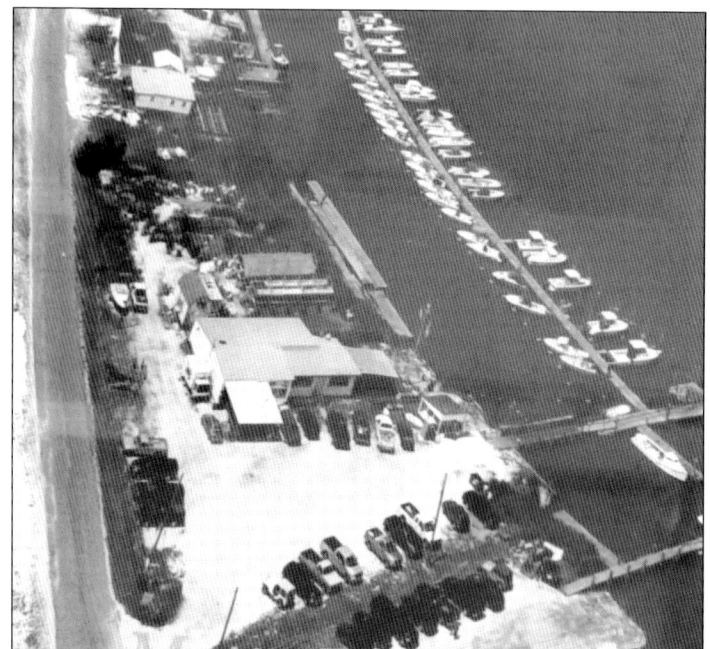

This is an aerial view of the marinas at Matts Landing on a busy summer day along the Maurice River. There is beautiful scenery on the water and in the area. Wildlife is abundant here. Bald eagles, egrets, blue herons, and cormorants are frequently spotted. (Courtesy of Joe and Donna Haase.)

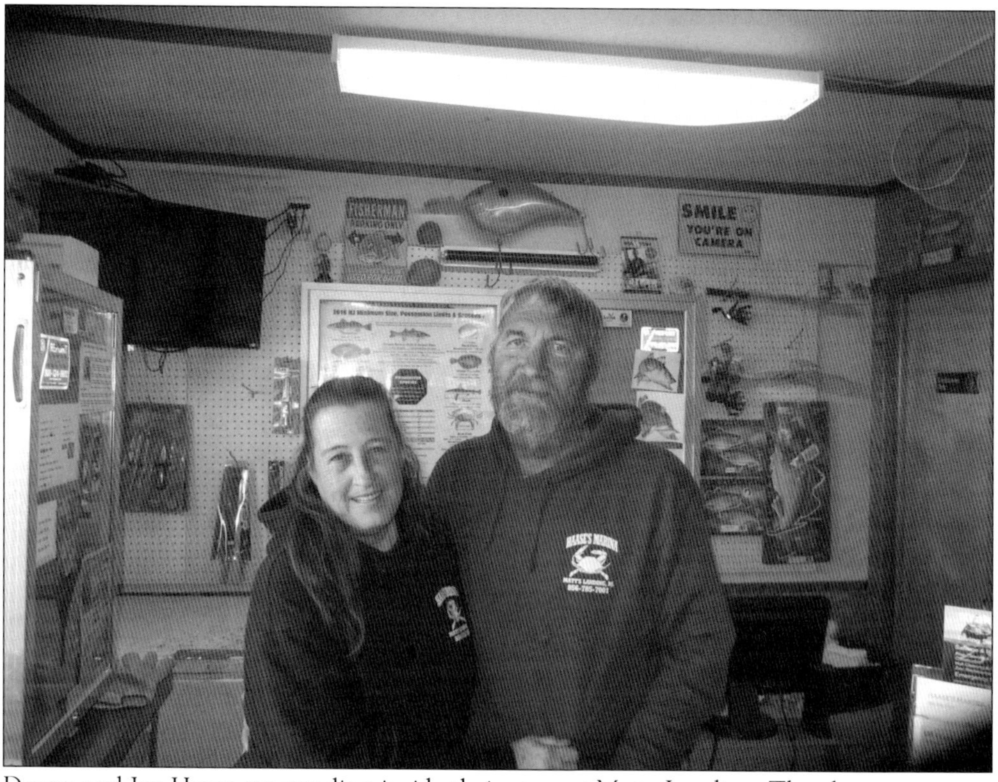

Donna and Joe Haase are standing inside their store at Matts Landing. They have numerous interesting and useful items for sale. Joe makes his living off the water as a commercial crabber. He loves the freedom and independence of his career. Donna works in the store and at the marina. (Author's collection.)

Seven

Delmont, East Point, and East Point Lighthouse

Delmont is a small village along Delsea Drive. It was known as Ewings Neck, after one of the founding families, until 1891. At that time, Sallie Henderson was instrumental in changing the name of the town to Delmont. For many years, the main industry was the hay business. One of the early public buildings there was the Union School, which was located on the road from Delmont to Hands Mill and was built in 1825. It was also known as Hands Schoolhouse. There was an earlier school building known as Friendship School, which was a one-room, wooden structure that was purchased in 1810 and served as a Methodist meetinghouse for several years. People would ride horses or walk for miles to attend meetings. Hands Mill was an old wooden structure that processed grain in the late 1800 to early 1900s. The town's post office was built in 1851. The mail would arrive by stagecoach, and later, by train.

Just a few miles down Glade Road from Delmont is East Point Beach. In the mid-1800s, there was a large wooden hotel with 29 rooms where passengers on ships could stay overnight. This structure burned to the ground in 1882. This quaint community has been the home of bayside dwellers since the 1930s. In fact, it was the location of a famous speakeasy, known as Captain Badgers, which thrived for decades in a dry township. East Point derives its name from the geography of the area. There is a jutting section of land at the eastern part of the mouth of the Maurice River that has been a landmark for boaters for hundreds of years.

Many fishermen, oystermen, and recreational boaters were guided through the waters by the beacon from the East Point Lighthouse. This lighthouse, built in 1849, is the second oldest in New Jersey. It was originally known as the Maurice River Lighthouse. The present name was adopted in 1913. It is a beautiful structure in a remote area that has been a source of inspiration for photographers and painters throughout its history.

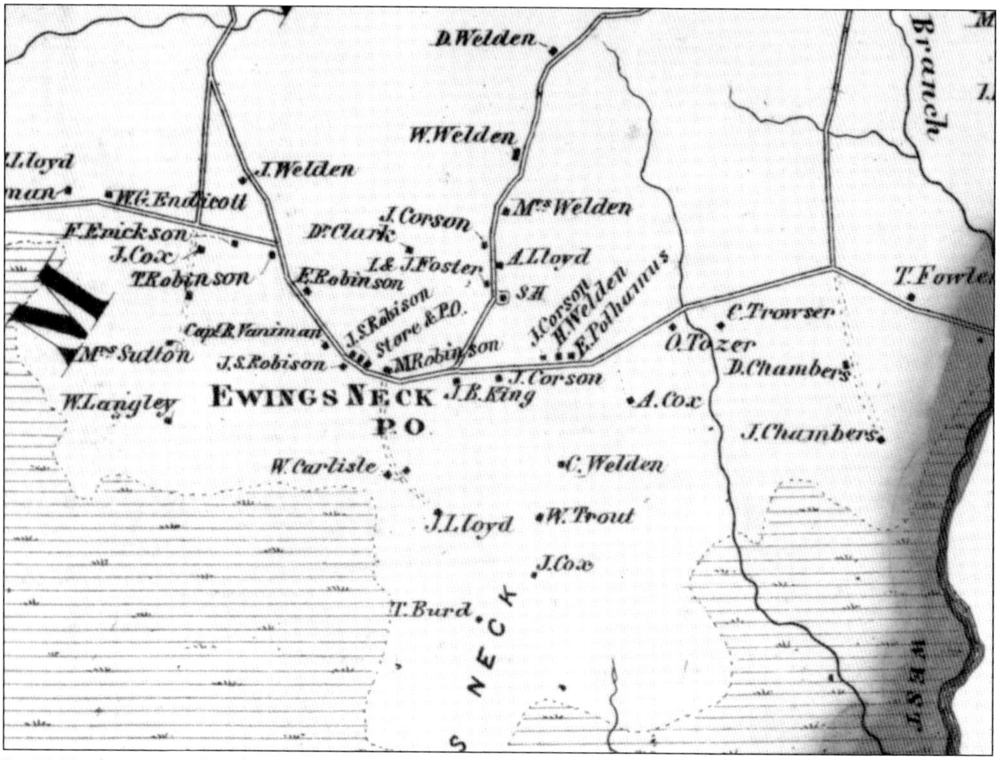

In 1862, the town of Delmont was known as Ewing's Neck. It was named after one of the founding families and for the geography of the land. There was at least one place of business at the time, J.S. Robison's store and post office. Mail would have come by stagecoach then. Some of the family names that are still in the area today include Corson, Cox, Foster, Polhamus, and Weldon. (Courtesy of the Library of Congress.)

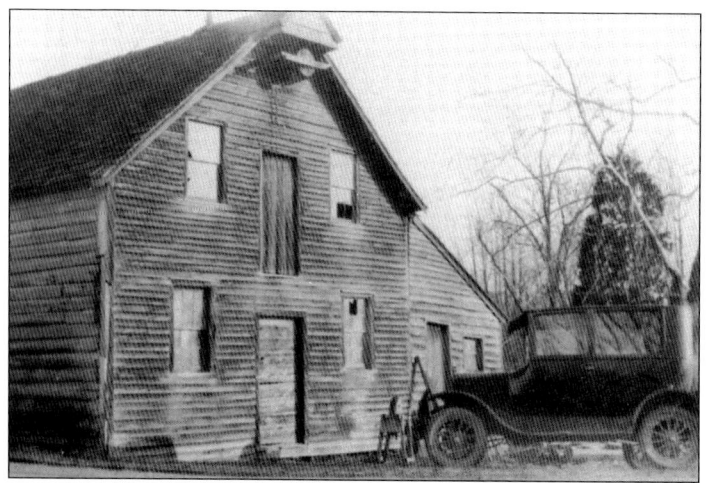

The Hands Mill in Delmont, on a road that bears its name, was active in the early 1900s. An early 1920s automobile is seen beside the structure. The technology for gristmills came to the country with the earliest settlers. The early mills, which ground grain into flour, were typically made from local wood. (Courtesy of the Maurice River Township Heritage Society.)

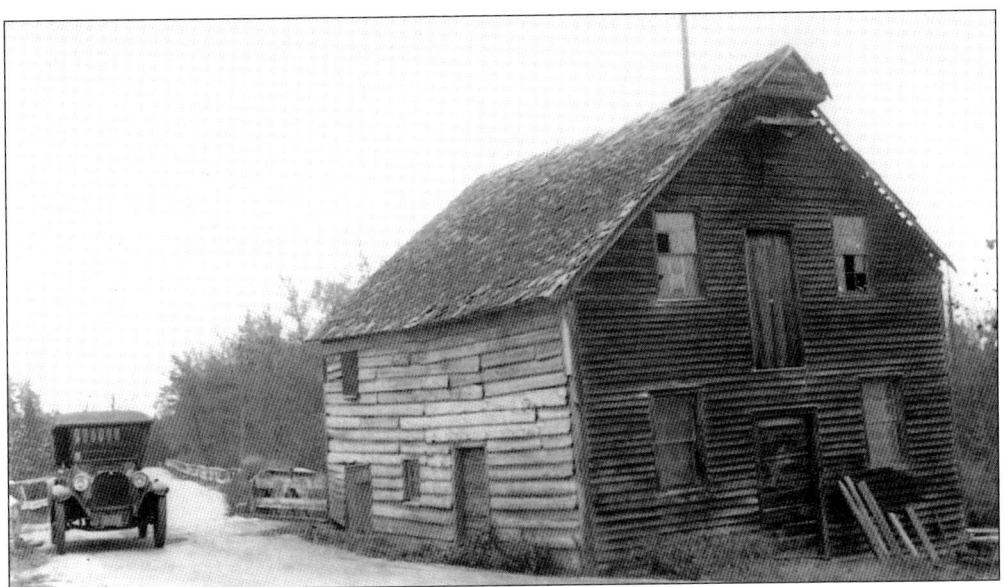

The mill has fallen into disrepair in this photograph. Broken windows are seen in the upper level, and the roof is in bad shape. Hands Mill was located on a branch of West Creek in Maurice River Township. Gristmills became a rarity by the mid-20th century. (Courtesy of the Maurice River Township Heritage Society.)

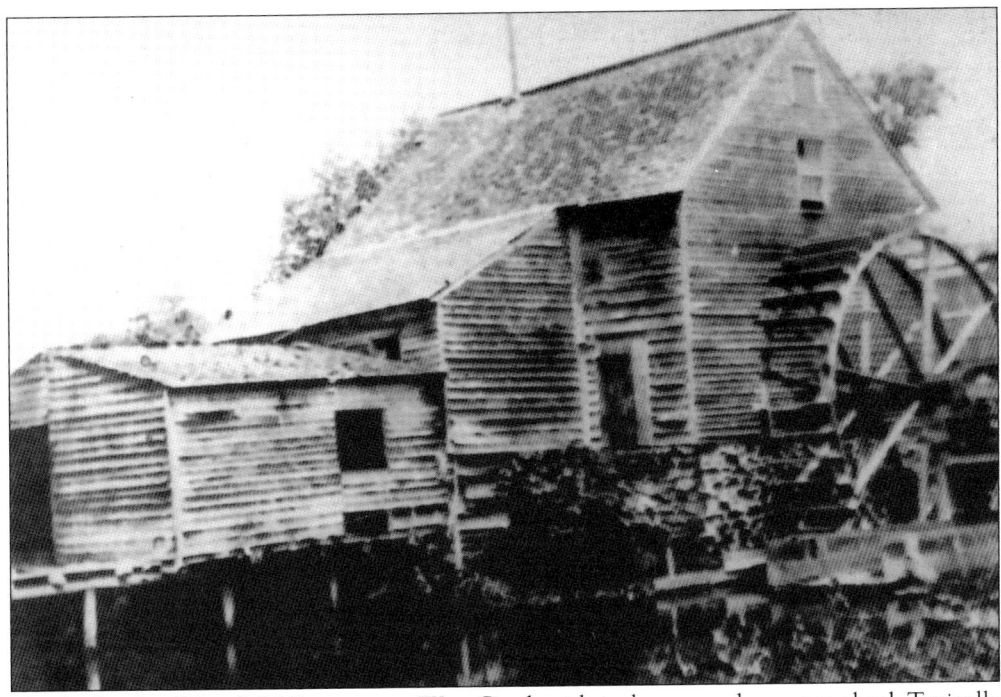

The back side of Hands Mill is seen on West Creek with its large wooden water wheel. Typically situated near streams, gristmills were self-contained and powered by water. (Courtesy of Drew Tomlin.)

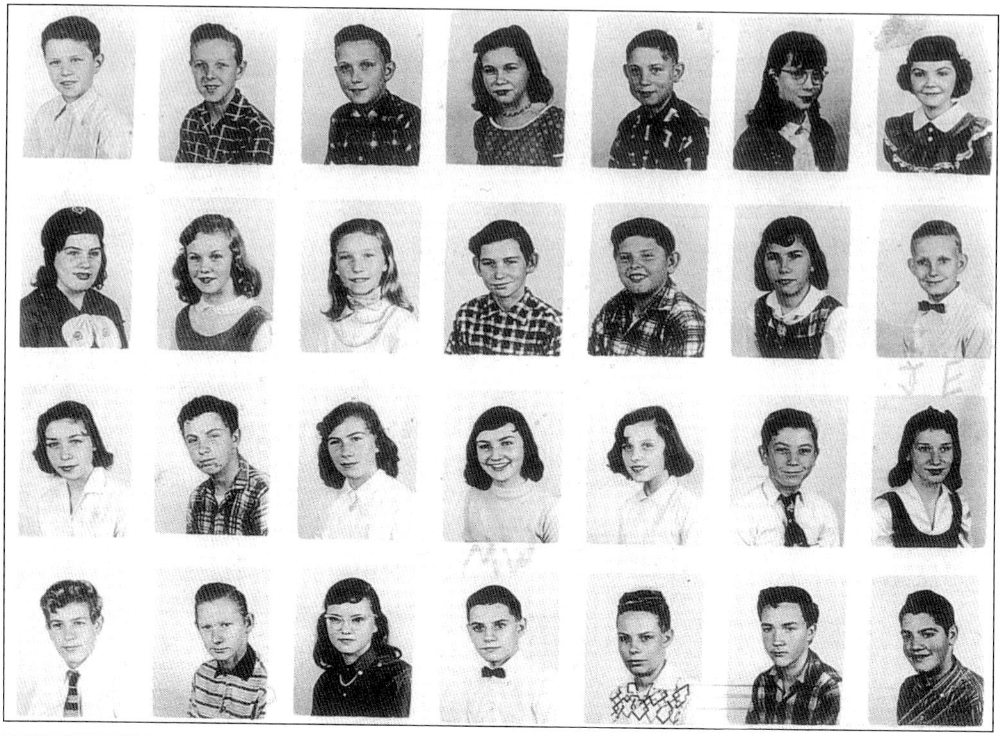

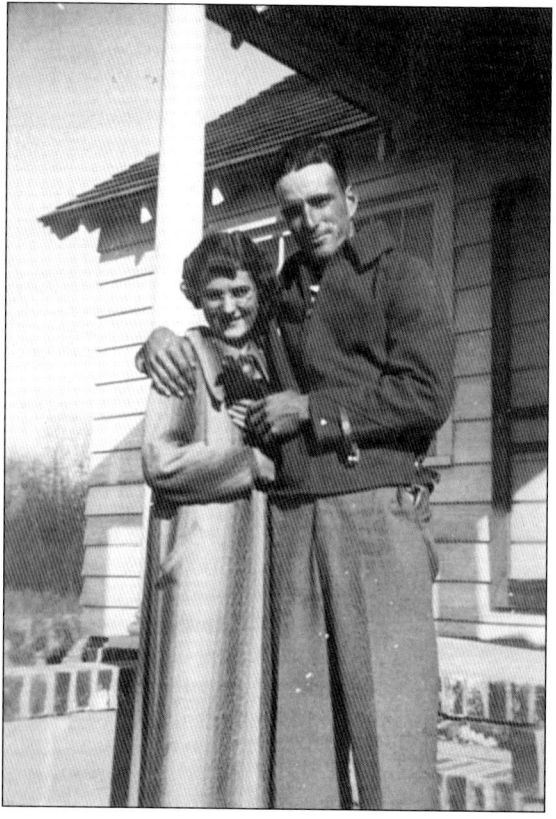

In this early 1960s picture are Delmont School students. Their beautiful two-story, wooden school building no longer stands. (Courtesy of Sonja Jordan.)

Ethel and Marvin "Jerry" Warwick are seen together in this picture taken around 1936. Their family has deep roots in Delmont. Their daughter Sonja Jordan lived next to her mother, Ethel, in the small village of Delmont. (Courtesy of Sonja Jordan.)

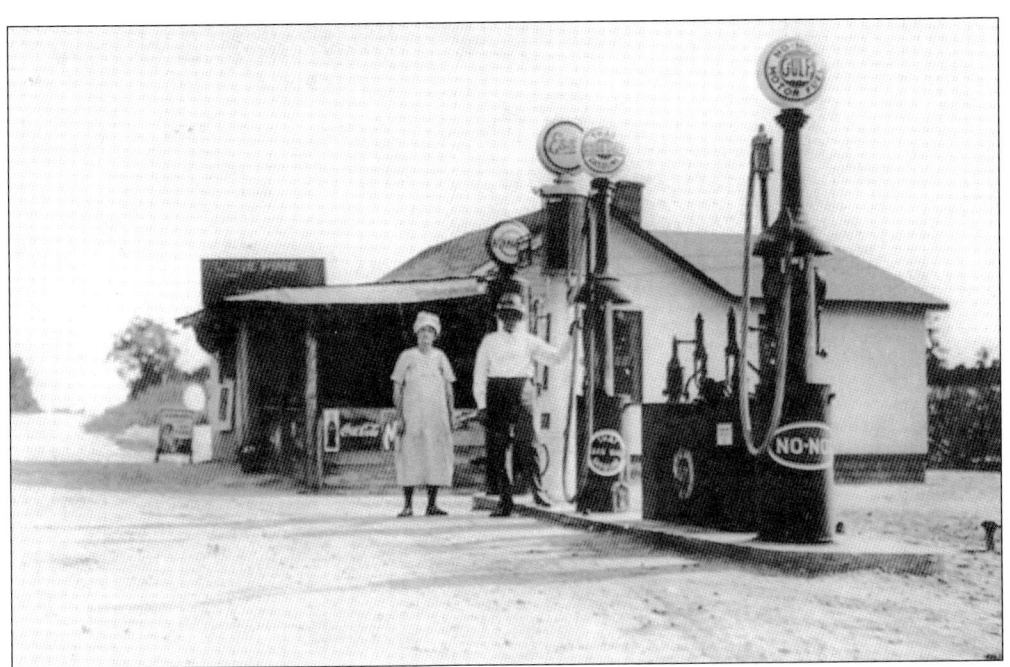

There was an Esso gas station in Delmont in the 1920s. This couple is standing by the visible-style gas pumps of the era. (Courtesy of the Maurice River Township Heritage Society.)

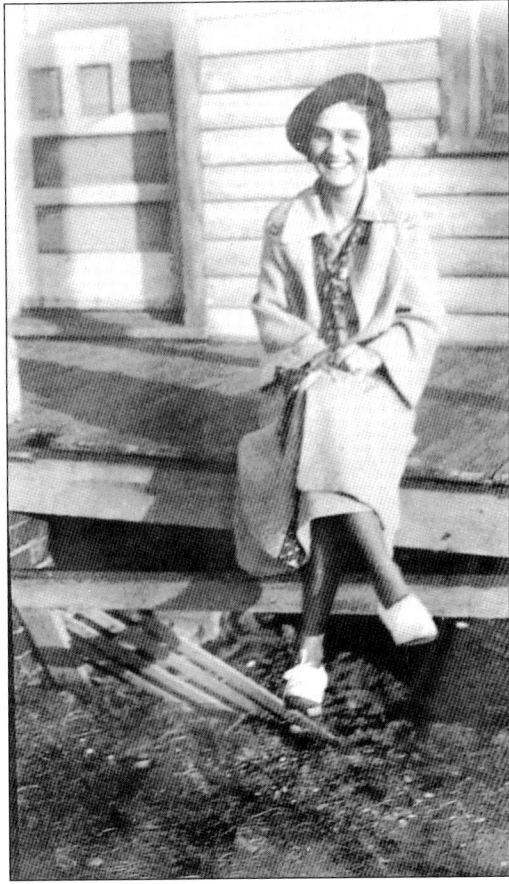

This young woman is Ethel Warwick, a lifelong resident of Delmont. She is sitting on the stoop of the family homestead. Ethel celebrated her 100th birthday in December 2016. (Courtesy of Sonja Jordan.)

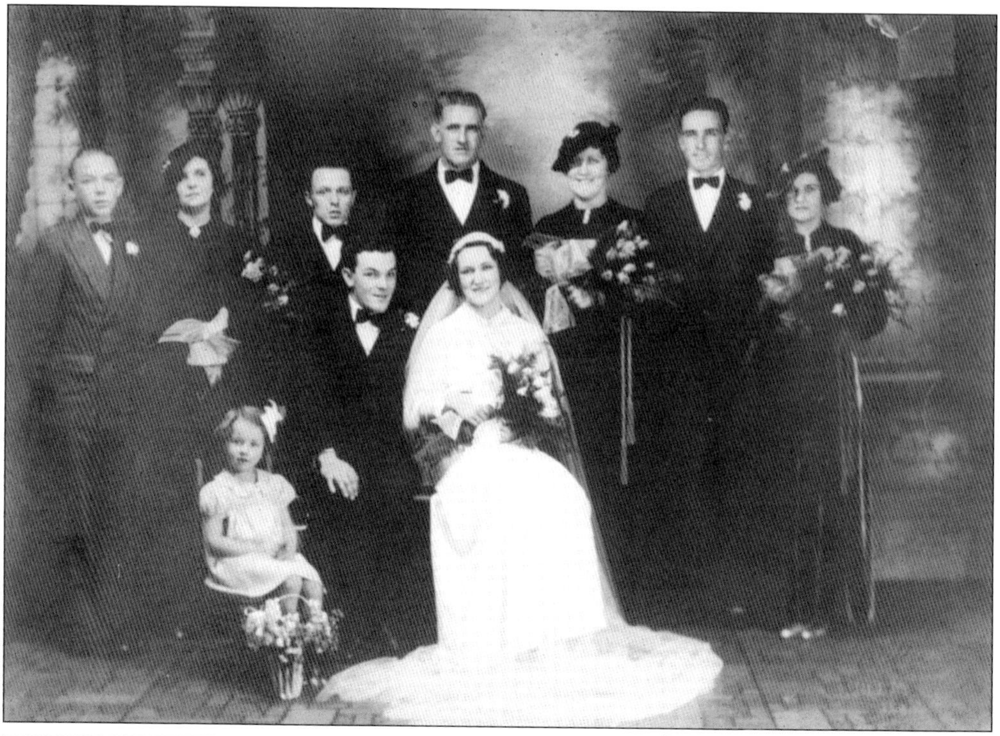

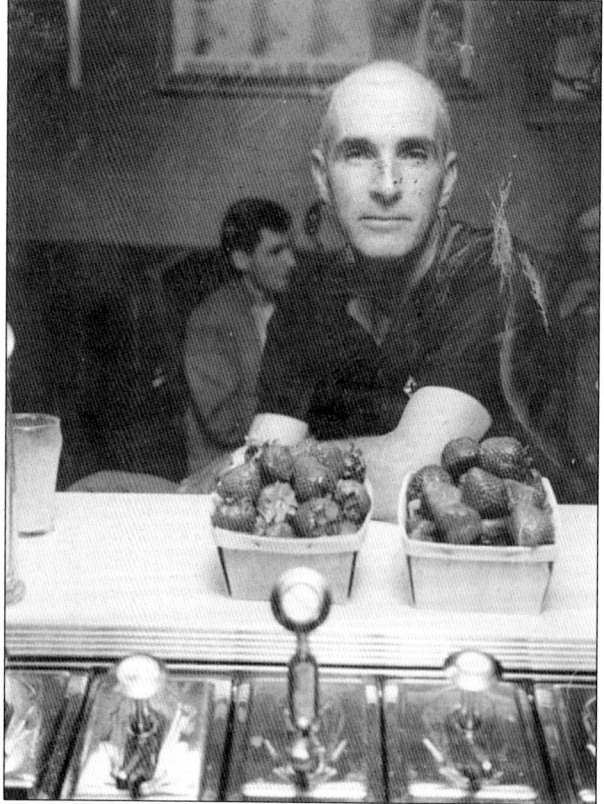

Willard and Dimples Johnson were married in the 1930s. Ethel and Marvin Warwick were in the wedding party and are the couple to the far right. The other members of the wedding party are unidentified. (Courtesy of Sonja Jordan.)

Marvin Warwick is seen sitting at the counter with his fresh strawberries around 1960 in Olsen's Ice Cream Parlor. The store and gas station are no longer in business in Delmont. (Courtesy of Sonja Jordan.)

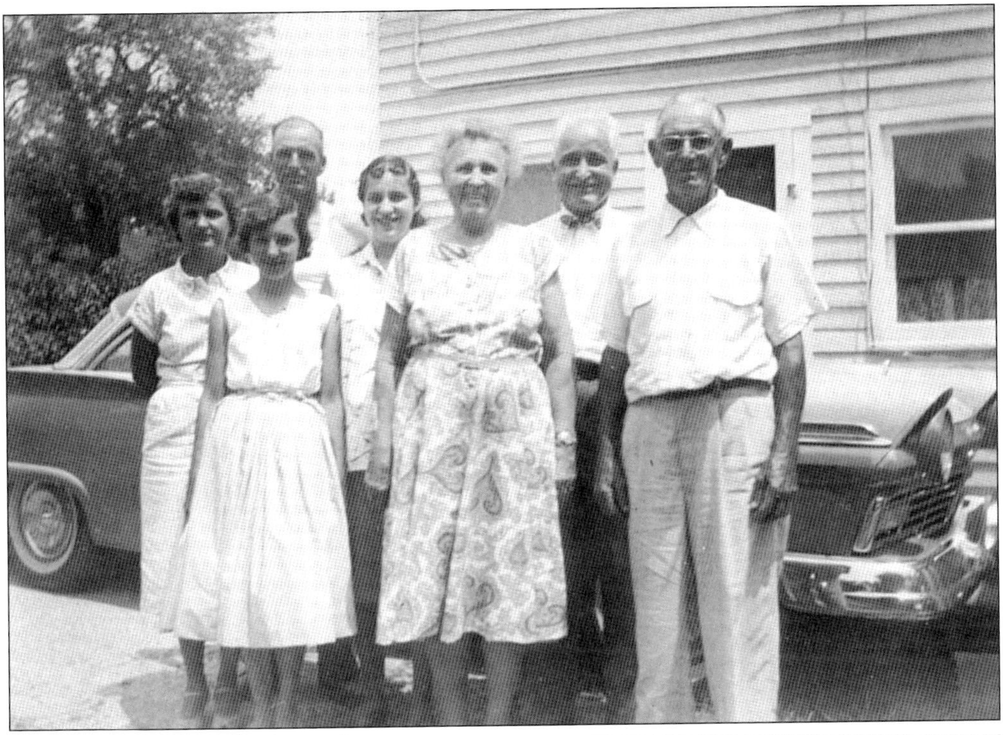

This 1950s photographs shows the Warwicks. From left to right are (first row) Marlyn, Carrie, and Thomas; (second row) Ethel, Marvin, Sonja, and Raymond. (Courtesy of Sonja Jordan.)

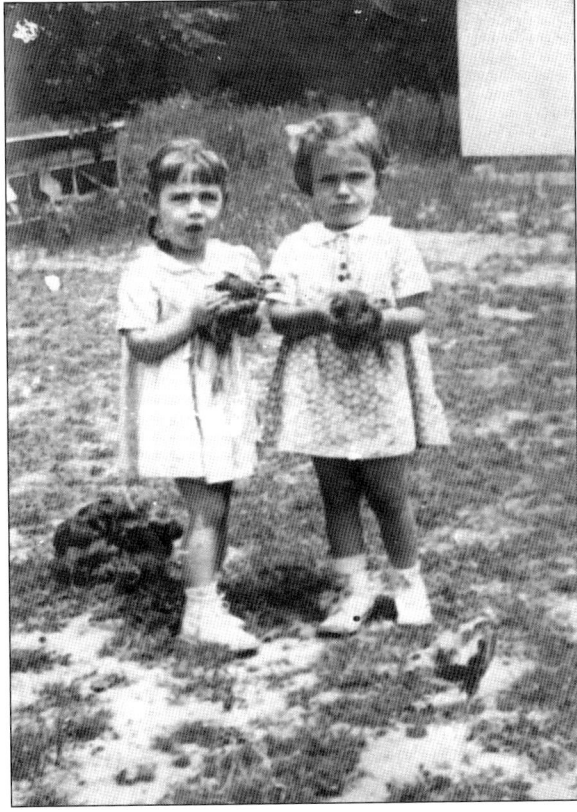

Friends Maryellen Hulitt (left) and Sonja Warwick are holding baby chickens. The c. 1943 picture was taken in the backyard of the Warwick homestead in Delmont. (Courtesy of Sonja Jordan.)

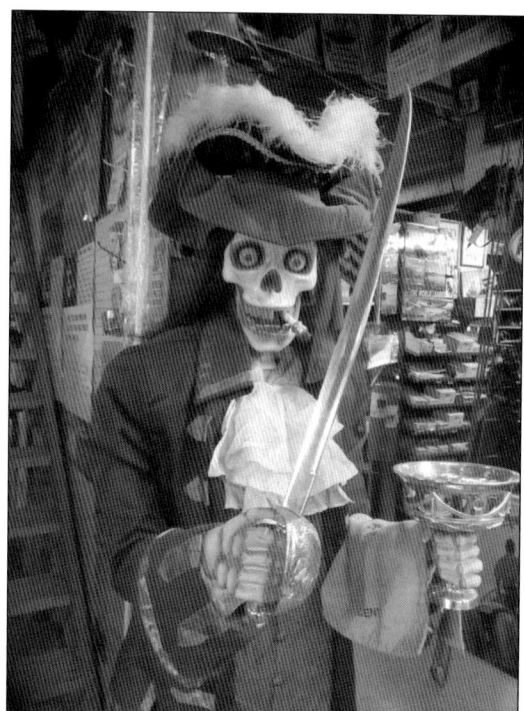

This unusual pirate greeter stands in Barnacle Bill's Marine Store. He is holding a sword and a silver bowl filled with candy and has a sparkplug in his mouth. Yvonne and Joseph Pekora own this business in Delmont. (Author's collection.)

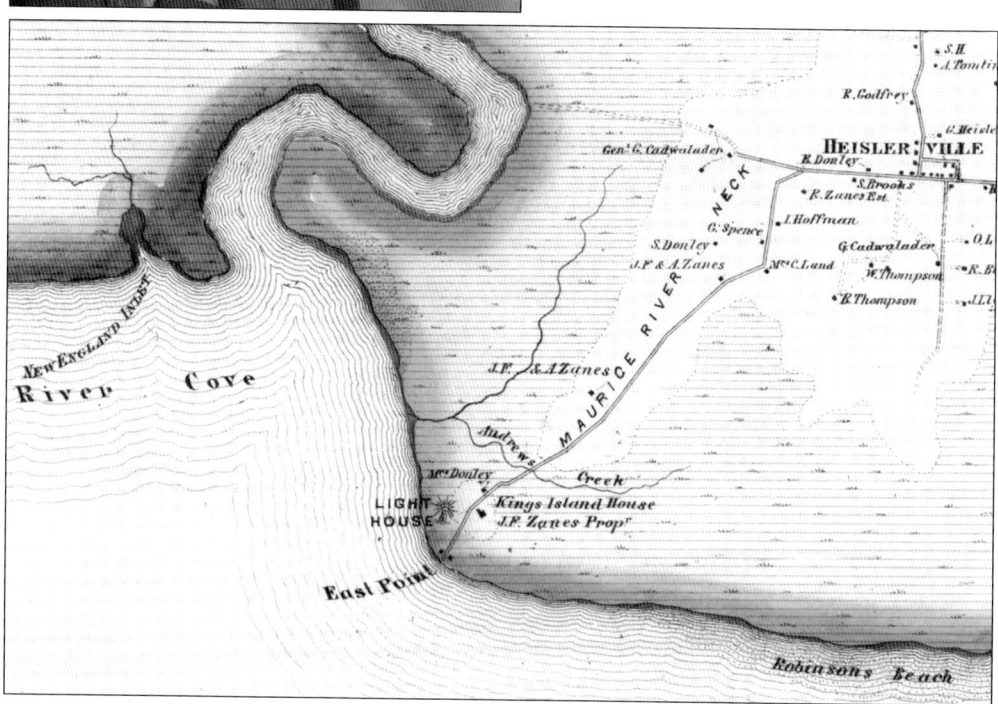

This is a map of East Point in 1862. It shows the King's Island House, which was a hotel on J.F. Zane's property in the late 1800s. The lighthouse is listed at East Point. The structure of the land is much different today due to significant erosion. Robinsons Beach is in an area that became Thompsons Beach later. Gen. George Cadwalader's property can be seen. Heislerville was still named Maurice River Neck. (Courtesy of Library of Congress.)

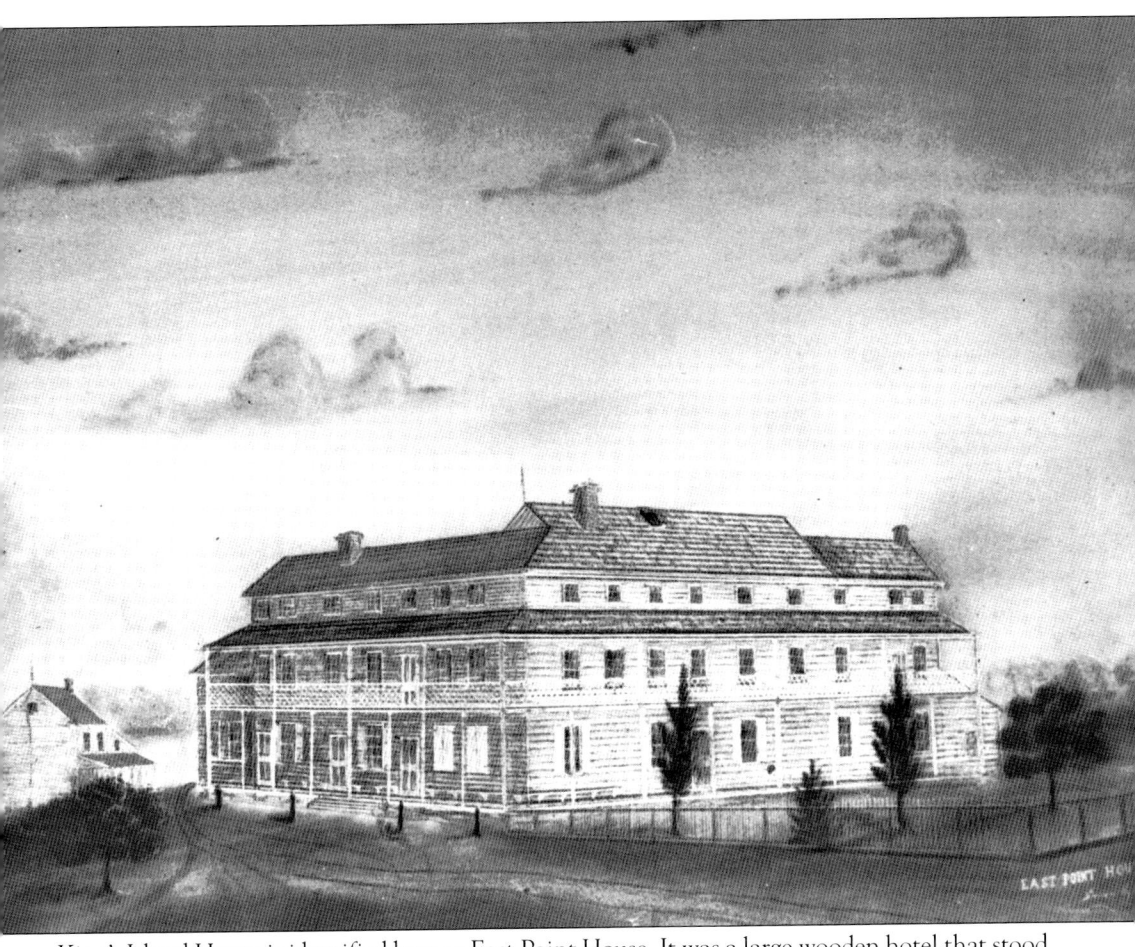

King's Island House is identified here as East Point House. It was a large wooden hotel that stood to the left of the lighthouse. The hotel had 29 rooms, a bowling alley, and a livery stable that held as many as 15 horses. The hotel burned to the ground in 1882. (Courtesy of Nelson Klein.)

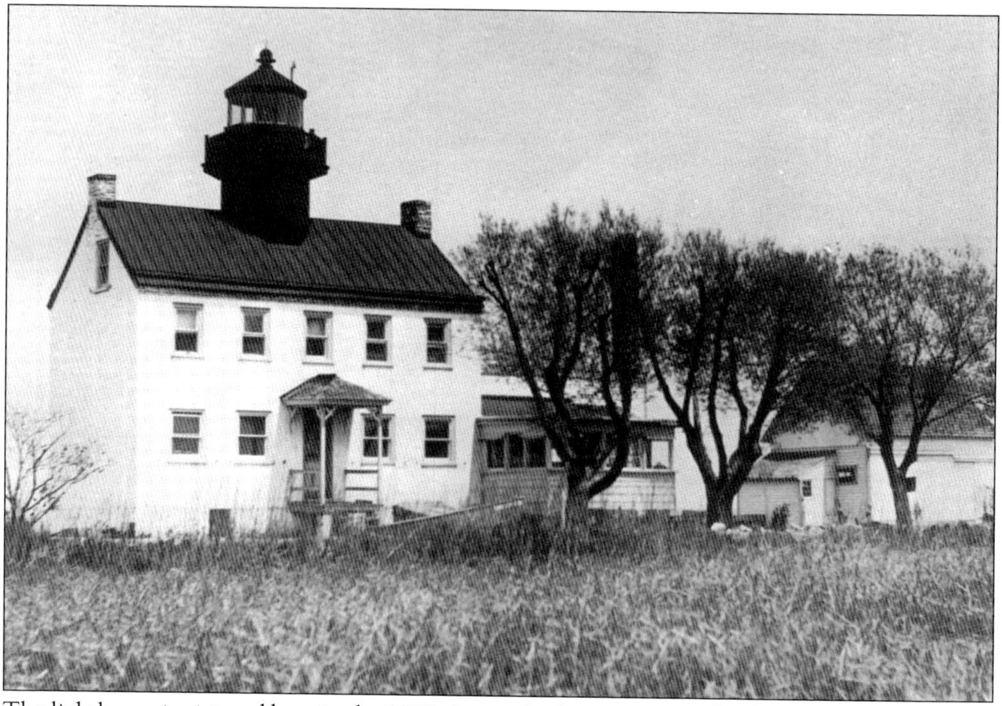

The lighthouse is pictured here in the 1930s. It was the living quarters for the lighthouse custodian and family. There were two bedrooms on the top floor, and the living room and dining room were on the first floor. The kitchen is on the right, with a closed-in porch. The boathouse storage and rental facility was on the far right. The last keeper was Linwood Spicer, who served from 1905 until 1911. At that time, custodians lived there rent free and were paid $1 per year. The last custodian was Gus Eulitz. (Courtesy of Friends of East Point Lighthouse.)

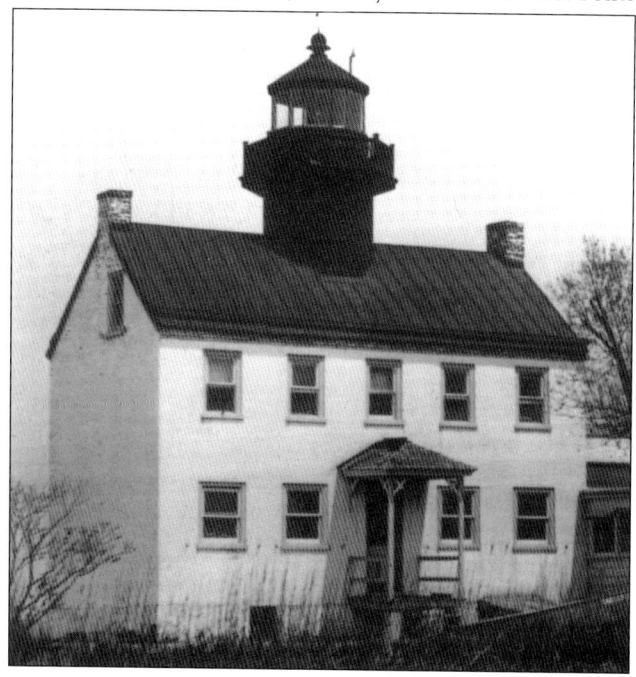

The front of the Cape Cod–style lighthouse is seen here. At the time, it was pure white in color. Currently, it has been restored to its original brick, whitewashed color with lead-gray trim and green shutters. (Courtesy of Friends of East Point Lighthouse.)

This is a side view of the East Point Lighthouse with one of the keepers standing at the side of the building in the 1930s. The light had a Fresnel lens, which was the latest technology at the time. It created a brighter light that went a farther distance. The lens was likely a fifth-order, the second smallest size. (Courtesy of Friends of East Point Lighthouse.)

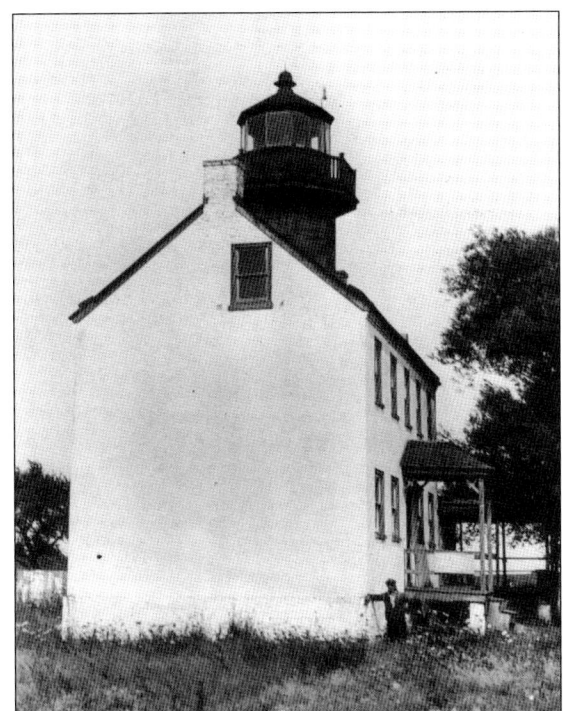

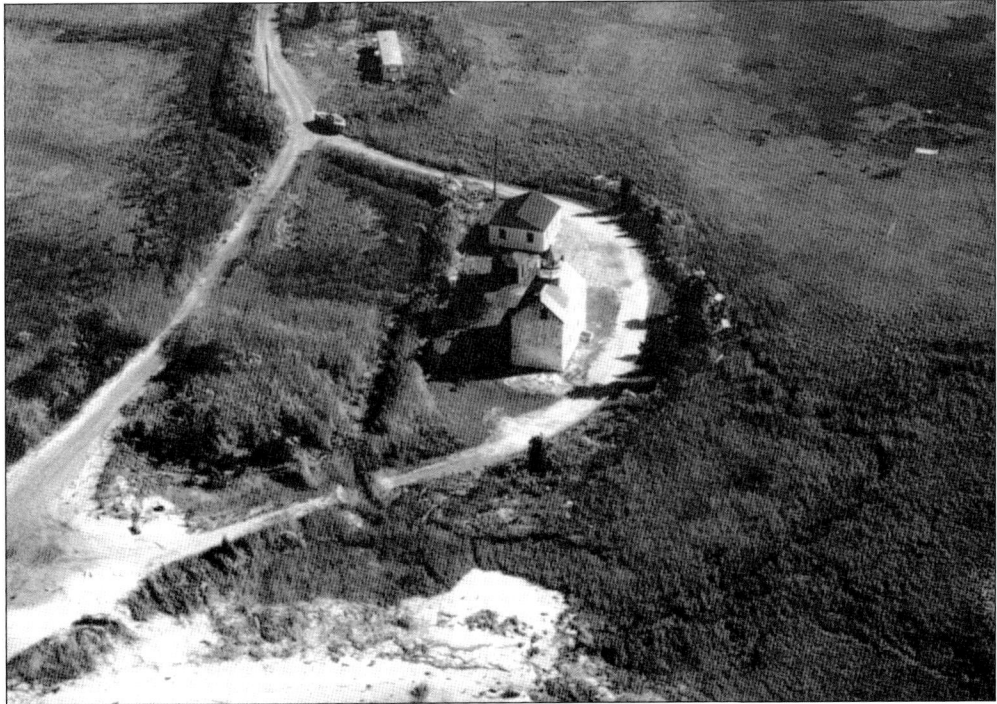

An aerial view of the lighthouse is seen here around 1970. At the time, a road went all the way in front of the building. What used to be the boathouse had been converted to a cottage. A trailer can be seen to the left of the buildings. It is no longer there. There was a lot more land surrounding the lighthouse at the time. (Courtesy of Friends of East Point Lighthouse.)

FISHING 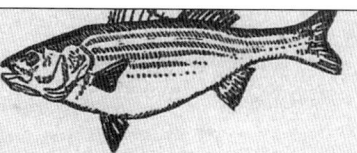 FISHING

The best grounds on Delaware Bay. Go to East Point and see the difference. Do not make no mistake go direct to Lighthouse.

ROW BOATS TO HIRE WITH 2 and 4 OARS $ 1.00 up

Special Built Boats for Outboard Motors, Free Parking, Refreshment Stand, Rest Room, Good Sanitary Accomodations, Bathing.

East Point best location on Delaware Bay. Special canal built for safety first. 40 good boats at your service, shortest row. Boats towed out to Fishing Grounds 25¢ extra. Yours for good boats good service and good fishing.

The Pioneer Captain

See **CAPTAIN PEACOCK**
East Point Box 68
HEISLERVILLE, N. J.

(OVER)

This is a postcard put out by Captain Peacock, who ran a boat rental facility at the East Point Lighthouse while he was there as a keeper from 1926 until 1938. He sold the business to the keeper who took over after him. Since the keepers were only paid a dollar a year along with a place to live, it was important to have an alternative means of making a living. The other side of the Captain Peacock postcard shows directions to the East Point Lighthouse boat rental facility. Route 47 went to almost all the surrounding areas. (Both, courtesy of Ronald Flynn.)

THIS SIDE FOR WRITING MESSAGES

EAST POINT, N. J. 56 Miles from Camden, N. J., via; the following towns and routes:

TOWN	ROUTE
1 Glassboro	47
2 Clayton	47
3 Franklinville	47
4 Malaga	47
5 Millville	47-49
6 Port Elizabeth	49
7 State Farm Leesburg	49

Next road below turn right through Heislerville to East Point.
P. S. Go direct to Lighthouse.

Boats Towed Out To Fishing Grounds 25c Extra

Place Stamp Here

Post Card

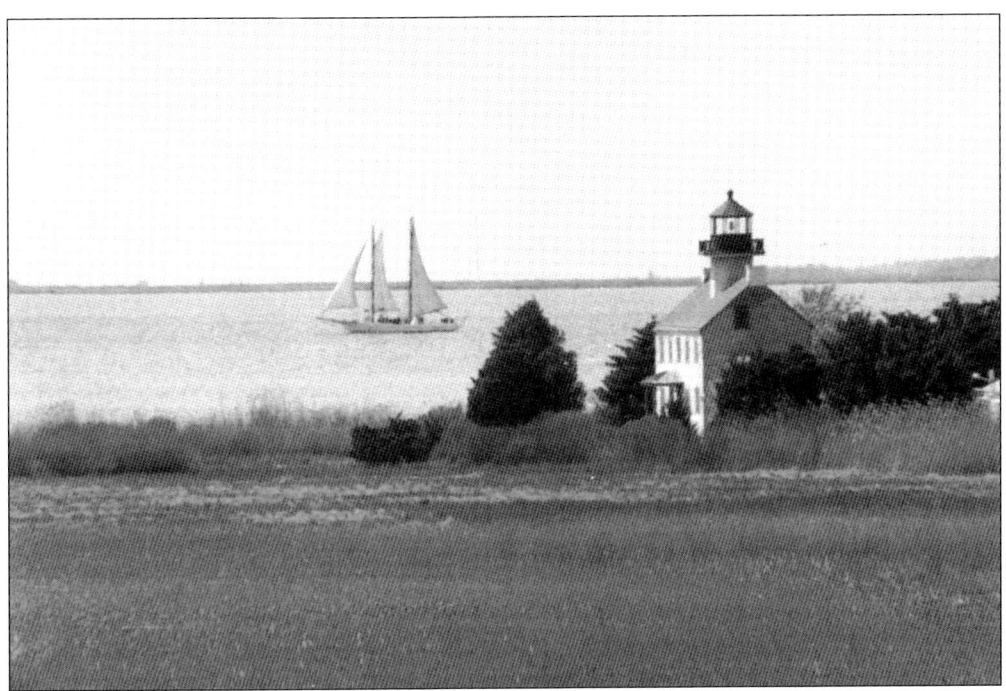

The *A.J. Meerwald* is seen sailing past the East Point Lighthouse. The tall ship's home port is at Bivalve, just across the river. (Courtesy of Richard St. Aubyn.)

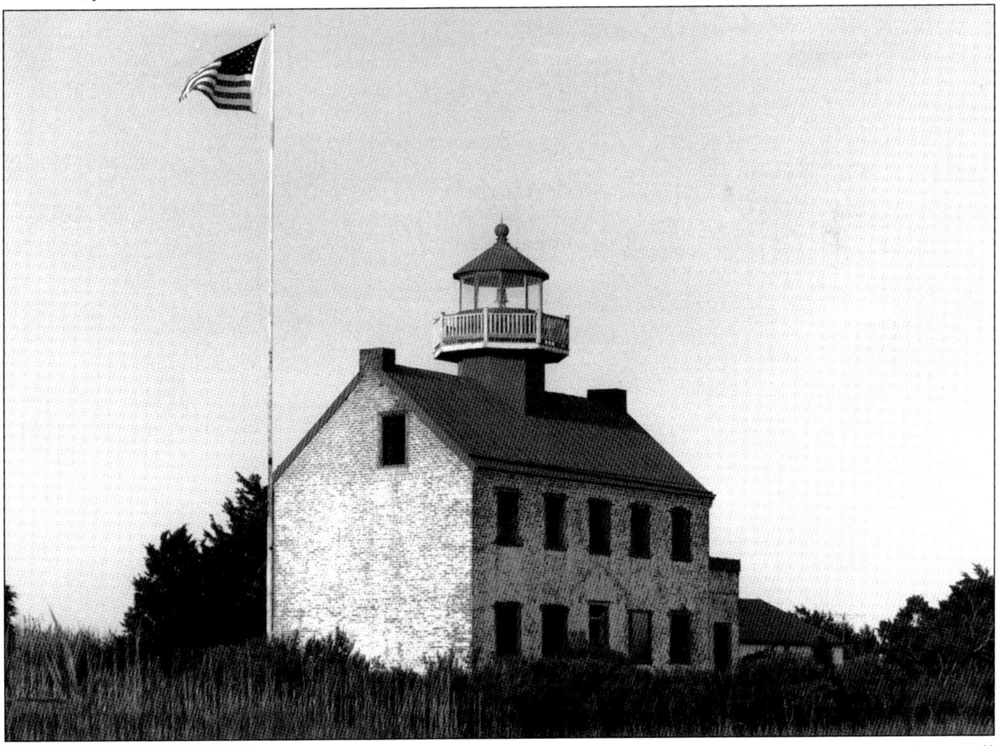

Although a flag is flying, the lighthouse stands abandoned here. This photograph was taken well before renovations began. (Courtesy of Friends of East Point Lighthouse.)

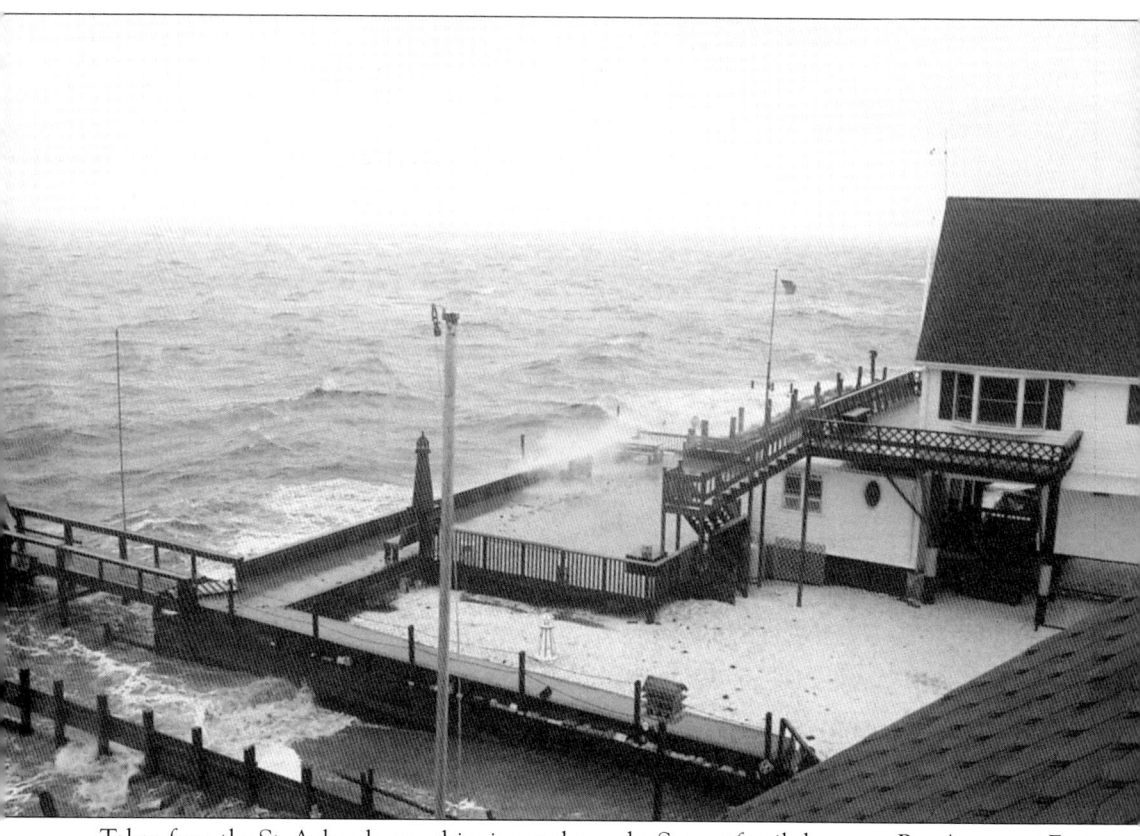

Taken from the St. Aubyn home, this picture shows the Secrest family home on Bay Avenue at East Point Beach. It looks like rough water on the bay on this day. (Courtesy of Richard St. Aubyn.)

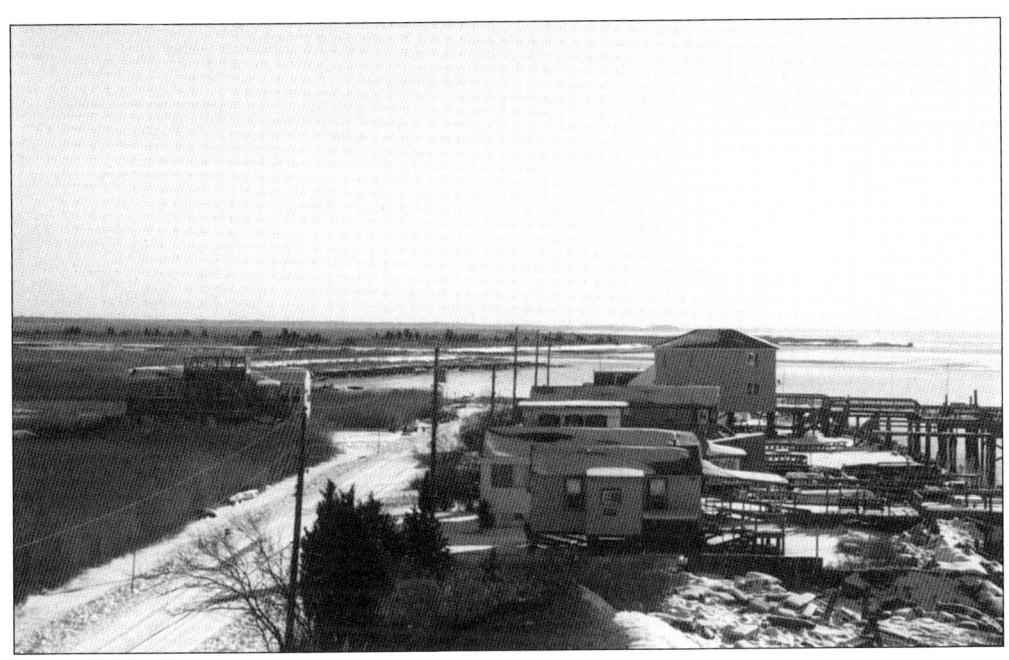

There is not a season without beauty at East Point Beach. Above, the neighbors' homes are seen from the top deck of the St. Aubyn residence, and what remains of Thompsons Beach can be seen in the background. Below is a side view of the St. Aubyn and Secrest homes on the bay at East Point. Peacefulness and serenity abound in this spectacular bayside community. (Both, courtesy of Richard St. Aubyn.)

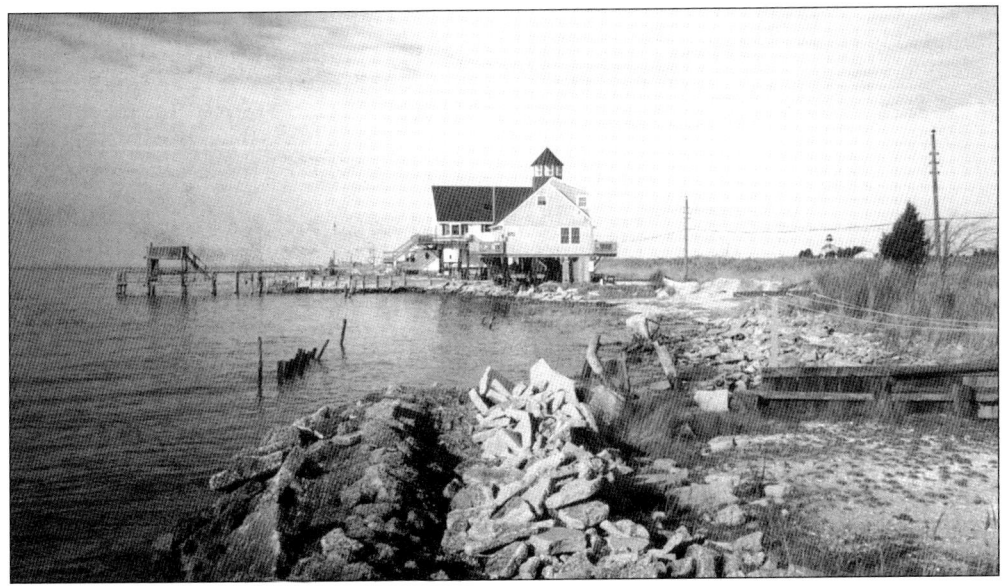

About the Organization

The Maurice River Township Heritage Society began with Facebook members of the Maurice River Township of NJ History Group. The group's page was started as a place to share photographs and information about Maurice River Township, and it quickly grew. Many people were interested in our area's history, and it was realized that there was a need for an organization and place to help preserve our stories, materials, and artifacts. Some meetings were held, and the group formalized by adopting bylaws and electing officers to the executive board. The Maurice River Township Heritage Society has monthly meetings where members have discussions and brainstorm new ways to share the area's history with others. Over time, the society became a Nonprofit 501c3 charitable organization.

The Maurice River Township Heritage Society's mission is to:

Collect, preserve, and exhibit any and all historical artifacts and materials associated with, or pertaining to, events, places, lifestyles, and cultures of the people of Maurice River Township, its villages, and surrounding areas.

Encourage the study of history and genealogy.

Provide historical and genealogical information to educate our members and the public through published and/or collected materials.

Obtain, operate, and maintain a building or buildings as a museum within Maurice River Township for the collection, preservation, and display of historical artifacts and materials related to Maurice River Township and surrounding areas for our members and the public.

Since organizing in September 2015, the society has provided and organized numerous displays of historical artifacts and information. The society has represented the township at an economical development meeting, contributed to the Maurice River Township Veterans Wall, and worked with many area historical organizations to help preserve our area's great history. For more information, please visit www.mrtheritagesociety.org.

BIBLIOGRAPHY

Beck, Henry Charlton. *Forgotten Towns of Southern New Jersey*. Boston, MA: E.P. Dutton and Company Inc., 1988.
Biographical, Genealogical and Descriptive History of the First Congressional District of New Jersey. New York, NY: Lewis Publishing Company, 1900.
Bowen, F.W. *History of Port Elizabeth, Cumberland County, New Jersey*. Philadelphia, PA: J.B. Lippincott, 1885.
Cushing, Thomas, and Charles Sheppard. *History of the Counties of Gloucester, Salem, and Cumberland Counties, New Jersey*. Philadelphia, PA: Everts & Peck, 1883.
Elmer, Lucius Q.C. *History of the Early Settlement and Progress of Cumberland County*. Bridgeton, NJ: George F. Nixon, 1869.
Gowdy, Jim, and Kim Ruth. *Guiding Lights of the Delaware River and Bay*. Egg Harbor City, NJ: Laureate Press Inc., 1999.
Harrison, Charles. *Cumberland County New Jersey: 265 Years of History*. Charleston, SC: History Press, 2013.
Maurice River Township Bicentennial: 1798–1998. NJ: Maurice River Township, 1998.
Mints, Margaret Louise, and Alex Ogden. *Man, the Sea, and Industry: A History of Life on the Delaware Bay from 1492 to 1992*. Port Norris, NJ: Mints and Ogden, 1992.
Reeves, Joseph S. Jr. *Maurice River Memories: Cumberland County, New Jersey, 1937–1947*. Baltimore, MD: Gateway Press Inc., 1993.
Rolfs, Donald H. *Under Sail: The Dredge Boats of the Delaware Bay*. Wheaton Historical Association, 1971.
The Trail of the Blue Comet: A History of the Jersey Central's New Jersey Southern Division. NJ: West Jersey Chapter of the National Railway Historical Society, 1994.
Vanaman, Herbert. *Maurice River Town*. Vineland, NJ: Cumberland County Historical Society, 1976.

Discover Thousands of Local History Books Featuring Millions of Vintage Images

Arcadia Publishing, the leading local history publisher in the United States, is committed to making history accessible and meaningful through publishing books that celebrate and preserve the heritage of America's people and places.

Find more books like this at
www.arcadiapublishing.com

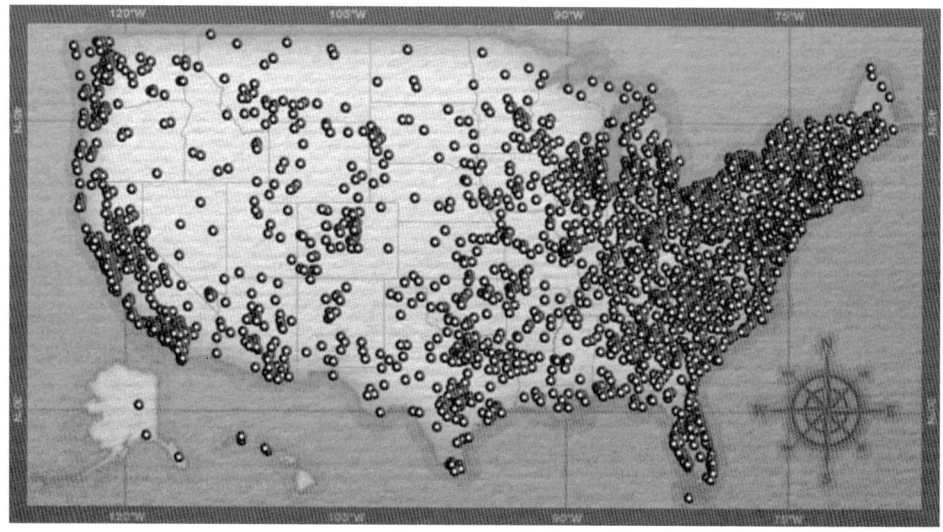

Search for your hometown history, your old stomping grounds, and even your favorite sports team.

Consistent with our mission to preserve history on a local level, this book was printed in South Carolina on American-made paper and manufactured entirely in the United States. Products carrying the accredited Forest Stewardship Council (FSC) label are printed on 100 percent FSC-certified paper.

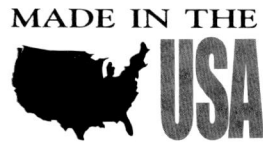